INSIDE THE NYPD'S

SECRET SPYING UNIT

AND

BIN LADEN'S FINAL PLOT

AGAINST AMERICA

ENEMIES WITHIN

MATT APUZZO

AND

ADAM GOLDMAN

A TOUCHSTONE BOOK

Published by Simon & Schuster

New York   London   Toronto   Sydney   New Delhi

Touchstone
A Division of Simon & Schuster, Inc.
1230 Avenue of the Americas
New York, NY 10020

First Touchstone hardcover edition September 2013

TOUCHSTONE and colophon are registered trademarks of Simon & Schuster, Inc.

For information about special discounts for bulk purchases, please contact
Simon & Schuster Special Sales at 1-866-506-1949
or business@simonandschuster.com.

The Simon & Schuster Speakers Bureau can bring authors to your live event.
For more information or to book an event contact the
Simon & Schuster Speakers Bureau at 1-866-248-3049
or visit our website at www.simonspeakers.com.

Designed by Joy O'Meara

Manufactured in the United States of America

1   3   5   7   9   10   8   6   4   2

Library of Congress Cataloging-in-Publication Data
Apuzzo, Matt.
Enemies within : inside the NYPD's secret spying unit and bin Laden's final plot
against America / Matt Apuzzo and Adam Goldman.
pages   cm
"A Touchstone Book."
1. New York (N.Y.). Police Department.   2. Terrorism—New York (State)—
New York—Prevention.   3. Terrorism—United States—Prevention.
4. Intelligence service—New York (State)—New York.   I. Goldman, Adam.   II. Title.
HV6432.44.N7 A67 2013
363.32509747'1   2013015663

ISBN 978-1-4767-2793-6
ISBN 978-1-4767-2795-0 (ebook)

To our wives. Without you, nothing is possible.

Beware of the words *internal security*,
for they are the eternal cry of the oppressor.

—VOLTAIRE

CONTENTS

ENEMIES WITHIN

PROLOGUE

The bomber handled the chemicals carefully, just as they'd taught him. No need to rush anything and blow off his hand, or worse. A few years earlier, a curious college student in Texas had tried the same thing in his kitchen. A 911 dispatcher listened to him die howling, begging for help as flames engulfed his body.

Mix hydrogen peroxide and acetone, and nothing happens. The chemicals swirl around next to each other. In the presence of acid, though, they form the basis for a powerful explosion. The bomber's acid of choice was muriatic acid, which he bought at a Lowe's. Muriatic acid is used to treat swimming pools and clean concrete. But when it's poured slowly into a mixture of hydrogen peroxide and acetone, clumps of white crystals appear. It looks like sugar, but it is as explosive as it is unstable.

The bomber used the Homestead Studio Suites kitchenette as his lab. He'd tried working in his aunt's garage, but when she saw all the chemicals, she and her husband got suspicious and made him pour them down the drain. Nobody would bother him here. Unable to pay their rent, many residents had recently been kicked out of their apartments. Cats slept in windows. Children played in the parking lot alongside cars packed with furniture and clothes.

Forty dollars cash for a night in room 207. The bedspread was rough, and only the whir of the refrigerator drowned out the pulse of the highway. But he was not there to rest. He chose the motel because of its kitchen. It was a simple setup: builder-grade cabinets, a dingy white laminate countertop, and, most importantly, a stainless-steel, two-burner electric stove.

He had everything he needed. For weeks he'd been visiting beauty supply stores, filling his carts with hydrogen peroxide and nail polish remover. At the Beauty Supply Warehouse, among the rows of wigs, braids, and extensions, the manager knew him as Jerry. He said his girlfriend owned hair salons. There was no reason to doubt him.

On pharmacy shelves, in the little brown plastic bottles, hydrogen peroxide is a disinfectant, a sting-free way to clean scrapes. Beauty salons use a more concentrated version to bleach hair or activate hair dyes. At even higher concentrations, it burns the skin. It is not flammable on its own, but when it reacts with other chemicals, it quickly releases oxygen, creating an environment ripe for explosions. At its highest concentrations, hydrogen peroxide can be rocket fuel. Even with a cheap stove, it's easy to simmer water out of hydrogen peroxide, leaving behind something more potent. It takes time, and he had plenty of that.

He added the muriatic acid and watched as the chemicals crystallized. The crystals are known as triacetone triperoxide, or TATP. A spark, electrical current, even a bit of friction can set off an explosion. If there's too much acid, or the balance of acetone and hydrogen peroxide isn't quite right, the reaction will speed out of control and trigger a chemical blast.

This was the moment when things often went wrong in basement laboratories, but he had done this before. A year earlier, he made his first batch under the watchful eye of his mentor. Then, a week ago, he made a practice sample in this same hotel. He took the finished product to an out-of-the-way spot, ignited it with a strand of Christmas tree lights and a battery, and watched it explode.

PROLOGUE

The white crystal compound had been popular among Palestinian terrorists. It was cheap and powerful, but its instability earned it the nickname "Mother of Satan." Once, an amateur bomb maker in the Mojave Desert had walked under a stretch of power lines. The electrical charge in the air was enough to detonate his TATP blasting caps and send paramedics rushing to his aid. Now most professional terrorists preferred to use it in only the smallest of quantities as the detonator for a bigger bomb. Even the average suicide bomber didn't want to carry around large amounts.

The volatile reaction was precisely the reason that all but the tiniest containers of liquids were banned on airplanes. A terrorist who boarded with a large shampoo bottle full of the right chemicals could conceivably create TATP in midair. It was unlikely, but the US government concluded that it was too risky to chance. One tablespoon of crystals was enough to blow through a cinder block. One cup could rip open the hull of an airplane.

The young bomber wanted to cook up two pounds.

When he was done mixing, he rinsed the crystals with baking soda and water to make his creation more stable. He placed the finished product in a wide-rimmed glass jar about the size of a coffee tin and inspected his work. There would be enough for three detonators. Three detonators inside three backpacks filled with a flammable mixture and ball bearings—the same type of weapon that left 52 dead in London in 2005.

There was more work to be done. He had to finish the main charge, a mixture of flour and cooking oil. Concealed in a backpack and ignited by the TATP, these household ingredients would create a massive dust explosion and fireball. That could come later. The hardest part was complete.

He was ready for New York.

3

1

THE MARRIAGE IS READY

NEW YORK
Wednesday, September 9, 2009

The address of the Federal Bureau of Investigation's Joint Terrorism Task Force in New York, the hub for all law enforcement intelligence in America's most populous city, is not advertised. The office is in a block-long brick–and–terra-cotta building at the western edge of Manhattan's gentrified Chelsea neighborhood. A half century ago, it was part of a Nabisco factory complex producing Oreo cookies and saltine crackers. Today the giant rows of industrial ovens on the tenth floor have been replaced by a sterile government office suite, unadvertised and unremarkable.

From that floor, Assistant Special Agent in Charge Don Borelli had one of the most spectacular views in the city. Sitting at his desk, he could see the Hudson River, Lower Manhattan, and the construction cranes clustered around ground zero, where terrorists destroyed the World Trade Center on September 11, 2001. On a clear day, he could see the Statue of Liberty in the distance.

At forty-eight, Borelli retained the laid-back cool of his Southern California childhood. He had a strong jaw and a full head of dark hair.

His office was decorated with mementos of a nearly twenty-four-year FBI career. Plaques noted his tenure as one of the FBI's top agents in Jordan. Souvenir rugs commemorated his time in Pakistan. There he interrogated and won a confession from a scientist working to obtain anthrax for the terrorist group al-Qaeda. And he had fingerprinted and photographed senior al-Qaeda member Ramzi bin al-Shibh, a would-be hijacker who was whisked off to a CIA secret prison. On his desk, Borelli kept a prescription bottle labeled "Prozac." He'd gotten the container from a pharmacist friend and filled it with M&M's, a bit of dark humor aimed at newcomers who dropped in and saw the boss hard at work, apparently crunching away on antidepressants.

It was an unremarkable late-summer Wednesday, a bit cloudy with a gentle breeze. Borelli occupied the morning by looking at intelligence reports indicating that a terrorist named Saleh Ali Saleh Nabhan might soon emerge from hiding in Africa. The FBI had been looking for Nabhan since 1998, when Borelli was sent to Kenya as part of the team that responded to al-Qaeda's twin bomb attacks on the US embassies in Nairobi, Kenya, and Dar es Salaam in Tanzania. The attacks left hundreds of local civilians dead, along with the targeted Americans. More than a decade later, he didn't see anything in the new reports to suggest that a break in the case was imminent. Rumors circulated all the time. Everyone would get spun up, but leads like this one almost always turned out to be nothing.

The phone on his desk rang.

It was Bill Sweeney, calling from the Counterterrorism Division at FBI headquarters in Washington.

"You up to speed on High Rise?" Sweeney asked.

Borelli had the highest level of security clearance and was privy to intelligence from across the globe that had anything to do with New York. As a supervisor of the country's largest counterterrorism task force, the one designated to protect America's number one target, Borelli was expected to know about problems before headquarters called. But there were thousands of open cases, and he'd never heard of this one.

"What's High Rise?" he said.

Sweeney paused. They were talking on the general line, not the secure, encrypted phone.

"You better get up to speed," Sweeney advised. "It's coming at you, ninety miles per hour."

Even as one of the office's most senior people, Borelli could not access top-secret intelligence at his desk. Though everyone in the FBI office suite had passed background checks and polygraphs, federal regulations require that the nation's most highly classified information be stored in special rooms accessible only to those with the right clearances and a need to know.

The rooms are called Sensitive Compartmented Information Facilities, or SCIFs. They can't be found on any public blueprint or building schematic. But there are thousands around the country, in federal buildings, on military bases, and in the offices of private security contractors. The White House Situation Room is one, as is the Joint Chiefs of Staff conference room known as "the tank."

Whether they are the size of an auditorium or a broom closet, everything about these rooms is governed by strict rules. The walls are three layers of drywall thick, stuffed with acoustic batting and coated with a sound-dampening sealant. Ceilings and walls are permanently joined together, eliminating tiny seams through which a spy might coax a microphone. Even hanging a picture is nearly always prohibited because it requires putting a hole in the wall. The heating and air-conditioning ductwork is soundproofed and guarded by steel, either by heavy grilles or half-inch-thick bars welded both vertically and horizontally in six-inch intervals. The plumbing is designed not to carry electric signals, lest someone use the pipes to detect conversations. Utility lines for the rest of the building are not allowed near these rooms. And every cable that serves them is threaded through a single opening. Cell phones are prohibited.

In Chelsea, the room was down the hall from Borelli's office, protected by a numeric lock. The keypad looked like the numbers on a telephone, only with a digital display. When the keypad was activated, the numbers rearranged themselves randomly, so even if someone nearby were trying to sneak a peek, he wouldn't be able to crack the code by memorizing the order.

New York's secure room was cavernous. Roughly a hundred agents spent most of their working hours there, organized in cubicles, with supervisors seated in small offices around the windowless perimeter. For most, there was no point in having a work space in the main office. Just about everything they said or did each day was too sensitive to share with their spouses, friends, and even most of their coworkers on the other side of the locked door.

Borelli found an empty cubicle. Each workstation contained three computers: an unclassified system for everyday work and email, one that contained intelligence marked secret, and one that stored top-secret information. The systems were kept separate so a hacker or a tech-savvy employee with a low-level clearance couldn't worm his way into the top-secret network. It was this last computer, the most secure of the three, that contained the Operation High Rise files. He logged in and began to read.

The High Rise files showed that, three days earlier, government eavesdroppers had intercepted emails sent from the United States to a Yahoo account in Pakistan linked to an al-Qaeda operative. U.S. intelligence officers had been monitoring the account as part of their own terrorism investigation.

The first email began innocuously but took a cryptic turn. The sender, using a computer in Aurora, was trying to get the measurements right for what seemed like a recipe involving flour and ghee, a thick, clarified butter used in Pakistani cooking. He included his phone number and asked for help. When there was no immediate reply, the sender asked again minutes later. The second email had set off alarm bells.

"All of us here r good and working fine. plez reply to what i asked u right away. the marriage is ready flour and oil."

Marriage and *wedding* were among al-Qaeda's favorite code words for impending attacks. The 9/11 attacks had been code-named "the big wedding." It referred to the day that a suicide bomber met his brides, the maidens of the hereafter. Shortly before the millennium celebration on January 1, 2000, authorities intercepted a phone call in which a terrorist said, "The grooms are ready for the big wedding." That call helped disrupt a plot to bomb Los Angeles International Airport. It was a running joke in the counterterrorism world that the US was lucky al-Qaeda couldn't come up with a better code word.

FBI analysts had traced the Aurora email address and phone number to a twenty-four-year-old Afghan immigrant named Najibullah Zazi. He had spent most of his young life in New York, where he'd lived in Queens and run a coffee cart in the Financial District. He had been living in Aurora, a suburb of Colorado's capital, Denver, for only a few months. He'd followed his aunt and uncle out there, and his parents had recently arrived, too. Travel records already in the case file showed that last year Zazi had flown to Peshawar, a bustling city in northwest Pakistan on the border of Afghanistan with a long history of harboring al-Qaeda and Taliban operatives.

Using flight manifests and seating charts, FBI analysts in Washington had concluded that Zazi probably had not traveled alone. They were confident that two others joined him: Zarein Ahmedzay, a New York taxi driver, and Adis Medunjanin, a security guard in Manhattan.

Zazi had spent nearly five months in Pakistan. Now he was on the move again.

For nearly a decade, the FBI's biggest fear had been the formation of a terrorist cell trained by al-Qaeda and operating inside the United States. The most recent close call was fresh in Borelli's mind. A year earlier, the FBI had arrested a New Yorker named Bryant Neal Vinas, who had traveled to Pakistan and received al-Qaeda training. The US government hunted him down before he could return to America, but it left Borelli with a nagging worry: What if someone like Vinas managed to get training and come back undetected? A US citizen, radicalized at home and trained abroad, could wave his US passport at the airport and return home with the skills to carry out an attack.

With Zazi, that threat appeared to be unfolding.

"This is a no-shit real deal," Borelli thought.

If this really were an al-Qaeda cell, a single misstep could send the terrorists scurrying underground. Or worse, they might be spooked into carrying out their attack ahead of schedule, before the FBI even had a chance to stop it. Borelli didn't know who was involved or what they were planning.

What he did know from looking at the case file was that the Denver field office of the FBI had full surveillance on Zazi and his family. Agents watched the night before as Zazi's father, Mohammed, drove his son to a Hertz franchise not far from their house. Mohammed put down his credit card and rented a car for his son. Surveillance teams were in pursuit that morning when Zazi awoke early, got into the red Chevrolet Impala with Arizona plates, and pulled out of the town house subdivision where he lived with his parents.

Aurora is east of Denver, and it's the last area of traffic in and out of the city. From there Interstate 70 turns into a high-speed straightaway through farmland and empty Colorado grassland. Zazi gave the Impala some gas and pushed it upward of ninety miles per hour. The surveillance agents called back to the Joint Terrorism Task Force in Denver, warning that they risked losing him. And if they kept pace, Zazi might figure out he was being tailed.

Borelli's counterpart in Denver, a man named Steve Olson, asked the Colorado State Patrol to arrange for Zazi's car to be stopped. The be-on-the-lookout call went out on the radio and was picked up by Corporal Gerald Lamb, on patrol in the tiny town of Limon—more than an hour east of Denver—directly in Zazi's path. It wasn't unusual for a federal agency to ask for a stop like this, and Lamb, a trooper with sixteen years' experience, didn't think much of it. It might be a drug dealer or a fugitive. It didn't really matter.

Shortly after seven o'clock in the morning, Lamb spotted the red Impala and called the dispatcher. He asked to be put through to the FBI and was soon talking directly to Olson. "We just need to know where he's headed," the FBI agent explained.

He didn't tell Lamb why, and Lamb didn't expect him to. That was a routine practice, meant to keep local lawmen from inadvertently revealing the existence of a larger investigation.

For Lamb, finding probable cause to stop the car was easy. He figured that Zazi was going at least 90 miles per hour before he'd noticed the police cruiser in his rearview mirror and began slowing down. Still, the radar flashed 73 in a 65-mph zone, and Lamb flipped on his blue lights. Zazi eased the car to the shoulder of the road, alongside the tall grass and wilting brown wildflowers. Lamb approached the driver's side window and recited the usual script.

"Good morning. I'm Corporal Lamb with the Colorado State Patrol. I contacted you today for your speed."

Zazi handed over the rental paperwork, and Lamb was surprised to see that he was listed as a secondary driver. People rarely pay extra for that. Lamb asked the young man where he was headed.

"New York," Zazi replied.

Where in New York?

"Queens."

Zazi immediately started in on how he needed to meet the man who was running his coffee stand. The guy had been sending him $250 a month out of the profits, but business had been down, so Zazi was taking it back over himself. He figured he'd drive to the city rather than fly so he could run errands while he was there.

Lamb didn't know what the FBI wanted with this guy, but there was definitely something off about him. He was overly friendly and talkative, almost nervously so. Nobody volunteered that level of detail by the side of the road. Plus, given the cost of gas, it didn't make sense for Zazi to rent a car and drive to New York. On a normal day, Lamb would have kept Zazi talking to get to the bottom of it, but that wasn't the assignment. Ask too many questions, and Zazi might suspect that he was being tailed. He told Zazi that he'd only be writing him a warning and asked him to sit tight.

Back in his cruiser, Lamb took notes on the cardboard backing from one of his empty citation books. He knew the FBI would want to know exactly what was said. He didn't call Olson back, worrying that Zazi would glance in the rearview, see him on the phone, and speed off.

Lamb handed Zazi a written warning and decided to press the conversation ahead a little longer.

I know Queens, he said. Where in Queens?

He tried to make it sound casual. In his sixteen years with the state patrol, Lamb had worked his way up from a communications officer to the rank of corporal. He'd never been to New York, much less to Queens. He was raised in the central Colorado steel city of Pueblo. But he nodded knowingly when Zazi replied, "Flushing Meadows," the home of the New York Mets and the US Open tennis championship.

As Zazi's car pulled back into traffic, Lamb called the FBI again and relayed what he'd learned. Olson listened calmly. He didn't say much and thanked the trooper for his help.

Until that moment, Najibullah Zazi had been a big deal for the FBI in Colorado. He immediately became a major concern for the bureau nationwide.

In New York, Borelli sat back, feeling a weight settle on his shoulders. In the immediate aftermath of 9/11, the FBI would have plucked Zazi off the road right then. It would have locked him up, like so many Muslim men, on ambiguous charges. Or the agency would have declared him a "material witness" and toss him in jail. Better that than letting a potential terrorist remain on the loose for one second more than necessary. But those days were over. First, internal investigators had eviscerated the FBI for detaining so many people indiscriminately. And second, there was a growing belief inside the bureau that such tactics only increased the terrorist threat.

Lock up Zazi, and they might never know what he was up to. In his email to the al-Qaeda operative, the young man had written, "All of us here r good and working fine." Who else was involved? Was he planning something in New York or running from something already under way in Colorado? Assuming that he was a terrorist and working with others, arresting him could send everyone running into the shadows to regroup. The FBI knew nothing about Zazi and didn't have nearly enough evidence to charge him with any real crime. Whoever this guy was, it looked as though he'd be pulling into New York in less than twenty-four hours. In that time, Borelli needed to learn everything about this man: who he was, whom he planned to meet, and, most importantly, what he was capable of doing.

In forty-eight hours, it would be the eighth anniversary of 9/11. On that day, hijackers from the fanatical Islamic terrorist group al-Qaeda, based in Afghanistan, steered airplanes into the World Trade Center, the Pentagon, and a Pennsylvania field. Al-Qaeda, Arabic for "the Base," formed in 1988. Its leader, Osama bin Laden, declared war on the United States in 1996 for stationing soldiers in Muslim countries, but it would take a strike in the heart of Manhattan five years later for the public to take notice. Almost three thousand people died that day, prompting the invasion of Afghanistan and planting the seeds of fear that grew into a call for war with Iraq. The attacks changed how people voted, how they traveled, and how they looked at Muslims in their neighborhoods. Americans accepted a more powerful, secretive government that kept an intrusive watch on its citizens.

Some of these changes occurred in the open. Six weeks after the attacks, Congress overwhelmingly passed the USA Patriot Act, which expanded the government's ability to monitor phone calls, emails, even library transactions. New warrants, called "sneak and peeks," allowed federal agents to secretly enter people's homes without immediately notifying them. City police installed cameras on street corners.

Other changes, the government made in secret. The president authorized the National Security Agency to turn its wiretapping powers on Americans. The government kept tabs on bank transactions. It built classified watch lists that, once on, were nearly impossible to escape.

As this power grew, Americans could do little but trust that the counterterrorism programs were effective. They accepted the changes, both seen and unseen.

In exchange, they expected security.

• • •

Despite Borelli's growing sense of urgency, the office around him was quiet and calm. Many FBI agents were out working cases. When Borelli made it across the room, already reading the file was Jim Shea, the deputy chief with the New York Police Department. He was assigned to supervise the NYPD detectives who worked alongside the FBI on the Joint Terrorism Task Force each day. The task force is designed so federal agents are in the same room as state and local departments, allowing information to be shared quickly. The FBI runs the show, but everybody has a seat at the table, from the CIA to transit police. Everybody has access to the same files.

The JTTF was created in New York in 1980, when ten FBI agents and ten city detectives teamed up to investigate the Armed Forces of National Liberation, better known as FALN, a terrorist group seeking Puerto Rican independence. The group claimed responsibility for deadly bombings in New York, at the landmark Fraunces Tavern restaurant in 1975, and the headquarters of Mobil Oil two years later. Before the task force was formed, the FBI and the NYPD ran independent investigations. Witnesses were sometimes interviewed twice, and detectives and agents competed for access to evidence and to be the first to execute search warrants or make arrests. It was not only a logistical mess but also jeopardized investigations and made it easier for defense attorneys to punch holes in cases.

The formation of the task force was an attempt to solve all that. The NYPD detectives assigned to it had top security clearances and were deputized as federal marshals, which meant they could investigate outside the city's borders, where NYPD jurisdiction normally ended.

After 9/11, city task forces became the centerpiece of the nation's law enforcement response to terrorism. There were now roughly one hundred task forces, big and small, in cities around the country. But there was nothing like the New York JTTF. In any other major city, the municipal police department contributed maybe a handful of officers to the effort. In New York, more than one hundred NYPD officers participated. Shea oversaw all of them. He'd been there six or seven months and already had a reputation as all business, which the agents appreciated. A former US Marine, he was tall and lean, with a short haircut to match his temper.

"Have you heard about this case?" Borelli asked.

"Yeah, I know," Shea said.

By now there were signs of movement. Phones were starting to ring in the secure room. Emails were coming in. Through official channels and interoffice chatter, word spread that something was going on.

Borelli and Shea began assembling their teams, ordering investigators on the streets to get back to Chelsea. Zazi, in order to drive into New York, would need to take a state highway and either a bridge or a tunnel. Those were the purview of the New York State Police and the Port Authority of New York and New Jersey, two other agencies represented on the task force. The situation as they knew it was that an Afghan-American had spent five months in Pakistan, was in contact with a known al-Qaeda email address, used an al-Qaeda code word for an attack, and was speeding toward New York.

"This thing is going to unravel so fucking fast," Borelli said.

"Put out the warning order," he told his team. Nothing else mattered. Postpone all plans. "Christmas is canceled."

Bill Sweeney and officials at headquarters in the J. Edgar Hoover FBI Building on Washington's Pennsylvania Avenue had scheduled a video teleconference in about an hour to coordinate the operation. Agents from Denver were following Zazi across the country, and headquarters wanted to make sure that the responsibility passed seamlessly from one field office to the next as he approached New York. Denver had already tapped Zazi's cell phone, and agents were listening to his calls in real time. By the time the teleconference began, Borelli would be expected to have started surveillance on the men who'd traveled with Zazi to Pakistan: Zarein Ahmedzay and Adis Medunjanin. He'd need taps for their phones, too.

Dozens of FBI agents would soon be on the streets. Borelli needed someone who could keep track of them, plus the information coming from Denver and Washington. Running a command center was a thankless, stressful job. Borelli approached Ari Papadacos, a supervisor on the terrorism financing squad whose expertise predated 9/11. At the time, Papadacos was running an investigation into the Alavi Foundation, an organization that promoted Islamic and Persian culture. The FBI believed it was a front for the Iranian government. Based on that casework, the US Justice Department was preparing to confiscate Alavi's $600 million building on Fifth Avenue, which would be one of the biggest counterterrorism seizures in US history.

"Hey, buddy," Borelli said, all smiles as he strolled up to Papadacos. "Whatcha workin' on this week?"

Borelli took the elevator to the eighth floor and entered the large conference room known as the Joint Operations Center. It looked a bit like the sales floor in some boiler-room call center, with flat-screen televisions on the walls and computers set up on long tables. A row of digital clocks displayed the time in every US time zone. This was the room that the FBI used to oversee massive operations such as manhunts

16

and the New Year's Eve celebration in Times Square. It was now open for business.

There was one more organization to call. Besides the many city police officers assigned to the federal task force, the NYPD had its own intelligence unit, a separate squad that operated in near secrecy and fancied itself a miniature CIA for New York's five boroughs. Unlike Shea's cops on the task force, the detectives from the intelligence unit were not federal marshals. Most did not have security clearances. Often the task force was in the dark about the NYPD Intelligence Division's activities. That was by design. While Borelli and Shea favored a single, collaborative investigation led by the Joint Terrorism Task Force, the Intelligence Division went its own way. That occasionally enraged both the FBI agents and the NYPD officers assigned to the task force. The competitive, often adversarial relationship had bruised plenty of egos and even undermined investigations.

• • •

The division was the brainchild of the city's sixty-eight-year-old police commissioner, Ray Kelly, and his top intelligence official, David Cohen. There was a mythology surrounding the division, the result of Kelly and Cohen's eagerness to boast about its capabilities while simultaneously refusing to say how exactly it carried out its business. Even its organizational chart was a secret. And the secrets held, thanks to a city council that never asked questions and a New York media that spared the Intelligence Division much serious scrutiny.

Everyone knew, however, that Kelly and Cohen had built a deep roster of undercover officers, a web of informants, and teams of linguists and analysts that were unrivaled by any police department in the country. It was clear where Cohen saw his four-hundred-person division, with a budget of $43 million, in the city's law enforcement hierarchy.

"We've got the feds working for us now," Cohen had boasted in a fawning 2005 *New Yorker* profile of the new, post-9/11 NYPD.

NYPD Intelligence, or simply Intel, as both the FBI and NYPD often called it, was across the street from the FBI's office in Chelsea, above the upscale food court of Chelsea Market and near the New York offices of the Food Network and ESPN. There was even a footbridge connecting the FBI and Intel offices. But it was locked at both ends. The two organizations never quite seemed to be on the same team.

A year earlier, NYPD Intel had been keeping tabs on a Staten Island man named Abdel Hameed Shehadeh, whose anti-American views were taking an increasingly violent tone. He confided in a close friend that he hoped to wage violent jihad, or holy war in defense of Islam, and dreamed of dying a martyr. He said he wanted to fly to Pakistan and find his way to a terrorist training camp.

Shehadeh's friend was an NYPD informant, yet Cohen's detectives never crossed the footbridge to tell the FBI what they knew. They worked the case in secret for months, until Shehadeh was headed to the airport, his bags packed for an al-Qaeda camp. Only then did the FBI get a phone call. Cohen wanted to let Shehadeh into Pakistan and send an undercover NYPD detective there too. On the seventh floor of FBI headquarters, top counterterrorism agents were stunned. They knew nothing about this case and, with the clock ticking, they were being asked to help arrange an international covert operation for a municipal police department. Absolutely not. People could get killed.

Yet FBI agents had no probable cause to keep him off an airplane. They hadn't been involved in the investigation and hadn't developed evidence against Shehadeh. So the agents pulled strings with their Pakistani counterparts and had him turned back at the airport in Islamabad, the capital of Pakistan. That bought them time to build a case, but a much weaker one. The incident enraged the FBI and contributed to the perception that Cohen was more interested in making sure that his guys got the credit than in preventing another attack. On the other side of the footbridge, the Intel brass believed that the FBI wouldn't be happy until it was in charge of everyone.

Despite camaraderie with the NYPD detectives who worked under Shea, many in the FBI, including Borelli, did not trust Cohen. But the truth was, if anyone would have insights into Zazi and his accomplices, if anyone would have a neatly organized dossier or a well-placed informant, it would be NYPD Intel. Like it or not, Cohen and his team were going to be involved in the Zazi case.

NYPD Intel was emblematic of a post-9/11 mind-set. In the aftermath of the attacks, the government persuaded Americans that keeping them safe required new rules and a new way of thinking. To some US officials, the FBI seemed a relic. The bureau was designed to investigate crimes after the fact, but terrorists needed to be stopped before they attacked. Defeating them, Vice President Dick Cheney said days after 9/11, required going to the "dark side." That meant imprisoning people indefinitely without charges, locking them in secret jails and using interrogation tactics that the United States once considered torture. The FBI did not participate in such efforts and fended off arguments that it was not cut out to fight terrorism.

"FBI officials want arrests and convictions," William E. Odom, former head of the National Security Agency, wrote in a 2005 *Washington Post* opinion piece calling for the creation of a domestic CIA. "FBI operatives want to make arrests, to 'put the cuffs on' wrongdoers. They have little patience for sustained surveillance of a suspect to gain more intelligence."

The military instituted a new legal system for suspected terrorists captured abroad and held at the Guantánamo Bay naval base in Cuba. Hearsay evidence and coerced confessions were admissible and, even if you won your case, there was no guarantee that you'd go free. In an America where the government could eavesdrop without warrants and lock citizens in a military prison without charges, the FBI's reliance on indictments, respect for the accused's right to remain silent, and adherence to the rules of evidence seemed anachronistic.

Kelly and Cohen were in the vanguard of the new security elite.

They recast the Intelligence Division's role, didn't concern themselves with arrests and convictions, and focused instead on disrupting terrorist attacks.

The FBI and NYPD had spent eight years and billions of dollars preparing for this moment. Their strategies differed, but, thanks to nearly a decade without a successful al-Qaeda attack in the United States, the debate over what worked in the fight against terrorism was largely academic. For all the money spent, for all the informants recruited, and for all the emails and phone calls intercepted, most terrorism cases in the US since 9/11 followed a similar script: An undercover agent sold a fake bomb to a dim-witted, angry young man and then arrested him. Press releases followed. From the early hours of the investigation, it was clear that Zazi and his friends were different. They were going to test the government's programs and its philosophies.

Like most FBI agents of his generation, Borelli hadn't signed up to fight terrorism. Armed with a business degree from the University of Southern California in 1983, he'd landed a promising job at Arthur Andersen, one of the Big Five accounting firms. But he'd quickly grown bored of the minutiae of ledger entries, and he dreaded the certified public accountant exam. Borelli didn't want a life behind a desk, staring at numbers. He wanted excitement, and the FBI seemed like a good place to start. When he arrived at the FBI Academy in Quantico, Virginia, he was twenty-five years old—the third youngest in his class. He imagined that life as a G-man would mean kicking in doors, gun drawn. But as a young agent in Dallas, Borelli's first assignment was to investigate the savings and loan crisis that was wiping out hundreds of banks. There he was, sitting behind a desk, staring at numbers. He considered quitting but stuck it out. He learned to investigate real estate fraud and other financial crimes.

Finally, in 1988 Borelli he got the adrenaline rush he'd always wanted. He joined the Organized Crime Drug Enforcement Task Force, which was responsible for infiltrating Mexican drug cartels. He signed up for tactical training, which allowed him to join the SWAT team on predawn raids. Between shifts, he squeezed in classes that got him certified as a paramedic. In 1993, when federal agents stormed the Branch Davidian compound in Waco, Texas, to arrest cult leader David Koresh on weapons charges, Borelli was inside a Bradley armored fighting vehicle nearby, waiting to treat the wounded.

Legions of FBI agents were reprogrammed to fight terrorism after 9/11. It was a massive organizational change. For Borelli, though, it wasn't that big a shift. His work as a medic had made him part of a national initiative to counter the threat of weapons of mass destruction. That's what led him to Africa after the 1998 embassy bombings and to Yemen two years later, when al-Qaeda attacked the USS *Cole* Navy destroyer, killing seventeen American sailors. He'd become one of the bureau's go-to agents on terrorism and was part of a small group that had seen the al-Qaeda threat up close. So after 9/11, when headquarters put out the call for volunteers to go overseas, it was an easy decision. Borelli raised his hand.

Borelli, who was divorced, worked long, unpredictable hours. In his one-bedroom apartment, he drank out of plastic cups and ate off disposable plates so he wouldn't have to do the dishes. After two and a half decades at the bureau, most of the agents who'd worked alongside him through the height of the war on terrorism were packing it in. Some took cushy, high-paying jobs overseeing security at Fortune 500 companies. Others were making money in government consulting. In a year, he, too, would be eligible to retire, maybe start a second career.

The truth was, he lived for nights like this.

2

A SPY IN NEW YORK

David Cohen didn't come to the NYPD in 2002 to make friends with the feds. And in his seven years on the job as the NYPD's top intelligence officer, he certainly had not.

Prominently displayed on the wall of his office at One Police Plaza in Lower Manhattan was a framed copy of a newspaper article from 2007. The story described how, on Cohen's orders, the NYPD stopped Iranian president Mahmoud Ahmadinejad's motorcade at John F. Kennedy Airport. Ahmadinejad was in New York to attend the opening of the United Nations General Assembly, and, like the other world leaders, he arrived with an entourage of armed security guards.

All the details, including who would be there and how many would be armed, had been worked out in advance with the State Department. Ahmadinejad was hardly a beloved figure in Washington, but he and his colleagues were traveling on diplomatic visas and had to be afforded the same treatment that American diplomats expected overseas. No pat-downs, no delays. The Iranians were allowed to have eleven armed guards, and the State Department felt comfortable that's exactly how many they had.

But the Iranian motorcade had an NYPD escort, and that car refused to move. Cohen suspected that the Iranian delegation had brought more weapons than it had acknowledged. The NYPD wanted to run a handheld metal detector over each Iranian before the motorcade was allowed to leave. It was a flagrant breach of diplomatic protocol, and the Iranians wouldn't stand for it. It was ugly, too, for the State Department, which had no patience for the NYPD's meddling. The standoff lasted about forty minutes before police allowed the motorcade to leave the airport.

"Way to go, NYPD," the New York *Daily News* cheered afterward. Though the incident infuriated the State Department, it sent a message to the Iranians and to the Washington bureaucrats: In New York, David Cohen makes the rules.

The slight, bookish, and bespectacled Cohen had clashed with several arms of the government but most frequently with the FBI. In public, the NYPD and the FBI always wore their brightest smiles and sang each other's praises when talking about their partnership. But as the city approached the eight-year anniversary of 9/11, with word spreading through the top ranks of the NYPD about an apparent terrorist plot in motion, relations between the bureau and Cohen's Intelligence Division were especially chilly.

A few months earlier, Cohen had been caught running an undercover operation far outside his jurisdiction, out of an apartment near the Rutgers University campus in New Brunswick, New Jersey, forty miles from Manhattan. Using a fake name, an NYPD detective rented a first-floor apartment in a building filled with graduate students and young professionals. Ordinarily, when an officer conducts an investigation out of state, he coordinates with the local and state police. If it's a terrorism case, the FBI expects a call too. Cohen kept the NYPD operation secret. The undercover officer was there to manage operations around the state and, posing as a student, to keep tabs on the Muslim student group at Rutgers.

The whole thing fell apart when a building superintendent unlocked the apartment door to conduct an inspection. The place was nearly empty, with no sign that anyone had been there for weeks. Surveillance photos of nearby buildings and terrorist literature were strewn about the table. When the building manager called 911, he and the dispatcher sounded equally confused.

"The apartment has about—has no furniture except two beds, has no clothing, has New York City Police Department radios," the manager said.

"Really?" the dispatcher asked.

"There's computer hardware, software, you know, just laying around," the manager continued. "There's pictures of terrorists. There's pictures of our neighboring building that they have."

"In New Brunswick?" the dispatcher asked, her voice rising with surprise.

Fearing the apartment was the base for a terrorist cell, New Brunswick police officers and agents from the FBI's Newark, New Jersey, office rushed to the building. It didn't take them long to figure out what was going on. The local police closed the matter with a one-page report and a simple note: "Through Police investigation, it was determined there was no evidence of criminal activity found at that location."

At the FBI, the incident met with a mixture of anger and amusement. On the one hand, what was Cohen doing sending officers into New Brunswick without telling anyone? On the other, the operation was amateurish. What kind of detective leaves police radios and surveillance photos sitting in an unmanned safe house?

The FBI seized everything in the apartment, forcing on Cohen the humbling task of asking the agents for his stuff back. Though the story hadn't made the news, it was a complete embarrassment, even inside NYPD Intel. Cohen didn't mind when FBI agents pounded their fists in anger. But now they were rolling their eyes.

Despite this testy relationship, there was never any doubt that Cohen would be brought into the Zazi investigation. In any other city in America, the investigation would be the unquestioned responsibility of the FBI. State and local police would help, but it would all run through the local Joint Terrorism Task Force. But New York, with eight million residents, the stock exchange, the Statue of Liberty, and a permanent scar from terrorism, wasn't like any other city. No other city had an intelligence division like the NYPD's. And no department had anybody quite like David Cohen, backed by the most powerful figure in American policing.

• • •

Weeks after the September 11, 2001, terrorist attacks, when the residents of his Lower Manhattan apartment complex were finally allowed back into the building, Raymond Kelly and his wife, Veronica, went up to the roof. They lived in Battery Park City, on the Hudson River, a block from the World Trade Center. They looked out over the heap of twisted metal and watched it still smoldering.

The towers were part of their neighborhood. Back in February 1993, during the final year of Mayor David Dinkins's administration, Kelly was the police commissioner when terrorists detonated a truck bomb in the garage below the North Tower. Six people were killed and more than a thousand were injured in an explosion that left behind a 130-foot crater. Later, when the building was finally declared safe and the shops in the concourse reopened, Kelly was one of the first customers to return while the rest of the city was still on edge.

Through it all, Kelly was confident and reassuring, declaring, "We must remember that fear is a type of weapon as well, one to which we must not submit."

That was all in the past. He was out of government. He'd enjoyed a decadelong career with the NYPD and a stint with the US Customs Service. In the mid-1990s he directed an international police force in Haiti during the turbulent period after president Jean-Bertrand Aristide returned to power. Now Kelly was watching a crisis from the sidelines. He had a lucrative job as director of corporate security for the Wall Street investment bank Bear Stearns. But his city—his neighborhood—was shattered, and he felt powerless.

Though his name had been floated in the press as a possible candidate to return to his old job at One Police Plaza, that seemed unlikely. Two weeks before the mayoral election, his preferred candidate, billionaire Republican Michael Bloomberg, trailed Democrat Mark Green by 16 points in the polls. Besides, Kelly wasn't angling for a comeback. He'd made it clear that, on the off chance that Bloomberg won, he was going to persuade the current police commissioner, Bernard Kerik, to stay on the job.

Outgoing mayor Rudy Giuliani, though, would change Bloomberg's— and Kelly's—fate. With little more than a week left in the race, Giuliani, who was riding a wave of immense popularity after the terrorist attacks, endorsed Bloomberg on the steps of city hall. Bloomberg quickly flooded the airwaves with a sixty-second advertisement that was more of a farewell from Giuliani than a rallying call for Bloomberg.

"It's been an honor to be your mayor for eight years," Giuliani said in the ad. "You may not have always agreed with me, but I gave it my all. I love this city. And I'm confident it will be in good hands with Mike Bloomberg."

The man whom the media was calling "America's mayor" had spoken. Voters turned out for his handpicked successor. Bloomberg won by 2 percentage points. And when Kerik declined the offer to stay on the job, Kelly was the obvious pick for police commissioner. He was sixty years old, but he'd never lost the discipline or posture of his days as a marine lieutenant during the Vietnam War. He stood square shouldered and always perfectly upright, making the most of his roughly five-foot-eight height. With a barrel chest, buzz cut, and a smile that verged on a smirk, the native New Yorker had been compared to Popeye, if the comic strip hero ever traded his sailor uniform for a custom-made suit and pocket square.

There was more than a bit of irony in Giuliani's role in Kelly's reappointment. Back in 1993, it was Giuliani who had swept Dinkins from office by portraying the administration as weak on crime. Never mind that Kelly had inherited a department beset by corruption, losing the fight against crack and still smarting from its disastrous handling of a deadly 1991 riot in Brooklyn's Crown Heights. Never mind that it was Kelly—not Giuliani, as has been said repeatedly—who started the crackdown on the homeless squeegee men who harassed drivers at red lights and demanded money for washing their windows. And never mind that crime rates started ticking downward on Kelly's watch.

Giuliani dismissed Kelly's strategy of community policing. He thought it forced cops to act like social workers. In late 1993, Giuliani held a secret meeting at the Tudor Hotel on Forty-second Street to give Kelly a chance to argue for his own job. But as soon as Kelly mentioned community policing, the mayor-elect cut him off and ended the meeting. Kelly was finished.[1]

By putting more police on the streets and using computerized crime mapping, Giuliani oversaw a seemingly miraculous turnaround in crime, one that changed policing strategies worldwide. But now, weeks after 9/11, with Kelly poised to retake the NYPD's top job, the city was suffering from a very different malaise.

It was not the racially charged city that Kelly had patrolled as a young officer in 1968, back from Vietnam, where he had conducted coastal raids and search-and-destroy missions and saw battle in the Que Son Valley.[2] And it was no longer a city of two thousand murders a year, as it was when he was police commissioner the first time. When Kelly last led the force, six in ten New Yorkers said that crime was their top issue. Now the city was a safe tourist mecca but on edge nevertheless.

It wasn't only because of 9/11. On the heels of those attacks, anthrax started arriving in the mail. The day before Bloomberg was voted into office, a sixty-one-year-old hospital stockroom worker was buried in the Bronx. She'd died of anthrax inhalation, despite no known contact with any of the letters. Then, on November 12, 2001, the day after news of Kelly's imminent reappointment was leaked to the media, American

Airlines Flight 587, destined for the Dominican Republic, took off from JFK and immediately crashed in a Queens neighborhood, killing all 260 people on board and 5 more on the ground. It turned out to be an equipment failure, but the government closed airports, bridges, and tunnels all over the country as a precaution.

The threat of terrorism had changed America's views overnight. Television pundits debated the benefits of torturing prisoners or shipping them off to countries that would do it.

"Torture is bad," CNN's Tucker Carlson said, but then added, "Keep in mind, some things are worse. And under certain circumstances, it may be the lesser of two evils. Because some evils are pretty evil." [3]

FBI agents around the country, and particularly in New York, were rounding up hundreds of Muslim immigrants on suspicion of a connection to the 9/11 attacks. They were held in secret, typically without charges and without contact with their families or lawyers. Many were abused physically or verbally.

The suspects were held on immigration charges, but the reasons for suspicion were often dubious. One grocery store employee was arrested after someone called the FBI and reported that the store was being run by Middle Eastern men. There were two to three grocers on each shift, which the caller said was "too many people to run a small store." For this, the worker was treated as part of the 9/11 investigation. [4]

It was against this backdrop that Kelly prepared for his return to One Police Plaza, the first man to rise from cadet to police commissioner and the first person to hold the top job twice.

His encore performance called for a new approach. Kelly had been a cop all his adult life and, throughout his career, the NYPD was ready to respond to whatever came its way. It was one of his detectives, working alongside a Bureau of Alcohol, Tobacco and Firearms agent, who found a vehicle identification number in the debris following the 1993 World Trade Center bombing. That helped police locate the rental agency that owned the truck and, ultimately, the terrorist who'd rented it.

But the NYPD never had a chance to prevent that bombing. And that attack had done nothing to change the attitude of the federal government—specifically the FBI—which rarely gave local police the information it needed ahead of time. After 9/11, the debris field a block away from Kelly's apartment had crystallized the notion that as long as the federal government controlled all the information, the NYPD was merely waiting to respond to the next attack, helpless to prevent it.

That was unacceptable to Kelly. The NYPD needed its own intelligence unit, one that would rival the FBI in ability and focus on New York in a way the FBI never could. Kelly knew the man to run it.

• • •

In November 2001, two months before being sworn in, Kelly called Cohen and offered him a job as the NYPD's deputy commissioner for intelligence, a new position. The two men had never worked together, but they'd met back in the mid-1990s, when Kelly was working in the private sector and Cohen was the CIA's station chief in New York,

Like Kelly, Cohen had since left government for Wall Street. He was a vice president for the global insurance giant American International Group. He'd been in the job for only about a year, and he told Kelly he'd need a few days to think about it.[5]

It was a rare opportunity not just to return to intelligence work but also to build something from scratch. He'd joined the CIA in 1966 as a twenty-six-year-old economist, a slender young man with a firm jaw and conservative pompadour haircut in the style of a young Ronald Reagan. Cohen left in 2000, having served as the top operations officer in the entire agency. And during those nearly thirty-five years, he'd been at his best when he found opportunities to create something.

Back in the 1980s, he started an analytical team to investigate terrorism; the first of its kind at the agency. In 1991 he forced the merger of the CIA's two domestic units, believing that they would operate better as one, with him at the helm. Then in 1996, years before Osama bin

Laden entered the public consciousness, and at a time when many in the CIA regarded the scion to a wealthy Saudi family as little more than a moneyman, Cohen assigned a dozen officers to gather intelligence on him. That unit, known as Alec Station, built the foundation for everything the CIA would come to know about bin Laden.

But while Hollywood often portrayed the CIA as an all-knowing intelligence service capable of sophisticated espionage and cunning, the real CIA could be a bureaucratic morass. It was often reactive, rushing to respond to whatever crisis bubbled up in the world or whatever had upset some senator or congressman. Changing anything on its own meant dealing with micromanagers at the White House and meddling politicians on Capitol Hill. That meant real vision—real change—was seldom realized.

Cohen saw those forces at their worst. He was there for one of the most tumultuous times in the agency's history, a period that shaped his views on intelligence gathering.

On February 21, 1994, FBI agents arrested veteran CIA officer Aldrich Ames on espionage charges. In a decade of work for the Soviet Union, Ames compromised covert operations against the Russians and revealed the names of more than thirty spies. The betrayal caught the CIA by surprise, but it shouldn't have. Time and again, there had been signs that Ames was trouble. He failed polygraphs. He slept on the job. He had money and drinking problems. Once, he left a briefcase full of classified information on a New York subway. He walked out of the CIA with shopping bags full of classified documents. Yet his behaviors were explained away and tolerated in the insular, protective club of the nation's spies.

His arrest and guilty plea triggered a level of scrutiny of the CIA not seen since the 1970s. The case portrayed the agency as cliquish, secretive, and at times borderline incompetent. In December 1994, after enduring scathing reports about the Ames fiasco from Congress and the agency's inspector general, CIA director R. James Woolsey resigned.

President Bill Clinton replaced him with John Deutch, a senior Pentagon official and a Massachusetts Institute of Technology–educated expert in nuclear proliferation.

As if the Ames case weren't enough of a headache for Deutch to inherit, shortly before he took office, New Jersey representative Robert Torricelli revealed that a paid CIA asset in Guatemala had been linked to the killings of one American citizen and the husband of another. Worse still, the CIA kept the informant on the payroll even after it learned about his involvement. Congress had been kept in the dark for years about exactly what the CIA was doing in Guatemala, where the agency had been fighting suspected Communists for years.

Right away, Deutch announced that most of the agency's senior managers would be gone by the end of the year. He formed a committee to find a new deputy director for operations, the formal title for the nation's top spy. It had to be someone without deep ties to the clandestine service and the culture that led to Ames and Guatemala. The agency needed someone who could handle the rigors of running covert operations but who also represented a break from the past.

David Cohen, a surprising choice to many, was announced as the new deputy director for operations, on July 31, 1995.

Cohen was taking one of the most prized jobs in the CIA: the person overseeing every clandestine officer. But while he'd risen through the ranks during the height of the Cold War, when the agency battled the Soviet KGB in the greatest spy war the world had ever known, Cohen had never been a spy. He'd never worked overseas. He'd never evaded hostile intelligence agents, or tried to turn the tide of a war, or worked to undermine the spread of Communism. He came from a very different CIA.

At its core, the CIA is made of up two groups: spies and analysts. And they jockey fiercely for recognition and influence.

The Directorate of Operations, or DO, is home to the spies. (The section is now formally called the National Clandestine Service but is still colloquially referred to internally as the DO.) Their careers are the stuff of novels. They are the ones who travel on fake passports, pass coded messages, evade and conduct surveillance, and dress up to attend embassy parties. They encouraged dissent inside the Soviet Union, tried to recruit spies behind the Iron Curtain, and were constantly suspicious that the Russians had turned one of their own against them.

Cohen came from a much more staid, academic section of the CIA known as the Directorate of Intelligence. The DI, as it's known, is home to the analysts. They take all the information—from the spies, the satellites, the military, the wiretaps, and more—and stitch it together in hopes of making sense of the world. Erudite and patient, they toil quietly in secure rooms, reading what comes in and turning it into what's called finished intelligence, the reports that land on the president's desk. Unlike the CIA men of the movies, the analysts do not drive flashy sports cars. They wait in the long line of family sedans, minivans, and SUVs that forms each morning outside the gates of CIA headquarters in Langley. As per stereotype, the spies are the sharp dressers; the analysts less so. Once, one of Cohen's aides told him that he couldn't possibly go into an important meeting looking so unkempt. He wasn't even wearing a belt. Cohen demanded one from a subordinate and marched into the conference.[6]

The analysts see the spies as cowboys, more interested in the thrill of the mission than the pursuit of facts. The spies deride the analysts as professors who always want more, better information and don't appreciate how hard it is to operate in the field.

So when Cohen, a career analyst, was tapped to run the world's premier spying service, the longtime officers were stunned. Like any large office, CIA headquarters was prone to backstabbing and political maneuvering. Unlike your typical company, however, office politics at the CIA were played by people *trained* to lie, cheat, and manipulate. The best covert actions, officers said sardonically, were run inside the building.

The closest that Cohen had ever come to being a spy was in the late

1980s, when he was tapped to run the National Collection Division, the arm of the agency responsible for overt collection of intelligence inside the United States. Much like the NYPD Intelligence Division that he would inherit decades later, National Collection was seen as something of a backwater posting. Officers stationed in major US cities would identify and interview American professors or businessmen whose overseas travels regularly took them to hostile countries.

At the same time, there was another CIA division operating inside the United States. The Foreign Resources Division was considered the A team of domestic operations. These officers were in America as part of their normal rotation, meaning that they arrived from overseas postings, often in trouble spots. They knew how to spy, and they looked down on National Collection. In the United States, the Foreign Resources officers recruited foreigners to become paid informants, or assets. They excelled at a trade known as "spotting and assessing." They'd identify graduate students from, say, China or the Soviet Union, figure out if they were likely candidates to work for the agency, and then slowly develop them as assets. Eventually they'd return home, and the CIA stations overseas would pick up where Foreign Resources left off, managing the assets and giving them assignments to spy for America.

Cohen looked at these two CIA teams and came to the conclusion that the organization needed to be changed. Why were his officers politely asking for information or waiting for a helpful walk-in to show up while the Foreign Resources officers were out recruiting real spies? As an analyst, he understood the value of what the agency was learning from these professors and experts, but he believed there shouldn't be a wall between their work and that of Foreign Resources. The CIA could save money and streamline operations if the two divisions were consolidated. Cohen, with a bit of charm and often by force of will, began to merge and take charge of both divisions.

It helped that his deputy was Gustav Avrakotos, the legendary CIA case officer whose exploits arming Afghan Muslims in the fight against occupying Russian forces formed the basis of the book and movie *Char-*

lie Wilson's War. Avrakotos had run his generation's most successful covert operation; Cohen had never been part of one. His first operation of any kind came on Veterans Day 1987, when an officer took Cohen along for an informant meeting in a Washington-area hotel room. As an unexpected storm dumped a foot of snow on the region, the CIA men turned up the television to prevent anyone from eavesdropping or taping their conversation. Cohen was hooked.[7]

But as far as the career spies were concerned, Cohen's stint at National Collection hardly qualified him to take the top job in American spy craft. CIA veterans swiftly delivered their verdict—anonymously—in the pages of America's newspapers and magazines. One retired officer told *U.S. News & World Report* in 1995 that Cohen had a "management by fear" philosophy. Another described him as "a company man from the word go" who will "find out which way the wind is blowing and then go with it." In the *Washington Times*, a former officer said Cohen was a hard-nosed outsider who wasn't very well liked.

It didn't help that Cohen had a reputation for an acerbic leadership style and an abrasive personality. He liked to swear, and, in the words of one longtime colleague, "If he thought you were an idiot, he'd say so." That was one of his favorite words. For subordinates, it wasn't clear what was worse, being called an idiot in the middle of a meeting or wondering whether Cohen was calling them an idiot after they'd left the room.

He'd call subordinates at any hour to talk through whatever had popped up in his head. It kept people constantly wondering what issue they would be pulled onto next. But while Cohen could be intimidating and aggressive, he was also prescient. He had been one of the first people in the agency, well before the Berlin Wall came down in 1989, to talk seriously about globalization. Cohen envisioned a world where economies became intertwined, where multinational corporations blurred the political boundaries between nations, and where terrorists and criminals operated across borders.[8]

Colleagues called him a fast talker, a reference both to the speed with which he spoke and to the fact that some saw him as a confidence man, always playing the angles. Melvin Goodman, an expert on the Soviet Union who worked with Cohen in the 1980s, regarded him as a quick study and a hard worker but believed he was cooking the intelligence to curry favor with his hard-line anti-Communist bosses. "He's the kind of guy who, after you deal with him, you feel like you should wash your hands," Goodman would remark years later.[9]

John Deutch and Cohen got along well, however. Deutch, a native of Brussels, Belgium, who, like Cohen, was educated in Massachusetts, saw his new deputy as direct and plainspoken. As far as he was concerned, the fact that Cohen had never run a covert operation overseas and had spent most of his career as an analyst in no way disqualified him from overseeing the agency's worldwide spying efforts.

"Who the fuck cares" where someone comes from as long as he's qualified? Deutch said. "I think that's silly."[10]

Still, longtime operatives looked for any reason to dislike Cohen. Early in his tenure, he held a meeting with the senior leaders overseeing Middle East operations. As he talked, he referred to the citizens of Jordan—the Jordanians—as "the Jordans." The room was filled with the agency's foremost experts on the Middle East, who looked at one another with blank stares that reflected a shared thought: "What is this guy doing running operations?"[11]

Cohen's tenure could have been an opportunity to remake the clandestine service for a post–Cold War world. Ames and Guatemala forced an unusual level of introspection onto an agency that was institutionally averse to it. And Cohen was undoubtedly capable of anticipating the next big thing. But any interest that Cohen had in long-term planning was overrun by Congress and the White House.

• • •

Bill Clinton had come to office in 1993 promising to cut the roughly $30 billion annual intelligence budget. On Capitol Hill, the mood was even worse. The chairman of the Senate Intelligence Committee, Dennis DeConcini, thought the CIA's reports were too unreliable to justify such a hefty price tag. New York senator Daniel Patrick Moynihan introduced a bill to abolish the CIA. The Guatemala scandal had revealed that the agency was doing business with people who had awful human rights records. Congress demanded a reckoning.

In response, Deutch fired two longtime and well-liked agency veterans and ordered a top-to-bottom review of the CIA's books. Cohen and his team began examining the backgrounds of every asset on the CIA's payroll. Those with too much baggage, whose unsavory histories outweighed their value to the United States, were cut loose. The "asset scrub," as it was known, was tantamount to heresy. CIA officers made their reputations by recruiting informants. Now headquarters was opening the books on their careers' work and dismissing their accomplishments. The fact that Cohen, an analyst, was running it made it even worse.

Deutch, Cohen, and the agency's lawyers came up with new rules for recruiting. If you wanted to recruit someone with blood on his hands, you needed approval from headquarters. It was never intended to be an outright prohibition; it was supposed to provide some review before the CIA put a torturer or a terrorist on the payroll. But in the field, coming on the heels of Guatemala, the message was clear: Don't bother recruiting anyone with a distasteful history.

The asset scrub made Cohen's workforce risk averse. At the CIA, those words are the ultimate insult, a shorthand way of saying that the agency doesn't have the stomach for difficult operations. Cohen saw it as the result of a broken system. As soon as an operation went bad, Congress and the White House were quick with recriminations. Fear of being second-guessed led to stifling deliberations. The way Cohen saw it, by subjecting covert operations to review by a battery of lawyers, the government was signaling a clear disapproval for such missions.[12]

As budgets were cut and agency recruits slowed to a trickle, Cohen earned a new name that would stick with him long after he left the CIA. To his employees, he was often known as Fucking David Cohen or, in the alternative, David Fucking Cohen. He knew that carrying out Deutch's directives made him unpopular. He didn't care. A good leader was decisive; someone who made tough calls even when they were unpopular. But he came to believe that Deutch had made things harder by speaking so publicly about his intentions to overhaul the agency. The lesson Cohen took away was that if you want to make changes, do it. Strong leaders don't make changes by talking about them in the newspaper ahead of time.[13]

It would prove to be a disastrous time to make budget cuts and stop taking risks. The roots of Islamic terrorism were taking hold. The 1993 truck bombing, carried out by Muslim terrorists with the same grievances that would later inspire al-Qaeda, proved that terrorists could strike inside America. As the United States focused more on spy satellites and less on old-fashioned spy craft, Osama bin Laden was gaining power and influence.

Instead of devising a grand plan to address this changing world, Cohen was forced to spend much of his time fending off cuts or at least directing the ax to lower-priority programs. He fought efforts to close overseas stations and defeated attempts to absorb Alec Station's money into the general counterterrorism budget, where it would undoubtedly disappear. Cohen recognized that the CIA had little coherent counterterrorism strategy, but that hardly mattered. With limited Arabic language skills, few new recruits, and a reluctance to hire spies, the agency was ill equipped to carry out a strategy even if it had one.

For its part, Alec Station made progress despite the cuts. The team quickly learned that bin Laden was running his own terrorist group and was linked to several attacks against US citizens, including the 1992 bombing of a hotel where US military personnel were staying in Yemen and the 1993 shootdown of Black Hawk helicopters on a peacekeeping mission in Somalia. By the fall of 1998, two years after the team was formed, the CIA had bin Laden in its sights and was rehearsing a covert operation to swoop into Afghanistan and capture him.[14]

Cohen would not be around to see those drills—or to see Washington put the brakes on the plan. Deutch was forced to resign as Clinton prepared for his second term. In May 1997, with George Tenet ready to become the fifth CIA director in about as many years, the *New York Times* editorial board called on Tenet to make the agency more accountable and to rein in the clandestine service. In an unusual move, the newspaper called for Cohen's head.

"He needs a deputy director for operations able to make change stick," the paper wrote. "David Cohen, the incumbent, is wobbly and should be replaced."

Tenet sent Cohen packing for New York, a plum preretirement assignment that made him the CIA's primary liaison with Wall Street titans and captains of industry. After three decades in Washington, he had become one of the most unpopular and divisive figures in modern CIA history. He left feeling that the agency was hamstrung by the people overseeing it. The White House micromanaged operations, slowing down everything. And Congress used its oversight authority to score political points. The CIA was stuck in the middle, an impossible position.

Now Kelly was offering a chance to start something new in the New York Police Department, without any of the bureaucratic hand-wringing or political meddling. The World Trade Center attacks had changed the world. Cohen was being given an opportunity to change policing in response.

He didn't need a couple days to think about it. He called Kelly back two hours later and took the job.

Bloomberg and Kelly introduced Cohen as the deputy commissioner for intelligence at a city hall press conference on January 24, 2002. Cohen spoke for just two minutes, mostly to praise the NYPD. He had been raised in Boston's Mattapan neighborhood, and though he'd been gone for decades, he still spoke with a heavy accent.

"We need to understand what these threats are, what form they take, where they're coming from, and who's responsible," Cohen said.

He did not make the same mistake that Deutch had made. The new deputy commissioner offered no specifics about what he had planned. Weeks before his sixtieth birthday, he even declined to give his age, telling reporters only that he was between twenty-eight and seventy. The brief remarks from behind the lectern would amount to one of Cohen's longest media appearances ever.

"I look forward to just getting on with the job," he said.

Cohen's appointment was not front-page news. The *New York Times* put the story on page B3. The *Daily News* ran a 165-word brief on page 34. It was four months after 9/11, and the country was focused on doing whatever it took to prevent another attack. Nobody questioned the wisdom of taking someone trained to break the laws of foreign nations and putting him in a department responsible for upholding the rule of law. Nobody even checked out Cohen's hand-prepared résumé, which said he had a master's degree in international relations from Boston University. In fact, his degree was in government.[15] The misstatement itself was inconsequential. That it went entirely unquestioned was indicative of the lack of media scrutiny Cohen could expect in his new job.

It didn't take him long to realize that he was not walking back into the CIA. The NYPD had an intelligence division, but in name only. Working primarily out of the waterfront offices of the old Brooklyn Army Terminal, across the Hudson River, facing New Jersey, the detectives focused on drugs and gangs. They were in no way prepared to detect and disrupt a terrorist plot before it could be carried out. Mostly, they were known as the glorified chauffeurs who drove visiting dignitaries around the city.

Cohen knew that more was possible.

Force of will alone, however, would not transform a moribund division into something capable of stopping a terrorist attack. If Cohen wanted to remake the NYPD into a real intelligence service, there were four men—four graying hippies—standing in his way.

Martin Stolar first began hearing stories about the NYPD Intelligence Division in 1970 while working as a young lawyer for the New York Law Commune. A recently formed law firm for leftists, hippies, radicals, and activists, the commune operated entirely by consensus. It didn't take a case unless everyone agreed. They saw themselves as part of the New Left, lawyers who didn't merely represent their clients but who fully embraced their politics and were part of their struggle. They represented Columbia University students who'd taken over campus buildings during a protest in 1968. They stood beside members of the Weather Underground, the Black Panthers, and other radical groups, and activists such as Abbie Hoffman. And they never, ever, represented landlords in disputes with tenants.

It was a new way of thinking about the law. The firm pooled all its fees and then paid one another based on need, not ability or performance. Operating out of a converted loft in Greenwich Village, the lawyers paid the bills thanks to well-to-do parents who hired them to keep their sons out of Vietnam. But about half their time was dedicated to political, nonpaying clients.

Every now and again, one of the lawyers would come across something—a news clipping, a document, or a strong hunch—that suggested the NYPD was infiltrating activist groups and building dossiers on protesters. When they did, they'd add it to a plain manila folder, as something to revisit.

Stolar had no problem questioning government authority. In 1969 he applied for admission to the bar in Ohio, where he was an antipoverty volunteer. When asked if he'd ever been "a member of any organization which advocates the overthrow of the government of the United States by force," Stolar refused to answer. Nor would he answer when asked to list every club or organization he'd ever joined. The questions were holdovers from the Red Scare days of the 1950s. Stolar, a liberal New York lawyer, would have none of it. He took his case to the United

States Supreme Court, which, in 1971, declared such questions unconstitutional. "[W]e can see no legitimate state interest which is served by a question which sweeps so broadly into areas of belief and association protected against government invasion," Justice Hugo Black wrote.

Stolar had moved back to New York by then and never bothered to return to Ohio to take the bar exam. He'd proven his point.

In 1971 he was among the many lawyers working on the Panther 21 case, the trial of Black Panther Party members accused of conspiring to bomb police stations, businesses, and public buildings. While preparing their defense, the Law Commune attorneys came across something unusual: The case against the Panthers was built largely on the testimony of some of the earliest members of the New York chapter of the Black Panthers. There was Gene Roberts, a former security guard for Malcolm X who was present on February 21, 1965, when the Nation of Islam leader was assassinated in Manhattan's Audubon Ballroom. There was Ralph White, the head of the Panther unit in the Bronx who'd once represented the entire New York chapter at a black power conference in Philadelphia. And there was Carlos Ashwood, who'd sold Panther literature in Harlem.

They were founding fathers of the New York Panthers. And all three, it turned out, were undercover detectives. The NYPD had essentially set up the New York chapter of the Black Panther Party and built files on everyone who signed up.

That convinced Stolar that something had to be done with his manila folder. He called another young lawyer, Jethro Eisenstein, who taught at New York University. The two knew each other from their work with the liberal National Lawyers Guild, and Stolar regarded Eisenstein as a brilliant legal writer. If they were going to have a shot at challenging the NYPD, the lawsuit had to sing.

Together they put out the word to their clients and friends that they were looking for stories about the NYPD. The anecdotes came pouring in, both from activists and from other lawyers who, it turned out, had been keeping folders of their own. The mass of materials described a police department run amok. There was evidence that police were collecting the names of people who attended events for liberal causes. Detectives posed as journalists and photographed war protesters. Police infiltrated organizations that they considered suspect and maintained rosters of those who attended meetings.

•   •   •

On May 13, 1971, the Panthers were acquitted of all charges. At the time, it was the longest criminal trial in New York history, spanning eight months. Closing arguments alone had stretched over three weeks. But the jury was out only three hours before voting for acquittal. And the first hour was for lunch.

In the courthouse lobby, jurors milled about, congratulating the Panthers and their lawyers. Some exchanged hugs. Jurors said there wasn't enough evidence that the conspiracy was anything more than radical talk. Defense lawyer Gerald Lefcourt called the verdict "a rejection of secret government all the way from J. Edgar Hoover down to the secret police of New York City."

The *New York Times* editorial page read:

> *It is not necessary to have any sympathy whatever with Panther philosophy or Panther methods to find some reassurance in the fact that—at a time when the government so often confuses invective with insurrection—a New York jury was willing to insist on evidence of wrong-doing rather than wrong-thinking.*

Five days after the verdict, Stolar and Eisenstein filed a twenty-one-page federal lawsuit against the NYPD. It accused the department of widespread constitutional violations.

The plaintiffs represented a grab bag of the New Left. There were

Black Panthers, members of the War Resisters League, and gay-rights advocates. There were well-known figures such as Abbie Hoffman and obscure groups like the Computer People for Peace. One young man, Stephen Rohde, sued because when he applied for admission to the New York bar, he'd been asked whether he'd ever opposed the Vietnam War. He had once signed a petition in a basement at Columbia University, and his views had ended up in a police file.

The lawsuit became known as the Handschu case, after lawyer and activist Barbara Handschu, who was listed first among the plaintiffs. Stolar and Eisenstein argued that the NYPD was using its surveillance tactics to squelch free speech. Police Commissioner Patrick Murphy did not deny using those tactics. Rather, he said, they were necessary to protect the city. Murphy devoted eighteen pages to explaining to the court why the NYPD needed an effective intelligence division. He said the effort began in the early 1900s as a response to the Black Hand Society, an extortion racket run by new Sicilian immigrants. As the threat evolved over the decades, so did the unit. The 1960s, Murphy said, was a dangerous time to be in New York. Along with antiwar protests, student unrest, and racial conflicts, he cited a list of terrorist bombings and what he called "urban guerrilla warfare."

In response to that threat, Murphy explained, the NYPD stepped up its investigations of political groups that "because of their conduct or rhetoric may pose a threat to life, property, or governmental administration." It was true, Murphy conceded, that a portion of that rhetoric might be political speech, protected by the Constitution. But that was the reality of a world in which some people used violence to achieve political goals. The police needed informants and undercover officers to figure out whether political groups were planning criminal acts.

"Without an effectively operating intelligence unit, the department would be unable to deal effectively with the many problems that arise each day in the largest, most complex, and most unique city in the world," Murphy wrote.

The intelligence unit of that era was an early example of what would become known as mission creep: the slow expansion of a government program far beyond its initial goals. Originally the NYPD investigated Italians, and then anarchists. Germans and Japanese were next, during World War II. Then came the Cold War, which turned the NYPD's focus to Communists. From there it was easy to cast suspicion on union leaders, whose prolabor views suggested they might be Communist sympathizers. By the 1960s, police looked at antiwar protesters as subversives who needed to be watched. Peaceful groups such as Women Strike for Peace were infiltrated, not because of any actual intelligence but as a precautionary measure.[16]

As the Handschu case dragged on for years, the NYPD acknowledged more and more about its tactics. There was an NYPD "extremist desk" and an NYPD "black desk" to investigate African Americans. Police monitored labor disputes. They conducted surveillance on political organizations formed by future presidential candidate Lyndon LaRouche.[17] Police maintained a huge library of intelligence documents. There were hundreds of thousands of case files and more than a million index cards containing people's names.[18] And since the intelligence unit did not make arrests, police said it was impossible to know how many of those investigations actually led to charges and how many simply collected information on people.

As it turned out, these NYPD tactics were part of a nationwide domestic surveillance boom during the 1960s and 1970s. The FBI was running its own nationwide spying operation, known as Cointelpro, short for counterintelligence program, which fed the CIA thousands of reports on American citizens. The FBI spied on liberal groups, civil rights leaders, journalists, and critics of US policies. Together the FBI and CIA built what was called the "watch list," a roster that began with counterintelligence threats to the United States and grew to include antiwar groups, authors, publishers, scientific organizations, and scholars interested in the Soviet Union.

The CIA, too, was spying widely on the antiwar movement. Presidents Johnson and Nixon used the CIA to find out whether the New Left was part of a campaign by foreign governments to destabilize the US government. The agency developed Project Chaos, a program that collected intelligence on domestic protest groups. Hundreds of thousands of Americans were put into agency records. Another operation, known as Project Merrimac, infiltrated antiwar and black activist groups, ostensibly to give the government an early warning of demonstrations. A third operation, Project Resistance, compiled intelligence about student radicals on campuses nationwide.

As the CIA described it in a cable to overseas offices in 1968:

Headquarters is engaged in a sensitive high priority program concerning foreign contacts with US individuals and organizations of the "Radical Left." Included in this category are radical students, antiwar activists, draft resisters, and deserters, black nationalists, anarchists, and assorted "New Leftists." [19]

Every major report that came out of Project Chaos concluded that foreign agents were playing no significant role in the protest movement. But these were met with skepticism by the White House, which demanded that the CIA look harder. Often the information collected was innocuous. But senior CIA officers felt that, over time, even seemingly insignificant information might shed light on the intentions of these domestic groups. So the information was retained as a way to generate leads. Soon the names of roughly 300,000 Americans were indexed in CIA computers. About 7,500 had files on them. [20]

The Handschu lawyers didn't know it at the time, but their lawsuit against the NYPD was part of a changing tide in America. The Pentagon Papers (officially titled *Report of the Office of the Secretary of Defense Vietnam Task Force*), a secret history of the Vietnam War leaked to the *New York Times* in 1971, showed that the government had lied to the public. Then came Watergate, the scandal that revealed the dirty tricks of President Richard Nixon and forced him from office.

Americans were no longer willing to take it on faith that their government was acting honestly or in the nation's best interest. The country was asking difficult questions about what role intelligence agencies should play in a free, open society.

In 1974 *New York Times* reporter Seymour M. Hersh published a blockbuster story outlining how the CIA had violated its charter by spying on Americans. Under the headline "Huge C.I.A. Operation Reported in U.S. Against Antiwar Forces, Other Dissidents in Nixon Years," Hersh revealed one of the most invasive operations in the agency's history. In response, two congressional committees began investigating the CIA. Before that, congressional oversight of the agency was nonexistent.

The ensuing investigation, led primarily by Idaho senator Frank Church and ten colleagues, cast into the public light many of the agency's most embarrassing and controversial operations: a list known internally as the "Family Jewels." The Church Committee revealed assassination plots, illegal mail openings, a covert propaganda campaign in Chile, and the unauthorized storage of toxins such as anthrax and smallpox. But the transcendent issue was the one Hersh brought to light: the spying on US citizens.

Congress responded by forming intelligence committees in both the Senate and the House in 1976 and 1977. It gave itself oversight of the way that presidents carried out intelligence activities at home and abroad. It was the very bureaucracy that would so frustrate Cohen decades later.

It would take nearly another decade before the lawsuit over the NYPD's surveillance was resolved. In 1985 the city settled the Handschu case and agreed to court-established rules about what intelligence the NYPD could collect on political activity. Under the rules, the department could investigate constitutionally protected activities only when it had specific information that a crime was being committed or was imminent. Undercover officers could be used only when they were essential to the case, not as a way to keep tabs on groups. Police could no longer build dossiers on people or keep their names in police files without specific evidence of criminal activity.

To ensure that the rules were being followed, the court created a three-person oversight committee. Two senior police officials and one civilian appointed by the mayor would review each police request for an investigation. Only with the majority approval of that board could an investigation proceed into political activity.

There were four primary lawyers on the case now. Stolar and Eisenstein were joined by Franklin Siegel, another early member of the New York Law Commune, and Paul Chevigny, an attorney with the New York Civil Liberties Union. Even after the rules went into effect, the Handschu lawsuit remained open. That way, if the lawyers ever caught wind that the NYPD wasn't following the guidelines, they could haul the police department before a judge. And if the NYPD wanted to change the rules, it had to talk to these four men first.

Just as the legacy of the Church Committee was greater transparency at the CIA, the Handschu case put a check on the NYPD's powers. But the Handschu guidelines, as the rules became known, also withered the division that Cohen would later inherit

On the morning of September 11, 2001, Intelligence Division detectives rushed to Lower Manhattan, but when they arrived, they realized their helplessness. They stood there on the street for hours, waiting for someone to tell them what to do. "Stand by" was all they heard. They stood by as World Trade Center 7 collapsed in a plume of dust and smoke and they waited as darkness began to fall on New York. Some were sent toward ground zero to escort surgeons onto the pile, where they conducted emergency amputations or other lifesaving procedures. Others gathered at the Police Academy, where Deputy Chief John Cutter, the head of the Intelligence Division, put them on twelve-hour shifts. He told them to contact their informants.

It was both the right command and a useless one. Nobody there had informants plugged into the world of international terrorism. But the detectives did what they were told. They called dope dealers and gang members and asked what they knew about the worst terrorist attack in US history.

They worked alongside the FBI out of makeshift command centers aboard the decommissioned aircraft carrier and museum USS *Intrepid* and in an FBI parking garage, where some detectives sat on the concrete floor. They responded to the many tips called in by a jittery public. They questioned Muslims whose neighbors suddenly deemed them suspicious and visited businesses owned by Arab immigrants.

This was exactly the kind of reactive, aimless fumbling that Cohen wanted to do away with when he came aboard. He envisioned a police force that was plugged into the latest intelligence from Washington and that generated its own intelligence from the city. If an al-Qaeda bomber were ever to set his sights on New York again, Cohen wanted his team to be able to identify the plot and disrupt the plan. The rules needed to change.

• • •

Stolar, the attorney who'd brought the Handschu lawsuit decades earlier, listened on September 20, 2001, as President George W. Bush went to Congress and declared war on terrorism. He knew things were about to change. The way he saw it, once the government declares war on something—whether it be poverty, drugs, crime, or terrorism—the public quickly falls in line and supports it.

But this former radical, who witnessed police fire tear gas and beat antiwar demonstrators during Chicago's 1968 Democratic National Convention and who was part of some of New York's most turbulent times, was surprisingly naive about what was to come. He talked to his wife, Elsie, a public defense lawyer, and told her it was only a matter of time before the FBI hunted down the people who planned the World Trade Center attacks. They would be prosecuted in Manhattan's federal court, he said, and they would need lawyers. Even the worst people in the world deserved a fair hearing and staunch defense. If the choice presented itself, Stolar and his wife agreed, he should take the case. As it turned out, there would never be any criminal trials. The suspected terrorists would be shipped to a military prison in Guantánamo Bay, where the government created a new legal system.

Stolar and his fellow Handschu lawyers also misjudged the NYPD's response to the attacks. In early 2002, Eisenstein wrote to the city and said that, despite the tragedy, the Handschu guidelines represented an important safeguard of civil liberties. Eisenstein said that he and his colleagues were available if the city wanted to discuss the rules in light of the attacks. The city lawyers said they would consider it. Eisenstein didn't hear anything for months. Then, on September 12, 2002, a twenty-three-page document arrived from someone named David Cohen.

Cohen's name wasn't familiar to Stolar, but as he skimmed the document, it didn't take long to reach a conclusion: "This guy wants to get rid of us completely."

The document, filed in federal court in Manhattan, had been months in the making, and Cohen had chosen his words carefully. He explained his background; his thirty-five-year career in the analytical and operational arms of the CIA. Invoking the recent attacks on the World Trade Center, he said the world had changed.

"These changes were not envisioned when the Handschu guidelines were agreed upon," he wrote, "and their continuation dangerously limits the ability of the NYPD to protect the people it is sworn to serve."

Like Commissioner Murphy's affidavit about NYPD surveillance on radical groups in the 1960s, Cohen painted a picture of a nation— in particular a city—under siege from enemies within. Terrorists, he said, could be lurking anywhere. They could be your classmates, your friends, or the quiet family next door.

"They escape detection by blending into American society. They may own homes, live in communities with families, belong to religious or social organizations, and attend educational institutions. They typically display enormous patience, often waiting years until the components of their plans are perfectly aligned," Cohen said.

He recounted the 1993 World Trade Center bombing, the attacks on embassies in Africa, the 1995 bombing of the Alfred P. Murrah Federal Building in Oklahoma City, and plots against landmarks in New York.

America's freedoms of movement, privacy, and association gave terrorists an advantage, he said.

"This success is due in no small measure to the freedom with which terrorists enter this country, insinuate themselves as apparent participants in American society, and engage in secret operations," he wrote, adding, "The freedom of our society has also made it possible for terrorist organizations to maintain US-based activities."

The stakes, Cohen said, could not be higher.

"We now understand that extremist Muslim fundamentalism is a worldwide movement with international goals. It is driven by a single-minded vision: Any society that does not conform to the strict al-Qaeda interpretation of the Koran must be destroyed. Governments such as ours which do not impose strict Muslim rule must be overthrown through Jihad," he said.

Faced with this threat, Cohen said, the police could no longer abide by the Handschu guidelines. Terrorists, like the violent radicals of the previous generation, often cloaked themselves behind legitimate organizations. The police had to be able to investigate these groups, even when there was no evidence that a crime was in the works.

"In the case of terrorism," Cohen wrote, "to wait for an indication of crime before investigating is to wait far too long."

Inside the NYPD, the document was regarded as a masterwork, one that clearly spelled out Cohen's view of the threat and what it would take to fight it. It was the foundation for everything the department would build. It was part autobiography, part history, and part ideology. One senior NYPD official took to calling it Cohen's *Mein Kampf*.

In the federal courthouse blocks from ground zero, Cohen's words carried great weight. When the new deputy commissioner for intelligence said that waiting for evidence of a crime made it impossible to fight terrorism effectively, Judge Charles Haight said he had no reason to doubt it. Cohen said that the NYPD sought only the same powers, with the same limitations, that the Justice Department had recently given the FBI. Haight had presided over the Handschu case for decades and was the one who approved the original rules. But he concluded that 9/11 required a new ruling for a new era. Again and again, Haight deferred to Cohen's expertise. The old guidelines, the judge ruled, "addressed different perils in a different time." The world had changed, and so, too, should the rules.

Haight did away with the requirement that the NYPD launch investigations only when it had specific evidence that a crime was being committed. And he eliminated the rule that police could use undercover officers in political investigations only when they were essential to the case. Now police could launch an investigation, including one with undercover officers, whenever there was the possibility that a crime could be committed.

The three-member panel—the one intended as a check on police authority—was stripped of its power. The board could now investigate allegations of wrongdoing after the fact but no longer had authority to decide what police could investigate. That power was placed in Cohen's hands. He'd never been a cop, never made an arrest, never had to build a case or send someone to prison. But he was now the final word on how police collected intelligence in America's biggest city.

Cohen had been clear about what he intended to do. But not even the Handschu lawyers could envision how Cohen's new authority would alter the NYPD's mission. He had been given lenient rules and the sole authority to enforce them, exactly what he'd said he needed for the NYPD to detect and disrupt a terrorist plot.

He didn't yet know the name Najibullah Zazi, but he knew that was precisely the kind of person he needed to stop.

3

HEADING EAST

DENVER
Wednesday, September 9, 2009

Zazi continued east on I-70, past grain elevators and tiny frontier towns toward the Kansas plains and miles of sunflowers. It was mid-morning, and the top FBI officials in Colorado assembled in a glass-walled conference room known as the "fishbowl" in a downtown Denver federal building. The building, a relic of the 1960s, was overdue to be renovated. The wall-to-wall carpet, matted and worn in spots, was a leaf motif set in seafoam, khaki, and olive. It looked like something from a far-off-the-Strip Las Vegas casino. Depending on where you stood, the place smelled faintly of sewage.

Gathered were the field office's senior agents, who met on every big case. But on the morning of September 9, they were joined by two unusual visitors: a case officer and an analyst from the CIA. The email address that had been traced back to Pakistan was, without question, an operational al-Qaeda address. There was no doubt about that. The CIA officials did not reveal that the NSA had been using a highly classified program called Prism to monitor the address, but such details didn't matter to the FBI agents. Everyone in the room knew the government monitored suspicious foreign emails—sometimes with specific warrants, sometimes without.

The CIA made clear that officials had been watching the Sana_Pakhtana@yahoo.com account for months. Five months earlier, the British Security Service, better known as MI5, arrested twelve people in the English cities of Manchester and Liverpool on suspicion of being part of a terrorist plot. The suspected ringleader had been cheerfully emailing with the supposed Sana Pakhtana about his search for a wife and plans for a *nikah*, the Arabic word for wedding.

"I met with Nadia family and we both parties have agreed to conduct the nikah after 15th and before 20th of this month," read one email sent shortly before the arrests. "Anyways I wished you could be here as well to enjoy the party."

The Brits were fairly sure that Sana Pakhtana was linked, either directly or indirectly, to al-Qaeda's global operations chief, a man named Saleh al-Somali.[1] The case against the dozen men arrested in Britain had fallen apart for lack of evidence. But that didn't change the opinion, either in the United States or Britain, that one of al-Qaeda's most senior operatives was behind that email account. And anyone sending chummy messages to that account represented a threat.

Jim Davis, the FBI special agent in charge, was already convinced that the Pakistani email address was serious business. He'd understood that since Steve Olson from the FBI's Joint Terrorism Task Force first called him during a Labor Day cookout and told him about the suspicious email exchange. Davis was less certain about the Colorado email. And that's what he wanted to know more about. Could there have been some mix-up? Email routes can be faked. Was it possible the Yahoo computer server was located in Colorado but the sender was somewhere else? The FBI had a team of agents chasing a man across the country, all because of that email. How sure was everyone about the trace?

The CIA said it was certain. The email tracked back to a computer in an apartment in a gated town house community in Aurora, a diverse suburb that had ballooned into a city of three hundred thousand, making it equal in population to Saint Louis and Pittsburgh. A man named Mohammed Wali Zazi was renting the apartment, and the email address was registered in the name of Najib Zazi, the nickname of Mohammed's son, Najibullah. There was no mistake.

For their part, the FBI agents at the table had seen cases like this before, and they didn't always pan out. A surprising number of stupid but ultimately innocent people send emails to al-Qaeda addresses that they find online. Then there are the fantasists who trawl jihadist websites and talk tough in emails but who the FBI quickly determines are all talk. Everyone at the table agreed this was different.

Davis leaned forward in his chair. At nearly six foot ten, he cut an imposing figure. He had dark hair, a baritone voice, and the build of a basketball power forward. Though friends joked that he couldn't string a noun and a verb together without some variation on the word *fuck*, he was even-keeled and easygoing.

"I need you to tell me if you have any reason to believe this isn't what it appears to be," he said, looking around the table. Olson from the task force was there. So were two assistant special agents in charge, Mike Rankin and Lisa Rehak. And, of course, the two CIA men. They all shook their heads. Nobody could offer an alternative explanation. And Zazi was closing in on New York.

"Okay," Davis said. "We're all in."

The Denver office oversaw ten satellite FBI locations in smaller, far-flung Colorado cities such as Pueblo, Grand Junction, and Glenwood Springs. Call them in, Davis said. Open up the command center. Until further notice, this was the most important FBI case in Colorado. Two time zones away, at the FBI in New York, Don Borelli was giving the same command to his team.

For both men, it was an order that carried risk. Like all large organizations, the FBI operates by the numbers. An agent is judged by the quantity and quality of his cases. His supervisor is judged by his squad's numbers. Redirecting people, even temporarily, inevitably meant putting other investigations on hold. In some instances, the delay would mean that agents missed their window of opportunity, and investigations would wither and die. If too many cases don't pan out, the supervisor might be passed over for a promotion.

The first order of business in Denver was finding someone to relieve the surveillance team that had been on Zazi's tail since early that morning. On prairie highways, truck drivers and road trippers can activate cruise control, flip on the radio, and zone out for a few hundred miles. Surveillance, however, is exhausting. An agent hiding in plain sight on an empty interstate can never shut off his brain. The team of four to eight cars following Zazi had to choreograph everything but appear entirely unscripted. They had to keep pace with the speeding car without looking like they were trying to keep up. If Zazi slowed down abruptly, the agents couldn't slow down with him. They had to be part of the anonymous flow of traffic zipping by. But they couldn't let him fall too far behind and slip away.

Sometimes, like when the FBI is following a suspected spy, surveillance teams can keep a close tail because the target already assumes he's being watched. In Zazi's case, the agents didn't want to be spotted. If he realized he was being followed, he might abandon his plan, and the FBI wouldn't know who else was involved. So they needed to tail him, but not too closely. Even day-trippers with nothing to hide notice the car in the rearview mirror that won't pass.

If a target pulls into a rest stop, someone on the surveillance team has to be close behind. Two minutes alone can be enough to meet a contact, get instructions, pick up someone, or drop off a package. If a target uses a pay phone, one of the agents has to be the next person to use that phone. She'll call an FBI number, introduce herself, and tell the voice on the other end that she's "marking this phone." The FBI can then trace the call and subpoena the phone company to find out what number was dialed moments earlier. Meanwhile, someone else has to pick up the tail when the target pulls back onto the highway. There are times when an agent needs to race ahead, maybe to get gas or use the bathroom, and then catch up with his team and let someone else do the same. Other times, when stopping is impossible, surveillance agents—both men and women—turn to their empty coffee cups for relief and press on.

It was a bad day, though, for Davis to be asking for surveillance backup. The FBI was preoccupied with another terrorism case, code-named Black Medallion. Agents were closing in on two men from Chicago who'd plotted attacks overseas and helped scout locations for a systematic shooting and bombing spree in Mumbai, India. Around the country, field offices were chasing leads and conducting surveillance on potential accomplices. At FBI headquarters, the bosses told Denver that they simply had no backup team to pick up Zazi in the Midwest.

Davis had a solution. He had a team in Denver to spare, but they were many hours behind. Thanks to the traffic stop, though, they knew where Zazi was headed. There were only a few routes from Colorado to New York that made sense. He'd stay on I-70 for sure through Kansas and Missouri. The drive across those two states alone was ten hours, maybe a little less, given how fast Zazi was driving. If Davis could get his surveillance team to Missouri, it could pick up the tail as Zazi cruised by. As it happened, the Denver field office owned an old ten-seat Beech-craft King Air turboprop plane that agents used to respond quickly to remote areas of the state. Four Denver surveillance agents packed their radios and gear onto the plane, and, a few minutes after noon, they were bound for Saint Louis. Like tourists, they would rent cars at the airport. When Zazi finished crossing Missouri, they would be ready to pick up the chase.

It was well past midnight when Zazi pulled into the first rest stop in Ohio, east of the Indiana line, about forty-five minutes outside Dayton. It had been a grueling full day of driving both for him and his pursuers. There was no gas or fast food at the rest stop, just a building with bathrooms, vending machines, and tourist brochures. There were two small parking lots, and, in the predawn quiet, the surveillance agents had to be extra careful to work unnoticed. If a bunch of cars pulled into the lot at the same time, the whole operation could be blown. One of the drivers, an FBI agent from Cleveland, steered his car to the far end of the lot, where he could observe Zazi inconspicuously. He watched as Zazi pulled the Impala into a parking spot next to a large white van. Zazi got out and went to the bathroom, and, from the agent's vantage point, it looked like Zazi talked to the driver briefly. And though he couldn't be sure, the agent believed he saw the van driver slip into Zazi's car. It was a bad vantage point. He couldn't tell if Zazi and the van driver, a white man, exchanged anything. When the van pulled away, the surveillance team was faced with a choice: split up to follow the van or have everyone stay on Zazi.

Zazi was the priority. That much had been made clear from the top levels of the FBI. Art Cummings, the bureau's top national security agent, who sits a few doors down from the FBI director in Washington, was getting regular updates on the pursuit. Across the Potomac River, in a building known as One Liberty Crossing, Jim McJunkin oversaw the FBI's worldwide international terrorism operations. More than once, Cummings had told McJunkin, "Don't lose him, Jimmy." Cummings was asleep on the leather couch in his office. Nobody wanted him to wake up to a call that Zazi was gone because half the team had followed a white van.

As the white van disappeared onto the highway, the FBI stayed put.

Zazi was observed sleeping in his car, but the bearded young man was up a short time later to continue toward New York City.

Thursday, September 10, 2009

At a morning videoconference with FBI agents from New York, New Jersey, Washington, DC, and Denver, there were more questions than answers. They still did not know what Zazi was planning or why he was in such a hurry to get to New York that he would drive 1,800 miles in two nearly sleepless days. Certainly, on the eve of the 9/11 anniversary, the calendar was all but screaming at them. If Zazi was being directed by al-Qaeda and coordinating with a cell inside the United States, the FBI had no idea who was involved. And Cummings was ticked that the surveillance team had let the white van, maybe its best lead so far, vanish into the night.

Back in Denver, Davis and Olson had round-the-clock surveillance on Zazi's family. In New York, the walls of the command center were covered in growing patches of easel paper. A timeline of Zazi's travels and a map of his relationships was coming into focus.

They didn't know whether the young man had anything dangerous in his car, but they all agreed on one thing: They could not, under any circumstances, allow Zazi into New York City as long as there was any possibility that the car might contain a bomb. Unspoken was the fact that, if Zazi were to blow himself up in northern New Jersey, that was one thing. Blowing himself up on the east side of the Hudson River, however, was quite another. If word got out that the FBI had allowed a suspected terrorist to enter New York the day before the 9/11 anniversary, the bureau would look terrible. Even if Zazi never managed to launch an attack, the FBI could expect to be skewered by Congress and in the press. Somebody had to stop Zazi and get a look in his car.

But getting that look would have to be done in a way that didn't arouse his suspicion. He'd already been stopped once, and the FBI didn't want to press its luck and signal to Zazi that he was being followed. If it turned out that there was nothing in the car, the agents wanted him unsuspecting and relaxed, or at least as relaxed as anyone can be after driving for more than a full day.

All signs were that Zazi was headed for Queens. He used to live there. He'd told Corporal Lamb by the side of the road in Colorado that he was going there. And he'd text-messaged his friend Zarein Ahmedzay, who lived in Queens, that he would arrive Thursday.

The easiest, most logical route to Queens was to pass through the island of Manhattan. a fact that worked in the FBI's favor. Everyone agreed that the two most likely ways for Zazi to enter New York were through the Holland Tunnel, connecting New Jersey and Lower Manhattan, or the Lincoln Tunnel, which feeds traffic into Midtown. Since 9/11, police had occasionally set up checkpoints at bridges and tunnels. They could do it again and make Zazi's stop look random. Nothing could look out of the ordinary.

That meant the FBI could definitely not make the stop. Black unmarked cars outside the tunnel and men in dark suits would advertise that something serious was afoot. A curious driver, delayed by the inevitable traffic backup, might call in a tip to a reporter, and before Borelli knew it, he'd be watching the whole thing live from the TVs on the wall of the command center. Nearly a decade had passed since 9/11, but even a whiff of a security issue in New York was still big news.

The police contingent on the task force, led by Jim Shea, wanted the NYPD to make the stop. It could post task force officers in blue uniforms on the bridge, and nobody would suspect this was a counterterrorism operation. The detectives on the task force had top-secret clearances, meaning they knew exactly what the stakes were and what they were looking for.

But bridges and tunnels belonged to the Port Authority of New York and New Jersey, an agency that controls much of the region's transportation infrastructure. Its technological wizards and fearless construction workers were behind some of city's great engineering feats of the early twentieth century. They burrowed tunnels beneath the Hudson River, working in caverns so deep that they had to enter through a series of airlocks to survive the high pressure. And they balanced precariously hundreds of feet in the air, building bridges the likes of which the world had never seen.

Now those bridges and tunnels fell under the jurisdiction of the Port Authority's police department. Though the force was constantly overshadowed by the NYPD, the Port Authority boasted 1,700 cops, as many as the Atlanta Police Department. Nobody had more experience making stops at bridges and tunnels. In a conference call, George Albin, an assistant chief with the Port Authority, assured the FBI that his officers could make the stop. They'd walk a bomb dog around the car and, just like at airports, use cotton swabs to check for trace amounts of explosives. They would do it quietly, without raising suspicion.

At FBI headquarters, Michael Heimbach, the head of counterterrorism, wanted to know more about what was allowed legally. He would need to brief Cummings, who would then need to tell the director that everything was being done by the book. If Zazi were stopped and police found a bomb, that would be the key evidence in the case against him, meaning that someday a prosecutor would need to get it admitted at trial. Heimbach was an affable twenty-year veteran agent who, even after moving into senior management, retained his reputation as a dogged investigator. That was no easy task in the FBI, where the bosses at headquarters are often labeled paper pushers by investigators in the field. Heimbach wanted to make sure that there was nothing out of the ordinary about a traffic stop like this. As for the Port Authority, it was business as usual. A few months earlier, its police were stationed outside the tunnels looking for drunken drivers. Convinced that they were on solid legal ground, headquarters gave its approval. The Port Authority would stop the car.

By the afternoon, a surveillance team from New Jersey had picked up Zazi's tail on Interstate 78, headed east toward Newark, Jersey City, and Lower Manhattan, north of the World Trade Center site. The team was backed up by an FBI airplane above. In an area that is crisscrossed by airplanes to and from Newark, LaGuardia, and Kennedy airports, spotting the FBI plane as suspicious would be next to impossible. There was no video feed of the pursuit, just audio. All the radio traffic was fed into the FBI office in Newark and to the command center in New York.

Holland Tunnel traffic was reduced to one lane in anticipation of Zazi's arrival. It was three o'clock. Tens of thousands of commuters would soon converge on the tunnel.

But Zazi turned onto I-95 and headed north toward the Lincoln Tunnel, a route that would drop him off a few blocks from Times Square. The Port Authority told its cops at the tunnel to be ready.

Minutes later, the radios in the surveillance cars crackled again. Zazi had passed the Lincoln Tunnel exit. The FBI command center was buzzing.

"Oh, shit."

"He's going to the bridge! He's going to the bridge!"

Port Authority officers in the room dialed their colleagues on the George Washington Bridge. It was a more roundabout route to Queens, but it was the last move that made sense. If Zazi didn't take the bridge, then he wasn't going to Queens, and the FBI would have no idea what was going on.

Spanning the Hudson River, the George Washington has two levels, each with twelve lanes. When it opened in 1931, it became the longest suspension bridge in the world, nearly doubling the span of the Ambassador Bridge in Detroit, the longest at the time. At almost a mile long, it is a marvel of engineering. And with more than 280,000 cars and trucks crossing in and out of northern Manhattan each day, it is also a surveillance nightmare.

Thomas McHale was in the FBI field office in Newark, listening as Zazi moved closer to the bridge. McHale, a Port Authority detective, had survived the 1993 World Trade Center bombing despite being in the parking garage when the truck bomb went off inside. On 9/11 he helped evacuate the North Tower, narrowly escaping its collapse. He later spent months in Pakistan and Afghanistan with Borelli, hunting terrorists with the JTTF.[2]

The plan was for the Port Authority to start randomly stopping cars, to put on a bit of a show, and then politely ask Zazi to pull over too. As Zazi worked his way through traffic and toward the tollbooth on the New Jersey side of the bridge, the surveillance cars behind him signaled to the Port Authority cops waiting on the bridge.

"Red Impala. Arizona plates, DX 4015."

The bridge cops could not find Zazi among the sea of cars. The surveillance team called out his position, counting out traffic lanes from the right. Again, there was no confirmation from the bridge. The voice on the radio became more urgent. *"Red Impala."* More lane counting. He was getting closer. Still nothing.

The officers on the bridge were counting lanes from their right, facing oncoming traffic. The surveillance team, however, was counting from its right, headed toward the tolls.

They were looking at opposite sides of the highway.

The surveillance airplane's radios had died out, leaving the FBI agents and the Port Authority officers alone to find Zazi. McHale listened to the confused radio traffic, and with Zazi nearly at the tolls, he barked into his phone, "Kill the tolls! Kill the tolls!" The gates on the bridge came down, and traffic halted.

So much for the carefully crafted ruse.

The Port Authority pulled over a car or two, trying to salvage the deception, but it looked anything but random. It looked as though the police were waiting for Zazi.

Officers waved Zazi toward the right side of road, after the toll, near the Port Authority building and its inspection area. The officer asked him to step out of the car and began asking him many of the same questions he was asked a day earlier in Colorado. Where was he going? How long was he staying? He said he was going to Queens. He'd either be staying with a friend or at his mosque.

While Zazi waited, a Port Authority officer walked around the rented car, peering in the windows. The cop did not have top-secret security clearances, which meant that FBI agents could not tell him why they were investigating Zazi. But nothing seemed out of the ordinary. It looked like any car nearing the end of a road trip. There was some trash, a warning for speeding, a jug of water, a rental contract. The officer called for a police dog.

The dog circled the car. It sniffed at the passenger door and the trunk but detected nothing. The police let Zazi go.

Nobody swabbed the car and checked it for explosives residue. Despite Albin's assurances, the Port Authority did not have the equipment to conduct such a test. As far as the FBI knew, though, everything went according to plan. The message was passed to Borelli and through the ranks, to McJunkin and Heimbach, all the way up to Cummings on the seventh floor: Zazi was clean.

A few minutes before four o'clock, Zazi pulled back into traffic and onto the bridge. Edwin Anes, a fifteen-year NYPD veteran who'd been assigned to the FBI task force for five years, was waiting a few hundred feet up the road. Anes was "on the eye," meaning that, of the six New York surveillance officers assigned to follow Zazi from there, he was the one responsible for keeping the target in his sights, regardless of what happened. They would rotate this responsibility every hour, allowing other cars to pull ahead, catch up, or fade back into traffic and look inconspicuous. Anes made a note in his log and eased his car back onto the highway in time to catch Zazi entering the Bronx, on the way to his adopted hometown of Queens.

Queens is one of the most diverse spots on the globe, a place where half the population was born in another country. Before 9/11, New York boroughs were a wilderness of ethnic neighborhoods. Sure, the cops in the Sixtieth Precinct needed some familiarity with Russian culture to patrol Brooklyn's Brighton Beach. And the men and women of the Sixty-seventh knew about that borough's growing Guyanese population in Flatbush. But as long as crime rates stayed low, ethnic neighborhoods could remain sealed off from the outside. In many ways, such insularity was part of the American story. The Irish once had Bay Ridge in Brooklyn. The Jews once had Manhattan's Lower East Side. A young man could get a job, find a place to live, and disappear, sheltered by language and culture.

At the NYPD after 9/11, this fact of life became a terrifying problem.

4

DEMOGRAPHICS

As a young analyst at Langley, David Cohen had cut his teeth in the CIA's Office of Economic Research. He was surrounded by hundreds of smart, creative economists at a time when Washington decision makers wanted to know more about foreign economies. When he oversaw domestic collection, he had by his side Gustav Avrakotos, the veteran of the Soviet war in Afghanistan. When Cohen led the analytical branch, he had access to intelligence from officers at stations around the world, satellite imagery, and a battery of expert analysts to interpret it. Even during his term in the Directorate of Operations, as dysfunctional as that was, he had access to highly trained spies and unmatched technological capabilities.

At the NYPD, intelligence expertise was scarce. Analysis was built around solving crimes, not about recognizing patterns or predicting the next emerging threat. And the analysts were all cops, not the social scientists or foreign-nation experts who filled the CIA. The Police Academy churned out some of the best officers in the country, ready to patrol one of the most dynamic, complex cities in the world. But they didn't learn anything like the espionage training that young CIA operatives received at the Farm, the agency's spy school near Williamsburg, Virginia.

Cohen knew that he would need to remake the NYPD and, in many ways, remake it in the CIA's image. He would need to hire civilian analysts from top-flight schools and change the mission from fighting crime to preventing terrorism. But those changes would come slowly. In the meantime, if he relied on his officers, he'd be in the dark. He'd sit in the morning meetings with Ray Kelly and have nothing. Meanwhile, his counterpart in counterterrorism, former marine lieutenant general Frank Libutti, would have access to the latest intelligence from the federal government thanks to the officers working beneath him on the Joint Terrorism Task Force. That might be fine in other cities. But Cohen was building something different. And he wasn't about to rely on the FBI, which was notoriously stingy when it came to sharing information, to decide what he needed to know. He needed to find someone who could take a hands-on role in the daily operations and, most importantly, had access to the latest raw federal intelligence. The man he found was Larry Sanchez.

Like Cohen, Sanchez was a CIA veteran; an analyst who'd come up through the ranks. Unlike Cohen, however, Sanchez was still on the job. That meant he had a blue CIA badge and the security clearances that came with it.

Cohen and Sanchez had met during their days at Langley. When Cohen was deputy director of operations, Sanchez was the top assistant—essentially the chief of staff—to Cohen's immediate boss, CIA executive director Nora Slatkin. But the two really got to know each other in 1997, when Cohen became CIA station chief in New York and the CIA detailed Sanchez to the staff of United Nations Ambassador Bill Richardson.

When Richardson left the United Nations in 1998 to become President Bill Clinton's energy secretary, he took Sanchez with him, appointing him the department's chief intelligence officer. Again, he was on loan from the CIA, this time to help protect the nation's nuclear secrets and research.

When Cohen called in early 2002, Sanchez was in limbo. Though he'd been working for the CIA, he'd been answering to someone else for a long time. Now he was back under the CIA's roof and was looking for a new assignment. Cohen pitched him on another out-of-town job. And he pitched Sanchez's boss, CIA Director George Tenet, who gave his consent.

Cohen's idea, putting a CIA officer inside a municipal police department, had never been tried. The NYPD was a pure law enforcement agency, one whose primary function was keeping the city secure. The CIA, by its very charter, was prohibited from having any "police, subpoena, or law enforcement powers or internal security functions." But this was months after 9/11. The finger-pointing over who'd missed the warning signs had begun, and the only question that mattered was how the federal government could make the country—and particularly New York—more secure. New York could have asked for anything, and Washington would have had a hard time refusing.

Normally, when a CIA officer takes a temporary assignment inside another agency, the arrangements are spelled out in great, lawyerly detail. Who's going to pay the bills? Who exactly is in charge of the assignment? What are the job duties? Will the officer temporarily sever ties to the agency? The rules of Sanchez's unprecedented assignment were never committed to writing, much less submitted for review.[1]

Twenty-seven years after the Church Committee and the beginning of congressional oversight, nobody on Capitol Hill, in either of the intelligence committees, approved Sanchez's appointment. The authority for the move was murky. Under a presidential order signed by Ronald Reagan, the CIA was allowed to provide "specialized equipment, technical knowledge, or assistance of expert personnel" to local law enforcement, but only when the details were approved by CIA lawyers. Instead, Tenet sent Sanchez to New York solely on his say-so. As director of central intelligence, Tenet asserted the authority to move his people from station to station as he saw fit to protect the country. At a time when the CIA was immersed in plans to carry out a covert war against al-Qaeda and create a network of secret prisons to hold and interrogate suspected terrorists, the decision to send Sanchez to New York generated little discussion and no controversy.

To the extent that Sanchez had an official title, it was the CIA director's counterterrorism liaison to the state of New York. In reality, he was Cohen's personal liaison to the CIA. The agency was paying the bills, but it was not at all clear what his job duties were or to whom he answered. He had an office at the CIA station in Manhattan and another at NYPD. At both places, nobody was quite sure what he did. He'd start many mornings at his CIA office, reading the latest intelligence reports. Then he'd head for One Police Plaza to give Cohen a personal briefing that was far more expansive than the updates he could get from the FBI or CIA.

At the NYPD, the word was that Sanchez was a consultant. John Cutter, a veteran cop who served as one of Cohen's top uniformed officers, remembers his introduction. "This is Larry Sanchez. Larry's a consultant. Larry knows things that can help us, and Larry knows people who can help us." The fact that he was CIA spread quickly through the ranks. Whether he was retired or active was unclear.

Sanchez was easy to talk to and easy to like. He was a former amateur power lifter and boxer, and though he was nearly bald, with patches of hair above each ear, he still had thick biceps and a broad chest. Sanchez wore a diamond stud earring, and he told great stories about scuba and skydiving, about working overseas. He recalled parachuting into Iraq with army commandos from Delta Force. If you left a conversation believing that Sanchez was a covert officer, not a career analyst, he wasn't going to do anything to disabuse you of that impression.

In contrast to Cohen's aloof, sometimes combative personality, Sanchez was outgoing and friendly. One retired officer remembers Cohen making a rare appearance at an Intelligence Division Christmas party at a Chelsea steak house and awkwardly approaching two officers sitting at the bar. He congratulated them on a good, successful year and thanked them for their hard work. They looked at him, confused. They weren't members of the Intelligence Division. They worked for a different unit and happened to be having their party there too. Sanchez, by comparison, was a regular at police events. He knew the officers and was good at both mentoring and socializing.

In the early days, Sanchez and Cohen would meet at Cohen's highrise apartment building on the Upper West Side, off Central Park, and discuss their vision for the NYPD. The pockets of cloistered Middle Eastern and South Asian neighborhoods were a particular concern for the two CIA veterans. The 9/11 attacks had been planned in communities walled off from the police by language, religion, and culture. New York was dotted with similar enclaves, places where someone could rent a cheap room and remain inconspicuous.[2]

In New York, Cohen and Sanchez reviewed the dossiers that had been built on the 9/11 hijackers. Some of the intelligence came from government sources, but in the wake of the attacks, journalists from around the globe worked to piece together the lives of the terrorists aboard the airplanes that morning. Sanchez looked at the life of Mohamed Atta, the ringleader of the hijacking operation, and saw a learning opportunity for the NYPD. Here was a man who'd managed to fade into anonymity on three continents, someone who Osama bin Laden trusted to avoid detection while planning the most ambitious terrorist mission ever. He was a man who announced calmly, "Everything will be okay," and then steered American Airlines Flight 11 into the North Tower of the World Trade Center. And he was about to become a case study in how to prevent terrorism. Sanchez and Cohen believed the Atta case contained the clues that future investigators could use to identify people before they attacked.

· · ·

In Cairo, Egypt, Atta was raised in a family dedicated to scholarship, not prayer. His father, a lawyer, expected his son to learn. Atta and his sisters were not allowed to play outside. His parents timed the walk home from school and expected Atta to be back in the apartment studying without delay. In a densely populated, neighborly section of the city, his family seldom socialized or broke the fast with neighbors during the holy month of Ramadan.[3] Eventually Atta graduated from Cairo University with a degree in architectural engineering and then continued his studies in Germany.

Friends in Cairo don't recall seeing Atta's family at the mosque. They certainly weren't regulars. But when Atta arrived in Hamburg in 1992, he immediately sought out the nearest one.[4]

At the Technical University of Hamburg-Harburg, Atta applied himself to his studies. He also became increasingly religious and confrontational over moral and spiritual issues but never advocated violence.[5] When he moved into university housing, his strict religious practices and stern personality quickly isolated him from his two successive roommates. He started a Muslim student group, a daily prayer session where investigators believe he met two men who would become hijackers with him.[6] He began attending the Al Quds mosque, where a radical version of Sunni Islam was preached.

In 1998 he rented an apartment with two friends, Ramzi bin al-Shibh and Marwan al-Shehhi. They shared a growing anti-American sentiment that, at least at first, they were not shy about discussing at the local pub where they went to talk—never to drink.[7] The shopkeeper on the corner near Atta's apartment recalls him growing out his beard and dressing in traditional Arab robes, called dishdashas.[8] Al-Shehhi would go on to pilot United Airlines Flight 175 into the South Tower of the World Trade Center. Bin al-Shibh, who was unable to get a visa to join his friends on their mission, was later captured and imprisoned in secret CIA prisons. His cooperation provided the foundation for much of *The 9/11 Commission Report*.

When Atta and al-Shehhi arrived in the United States in 2000, they stayed in New York, moving from cheap motels to short-term leases in Manhattan's Hudson Heights and Brooklyn's Park Slope neighborhoods.[9] Al-Shehhi enrolled in an English class. They traveled the country, conducting premission surveillance, assembling their team, and training to fly jets. They attended mosques sporadically, visited internet cafés, and joined gyms.

For Sanchez, this was a road map for the new NYPD. The federal government was tightening security at airports, getting tough on visa requirements, freezing money used to finance attacks, and requiring background checks for foreigners attending flight schools. With Cohen, the NYPD could go further. The story of Mohamed Atta was one of missed opportunities. There were people who'd seen signs of trouble, radical ideology, and anti-American vitriol: housemates and roommates, shopkeepers and pub patrons, fellow students and mosquegoers. They didn't think anything of what they saw until it was too late.

If the NYPD had its own eyes and ears in those cloistered communities, maybe things could be different. They needed be in the shop to spot the next Mohamed Atta in his kaftan with his newly grown beard. They had to be at the restaurant to overhear the group of friends ranting about America. If NYPD detectives infiltrated Muslim student groups, maybe they could identify the young man with the seething fanaticism. If the cops had a better handle on what went on inside the mosques, or which internet cafés were nearby—or even which gyms a young Middle Eastern man would attend—then maybe they could piece together the clues. Maybe they could prevent the next 9/11.

The nearly successful effort by Richard Reid to detonate explosives in his shoes aboard American Airlines Flight 63 in December 2001 further validated the NYPD's plans. Reid, who later became known as the "shoe bomber," was a British citizen and Islamic convert who attended north London's fiery, anti-American mosques. He had spent days in Paris before his flight, staying in the diverse neighborhood near the busy Gare du Nord train station. He ate at many of the restaurants in the area and used an internet café to send his mother his will and a final letter: "What I am doing is part of the ongoing war between Islam and disbelief (and as such a duty upon me as a Muslim)." Only after the attempted bombing did French authorities unravel the terrorist organization in Paris that supported Reid. To Cohen, that underscored the crisis.[10]

Profiling is a loaded word in policing because it conjures images of white cops pulling over young black men and searching for guns or drugs. Racial profiling uses race as a stand-in for behavior: "That driver is probably up to no good because he's black." But racial profiling and behavioral profiling are different. The FBI, for instance, builds profiles of serial killers through its Behavioral Analysis Unit. And while such social science has not been immune from criticism, these profiles have been credited with helping solve crimes and catch killers.

Sanchez envisioned a similar role for the NYPD, but with an important difference: It would not wait until a crime was committed. He wanted NYPD detectives to be the surrogates for all the people who missed the significance of Atta's growing radicalization. It was an audacious plan, because the behaviors to be profiled were common not only to Atta and his murderous friends but also to a huge population of innocent people. Most café customers, gym members, college kids, and pub customers were not terrorists. Most devout Muslims weren't, either. Nevertheless, Cohen liked the idea. He compared it to raking an extinguished fire pit. Most coals would be harmless and gray. But rake them carefully, and you might find a smoldering ember—a hot spot waiting to catch fire.[11]

Like Sanchez's very relationship with the NYPD, there was nothing like what he was proposing anywhere in American law enforcement. People who kill abortion doctors or bomb clinics have common behavioral traits too. They tend to be Christian; usually fervently so. They attend church, often participate in protests outside clinics, and acquire weapons. There has been no known effort to establish police eyes and ears in Christian churches, antiabortion groups, and gun clubs in hopes of spotting the next abortion-doctor killer. But New York was not under attack by fanatical, antiabortion Christians.

There was, however, precedent for what Sanchez wanted to do. The surveillance abuses of the 1960s and 1970s were born out of a similar desire to identify trouble spots by monitoring lawful communities. Decades before that, in 1919, New York state senator Clayton Lusk led the Joint Committee Investigating Seditious Activities. He commissioned ethnic maps of New York. Irish, Germans, Russian Jews, Italians, and other groups were designated on color-coded charts to help authorities root out disloyalty and radicalism.[12]

But Sanchez didn't get his inspiration from New York's troubled past. Rather, he got the idea from one of America's closest allies, a country that had lived under the threat of terrorism for decades. Sanchez told friends and colleagues that the NYPD was taking its cue from Israeli officers' methods of keeping tabs on the military-occupied West Bank, the swath captured from Jordan in the 1967 Six-Day War.[13]

Sanchez's proposal ignored some important differences between the US and Israel. Brooklyn and Queens, for instance, were not occupied territories or disputed land. There was no security wall being erected in New York City. Israel does not have a constitution, and Muslims there do not enjoy the same freedom as Jews. In fact, they are routinely discriminated against.[14] And, most significantly, unlike Israel, New York was not trying to preserve a religious identity.

In the words of one former senior police official, reflecting on his role in transforming the NYPD, "Desperation breeds novel ideas." Besides, it was hardly unusual for Israel to serve as a model for a US counterterrorism program. In the months after 9/11, American politicians flew to Israel in droves and extolled the virtues of Israeli tactics. Twenty years before the CIA opened its network of secret prisons, Israel was operating its own black site, called Facility 1391, to hold and interrogate prisoners indefinitely. Like its CIA cousins, Facility 1391 permitted harsh interrogation and was off-limits to human rights inspectors with the International Committee of the Red Cross.[15]

The US looked to Israel, too, when crafting the rules for interrogation at black sites. In its memos, the Justice Department noted that the

Israeli Supreme Court had, in 1999, determined that sleep deprivation, painful stress positions, and intense, lengthy interrogations were cruel and inhuman but did not constitute torture. The Justice Department concluded that international law allowed "an aggressive interpretation as to what amounts to torture."[16]

In fact, America's signature offensive counterterrorism strategy not only replicated a tactic used by Israel but also used a strategy that the United States abhorred until 9/11. It was Israel that popularized the phrase *targeted killing* to describe its precise attacks on suspected militants. In July 2001 the American ambassador to Israel, Martin Indyk, had a different word for it. "The United States government is very clearly on the record as against targeted assassinations," he said. "They are extrajudicial killings, and we do not support that."[17] That was before 9/11, before the Predator drone became the CIA's signature weapon in the war on terrorism and before the word *assassination* was scrubbed from the US counterterrorism lexicon.

Once Cohen persuaded Judge Haight to relax the Handschu rules, Sanchez's vision could become a reality. The new rules made it explicit: "For the purpose of detecting or preventing terrorist activities, the NYPD is authorized to visit any place and attend any event that is open to the public on the same terms and conditions as members of the public generally." The only caveat was that police couldn't document and keep any information from these visits unless it related to potential criminal or terrorist activity. That rule was intended to prevent the NYPD from building files on innocent people, as it did during the 1960s. Cohen, however, took a very broad view of what qualified as information related to terrorist activity.

Cohen and Sanchez enjoyed one advantage at the NYPD that they never had at the CIA. The department drew recruits from one of the most diverse talent pools in America, and the force reflected that. The FBI and CIA struggled to recruit Arabic speakers and Middle Eastern agents. In part, that was because those jobs required top-secret security clearances, which meant passing background checks that look unfavorably on applicants who still had strong ties overseas. The NYPD didn't have that problem. The police force had long been a stepping-stone to the middle class for immigrants. One in five academy graduates were born overseas. So when Cohen went searching for officers who could blend into Muslim neighborhoods, he didn't have to look far. He recruited young Middle Eastern officers who spoke Arabic, Bengali, Hindi, Punjabi, and Urdu. They would be the ones raking the coals, and inevitably they became known as "rakers." [18]

The effort began simply enough, with a copy of the 2000 US census. The police did what anyone else could do with that data trove. They mapped the city based on ethnicity and ancestry. The NYPD was interested in what it called "ancestries of interest." There were twenty-eight, nearly all of them Muslim countries. There were Middle Eastern and South Asian countries such as Pakistan, Iran, Syria, and Egypt. Former Soviet states like Uzbekistan and Chechnya were included, too, because of their large Muslim populations. The last "ancestry" on the list was "American Black Muslim." [19]

Every day, the rakers would set out from the intelligence offices at the Brooklyn Army Terminal. They'd work in teams, usually of two, and visit businesses.

They were not officially working undercover. At the NYPD, that designation is reserved for officers who use an assumed identity, with fake paperwork and a cover story. But the rakers weren't advertising their police affiliation, either. Their job was to blend in and look like any other young men stepping in off the street.

The routine was almost always the same, whether they were visiting a restaurant, deli, barbershop, or travel agency. The two rakers would enter and casually chat with the owner. The first order of business was to determine his ethnicity and that of the patrons. This would determine which file the business would go into. A report on Pakistani locations, for instance, or one on Moroccans. Next, they'd do what the NYPD called "gauging sentiment." Were the patrons dressed in the clothing of observant Muslims? What were they talking about? If the Arabic news channel Al Jazeera was playing on the TV, the police would note it and also observe how people were acting. Were they laughing, smiling, or cheering at reports of US military casualties in Iraq and Afghanistan? Did they talk Middle Eastern politics? If the business sold extremist literature or CDs, the officers would buy one or two. Was the owner selling fake IDs or untaxed cigarettes? Police would note it. If customers could rent time on a computer, police might pay for a session and look at its search history. Were people viewing jihadist videos or searching for bomb-making instructions?

On their way out, the rakers would look for bulletin boards or fliers about community events. Was there a rally planned in the neighborhood? The rakers might attend. Was there a cricket league? The rakers might join. If someone advertised a room for rent, the cops would bring the flier back with them. That could be the cheap apartment used by the next Mohamed Atta.

• • •

In the beginning, raking was normally done by neighborhood. Sanchez had the NYPD carve the city up into about eighteen zones, and the rakers would visit Muslim businesses in each. They often picked their own targets, with a supervisor sitting in a parked car somewhere nearby in case of trouble. Sometimes they were sent to neighborhoods based on world events. If there was a car bombing in Lebanon, a Predator drone strike in Pakistan, or a firefight in Afghanistan, the rakers would be in those neighborhoods, gauging sentiment and reporting back. If people in a Pakistani barbershop were enraged over a drone attack that killed nearby civilians, it might be a warning sign that retaliation was imminent.

The rakers were in mosques too, gauging the sentiment of the imams and the congregations. They'd scan bulletin boards for scraps. They bought neighborhood newspapers and identified religious schools, community centers, hotels, and gyms. The NYPD was creating a new kind of map. Just as political maps showed the borders of New York City and topographic maps revealed the city's elevation, rakers charted New York's human terrain, mapping people and their attitudes.[20]

The idea of getting to know a community was a hot topic at the FBI too. And like the NYPD, the bureau had its own advisor on loan from the CIA, an analyst named Phil Mudd. He wanted the FBI to be more aggressive, to focus less on making isolated criminal cases and more on collecting intelligence. Inside the bureau, he was one of the biggest advocates of what became known as domain management, a process in which FBI offices nationwide compiled information on communities and assessed where terrorist threats might emerge. Like the NYPD, the FBI began with census data. It could then overlay other data—crimes, informant locations, potential targets—and create maps of neighborhoods. It used that information to find informants, assess threats, and decide where to conduct outreach to community leaders. Also like the NYPD, the FBI focused its efforts on Muslim neighborhoods. There was no FBI Catholic outreach program, nor was anyone interested in mapping Scottish immigrant neighborhoods. Domain management was controversial both inside the FBI and, when it became public, among civil libertarians.

While the NYPD and FBI had similar goals, they diverged at one important point. The FBI was prohibited, both under its guidelines and under federal law, from collecting and storing information concerning constitutionally protected activities such as religious and political speech unless related directly to law enforcement activities. That meant the FBI could not keep tabs on which pastry shop posted religious fliers on its bulletin board. Nor could the bureau put in its files that a Turkish couple owned a restaurant that served a "devout clientele." The FBI could not keep a file on an Egyptian travel agent who was "devout in appearance." And it could not send plainclothes agents into mosques to assess "sentiment."

NYPD did all of that. While Cohen had promised Judge Haight that his reinvented Intelligence Division would follow the same rules as the FBI, it did not. The newly created NYPD unit was explicitly instructed to "analyze religious institutions, locations, and congregations."[21]

Sanchez took a particular interest in the program's success, reading the reports and coaching the police on how to improve. Their daily dispatches were compiled into bound color reports that filled the bookshelves in Cohen's office. Mosques and religious schools were catalogued and hot spots were mapped by ethnicity for every precinct. The reports allowed police to visualize their city in a new way. If a group of young Muslim men were growing increasingly radicalized and planning an attack, these hot spots were the likeliest places to detect and locate them. There were hundreds of hot spots on the maps, all screaming for attention.

In a few years, the new unit had made New York's warren of ethnic neighborhoods seem much more manageable. There would be other programs; other trip wires to set. But with each new report, the chance of an al-Qaeda cell going undetected in New York seemed to diminish. Cohen's new squad embodied the change he'd hoped to bring to the NYPD. They were acting more like intelligence officers and less like cops.

Inside the NYPD, it was christened the Demographics Unit.

• • •

In late 2006, when Captain Steve D'Ulisse waved Hector Berdecia into his office in Chelsea and told him he was being assigned to oversee the Demographics Unit, Berdecia didn't know what he was inheriting. Berdecia was on leave from the Intelligence Division in 2003 when Cohen and Sanchez originally hatched the idea for the unit. On active duty in the US Army Reserve, he'd been in Iraq's Babylon Province, near the lawless area south of Baghdad dubbed the "Triangle of Death." He had been back a year and heard about a "Middle Eastern team" mentioned in passing around the office, but he didn't pay much attention.

On Cohen's orders, the sturdily built lieutenant with a shaved head and a broad, boyish smile had spent the past year creating and running the Citywide Debriefing Team. Each morning, the team would receive a list of people arrested in the past twenty-four hours and who were born in one of the NYPD's countries of interest. Men between sixteen and forty-five were of particular concern. Berdecia and his detectives tried to talk to every person on the list. They were interested in tips about terrorism, of course, but they were after more mundane information too. Did the Egyptian cabdriver know where a new immigrant could rent a cheap room? Could the Moroccan student tell you where to buy a fake ID? Where do you learn English? What mosque do you pray at? Where's a good gym? When you get to America, who helps you get on your feet?

The tactic had worked well in the 1990s, when everyone arrested on gun charges would get asked where to buy weapons. Even nonviolent criminals were asked. In the post-9/11 era, police were asking every Muslim what he knew about terrorism.

The debriefing job suited Berdecia. He'd spent nearly his whole career in plain clothes, rising through the ranks on his signature skill: sitting across from someone and getting him to talk. Berdecia had a knack for spotting what mattered to people. The father of two knew whether to play to their sense of family ("Do you really want to spend three summers away from your children?") or to their manhood ("If you go upstate, do you want another man coming into your house taking care of your old lady?"). Out in the Seventy-second Precinct in Brooklyn's Sunset Park neighborhood during the early 1990s, Berdecia would buy a four-pack of miniburgers, fries, and a soda from the White Castle down the street and slide them across the table. I'm not your enemy, he'd say. No hard feelings. I just want to talk.

That was his strategy in Iraq, too, where he was a military police officer responsible for debriefing prisoners picked up by Iraqi authorities. He worked through a translator, but the tactic was the same. In December 2003, when US Special Forces were hunting for a former Iraqi brigadier general believed to be training an al-Qaeda cell, it was Berdecia who caught him, and without firing a shot. He had an informant tell the general that the US government was prepared to pay him $50,000 in reparations for bombing his land. All he had to do was show up and claim the money. And he'd receive an official apology, too. When the general arrived, he and Berdecia chatted over tea until the general was hauled away, hooded and cuffed, in the back of a military gun truck.

In his new job at NYPD, the debriefings were much easier. Many people were willing to talk. In most cases, cooperating didn't involve ratting anybody out. It meant explaining a little bit about daily life in their neighborhoods.

D'Ulisse, whose glasses, bushy eyebrows, and mustache earned him comparisons to Groucho Marx, told Berdecia that day he wouldn't have to give up debriefing. Cohen was giving him the Demographics Unit on top of his other responsibilities. The captain didn't get into what the new job entailed, and Hector didn't ask why he was getting the assignment. He just accepted. He was a keep-to-yourself kind of guy. He'd earned an Army Commendation Medal for heroism and combat valor during a firefight in Iraq. But rather than display it, he kept it in his garage, placed inconspicuously atop a dusty metal locker. He didn't talk about what he'd done to earn it, not even with family and friends.

"Good cops make their bosses look good," cop-turned-author Edward Conlon wrote in his memoir, *Blue Blood*. "And Hector was a one-man beauty school."

Berdecia knew firsthand how New York had a way of hiding itself in plain sight. He was a Brooklyn native, the son of a longshoreman and the youngest in a home with four sisters. A family of Puerto Rican heritage, the Berdecias lived for a time in Wyckoff Gardens, a high-rise housing project with 1,200 residents. He grew up in the traditionally

Italian neighborhood of Carroll Gardens. He'd been in and around the city all his life, but it was only now—after what he saw in Iraq—that he really started to notice the Arabic storefronts all around New York.

In Iraq, he had met lots of wonderful Iraqis and even started a Cub Scout troop there, using his son's old troop banner. But, frankly, looking around his city, he was suspicious. He'd lost friends to terrorism: First there was John Chipura, who'd survived a 1983 Hezbollah bombing as a marine in Beirut but who died as a firefighter in the World Trade Center. Then came the commanding officer of his military police battalion, Lieutenant Colonel Kim Orlando, who was killed enforcing a curfew in Iraq.

Berdecia got his introduction to the Demographics Unit from one of his sergeants, Timothy Mehta. A burly, likable man of Indian ancestry, Mehta ran through some PowerPoint slides and reports explaining the unit and how it gathered information. Berdecia was impressed.

He believed there was an al-Qaeda cell hiding somewhere in New York's ethnic neighborhoods, planning to strike the city again. And as he thumbed through the Demographics reports, looking at shopkeepers identified by name and ethnicity, at restaurants catalogued by the nationality of their clientele, he felt safer.

Not everybody agreed. Berdecia didn't know it, but Cohen and Sanchez were sharing their innovative new model with a select group of outsiders. And some had serious doubts.

In the fall of 2005, for instance, a senior CIA officer named Margaret Henoch flew to New York to smooth over a dispute over another of Cohen's new initiatives. With Kelly's blessing, Cohen had begun stationing officers in foreign police departments so that in the event of a terrorist attack in, say, Paris or Toronto, the NYPD would have a direct line to information about the bomber and the device used. That information normally passed through the Joint Terrorism Task Force, but Cohen and Kelly believed that route was too slow. More importantly, they believed that the JTTF was too focused on the big picture. They wanted granular information that could help protect New York. They wanted someone who could, as Kelly would often say, "ask the New York question."

Even with an annual budget of more than $3 billion, Kelly knew that obtaining approval to send officers overseas would be a tough sell in front of the parochial New York City Council. So he asked the New York City Police Foundation, a private nonprofit group, to pay for the program. The foundation was formed in the 1970s to help support the department. And since 9/11, it had become flush with cash. The city's corporate titans eagerly opened their checkbooks to donate, especially when fund-raisers mentioned terrorism. The foundation's gala dinner brought in more than $1 million each year. The mixing of corporate money and municipal policing created some unusual arrangements. For instance, an NYPD undercover operation into counterfeit merchandise was paid for by the foundation, courtesy of New York's fashion industry. With their donations, companies were able to hire the NYPD to investigate the crimes most important to them.

Paying police to work overseas, however, raised eyebrows even among the foundation's board members. If it was such a good idea, they asked, why not put it before the city council? In a meeting with the foundation's leadership in 2002, Kelly said that the council would never go for it. Every time crime rates inched up in some council member's neighborhood, he'd get questioned about why the city was paying to keep a cop in Lyon, France. "I don't like to be told no," Kelly said. "So I just don't ask." [22]

The foundation agreed to foot the bill, with a goal of building relationships overseas to gather information and identify threats to New York. [23]

But the NYPD's new arrangement quickly frustrated the FBI and the State Department, which had official relationships with foreign governments. After London's subway and a bus were bombed in July 2005, Cohen's man in the United Kingdom, Ira Greenberg, passed information from Scotland Yard back to NYPD about the bomb's chemistry. Kelly then announced that information publicly, enraging the tight-lipped Brits. The incident strained relations between the FBI and British authorities, who threatened to withhold information from all their American counterparts. At the FBI, it was yet another reason to speak Cohen's name through gritted teeth.

NYPD and FBI officials privately worried that the detective in Tel Aviv, Mordecai Dzikansky, was being used by Israeli intelligence officials to influence thinking in New York. Not that he had any secrets to spill or would ever betray any if he did. But Dzikansky had a drinking problem, and in a country where Israeli intelligence agents regularly try to recruit their CIA counterparts, an NYPD officer could be a useful pawn.[24] From time to time, Dzikansky would get his colleagues to do favors for the Israelis, such as conducting surveillance in New York at their request.[25]

In France, the CIA station chief, Bill Murray, rolled his eyes over the NYPD's arrival. On his way out the door, he told Cohen that he'd seen some of the police reports coming out of Lyon. "They're shit," he said. Cohen explained that he had to start somewhere. He had to do whatever was necessary to protect New York, and that meant having eyes and ears around the globe.[26]

In Canada, the first country to host the NYPD, the relationship had become a source of friction at the CIA station in Ottawa. That's why Henoch went to Manhattan. With three CIA officers from the New York station, she met with the NYPD Intelligence brass in hopes of resolving that tension. Cohen wasn't there, so Sanchez conducted the meeting. His assignment as Tenet's representative to New York had ended in 2004, but CIA headquarters granted him unusual permission to take a leave of absence and officially become Cohen's deputy. He no longer had access to the CIA's intelligence files as an NYPD assistant commissioner, but Cohen and Sanchez still had their network of agency contacts in Virginia and New York.

Sanchez began by trying to allay any concerns about the overseas program. The NYPD guys in Canada were going to answer to Cohen, and, if they came up with something the CIA needed to know, the police said, they would call. It became clear to everyone in the room that the issue wasn't going to get resolved. The department's role overseas would continue to be a source of friction with the federal government for years, but it remained one of Kelly's signature programs, even though it never produced a single tip related to terrorism in New York.[27]

As the conversation with Henoch continued, however, it veered away from the dead end that was the international program. It became a wide-ranging briefing on the NYPD's new capabilities, including its Demographics Unit.[28]

Ira Weiss, a police detective and a dual US-Israeli citizen who was instrumental in setting up the Demographics Unit, explained that the NYPD had carved the city into zones and mapped each area based on a number of factors: religious affiliation, nationality, profession, and others. They knew where all the mosques were. They knew where the Sunni Moroccan barbers were, where the Shiite Lebanese butchers were, and where they prayed.

Henoch had a reputation as a skeptic. During the run-up to the Iraq War in 2002–03, when CIA analysts concluded that Saddam Hussein possessed weapons of mass destruction, they put a lot of stock in statements by an Iraqi defector code-named Curveball. Henoch was one of the agency's most vocal critics questioning Curveball's reliability. She said the agency had fallen in love with its own analysis and hadn't conducted a dispassionate review. By the time Henoch would be proven right, however, the US was stuck in the quagmire of Iraq.

Now, sitting with the NYPD, she felt a similar skepticism. She was impressed with the level of detail but didn't see how it could be used to draw any conclusions.

"I think this is a really impressive collection of what's where, but I don't understand how it helps you," Henoch said. If it was useful, she figured, maybe the CIA could replicate it. But she didn't understand how collecting troves of information on local businesses and religious affiliations helped find terrorists. "You know what kind of people are in what neighborhoods. But you don't actually know who's in your city."

She pressed them for an example. Was there some success story that summed up the program's usefulness in its first two years? When she didn't get it, she assumed that the NYPD was playing coy. Even in the post-9/11 era, intelligence agencies often jealously guarded their secrets. "I figured they were just lying to me," Henoch recalled years later.

It did not occur to her that there might not be any stories to tell.

After nearly three hours, she left the meeting, angry that the disagreement over the international program was unresolved and confused about what the NYPD was doing. It seemed so backward. It would be like hanging out in all the churches, coffee shops, and bars in northern Virginia to figure out who worked for the CIA. It seemed to her like a huge waste of time, and Henoch was stunned that it was legal. But she figured that the NYPD wouldn't be doing it if it wasn't both productive and legal.

Berdecia assumed the same thing. There must have been something useful about his team that he didn't understand, something to justify all the time and money being spent. Every now and then, rakers would complain to Berdecia about their assignments. They felt conflicted. They were cops, eager to protect the city. But they also knew that they were building files on fellow Muslims—immigrant business owners and members of their communities who'd done nothing wrong. Berdecia would reassure them. There was nothing insidious about what they were doing, he said. They weren't collecting anything that couldn't be observed by any other member of the public.

"At the very least, we can eliminate this guy from our list if he's not a terrorist," Berdecia said. "And we can find out who the terrorists are. And that's your job."

The truth, though, was that raking didn't eliminate anybody from a list. It contributed to the NYPD's growing files. One Brooklyn business that the NYPD labeled a Bangladeshi hot spot, for instance, was a restaurant named Jhinuk. The list of "alleged activities" included being a "popular location for political activities" and attracting a "devout crowd".[29] The Nile Valley Grocery in Brooklyn was noted simply as a "medium-size grocery owned by a person of Syrian descent."[30] Milestone Park, in Brooklyn's Bensonhurst neighborhood, was labeled a "location of concern" because it attracted middle-age Albanian men from the neighborhood: "This location is mostly frequented during the early afternoon hours when Albanians get together for a game of chess, backgammon, or just to have a conversation," the rakers noted.[31]

Though it was against the law for the federal government to collect such information, Washington helped pay for the NYPD to do so. The Demographics Unit, like many Intel operations, benefited from a little-known White House antidrug grant that provided millions of dollars for cars and computers.[32]

There was pressure on the rakers to produce. When a Muslim detective wasn't delivering enough information about community events or overhearing enough suspicious conversations, his sergeants wrote him up.[33]

When the Intelligence Division's lawyer, Stu Parker, raised concerns that the Demographics files posed a potential problem for the department even under the new Handschu rules, the department set up a stand-alone computer at the Brooklyn Army Terminal for the files. It was walled off from the rest of the NYPD's computer systems.

Under the new Handschu rules, the NYPD could keep those files only if they related to potential criminal or terrorist activity. So the very fact that the Demographics files existed showed that either the NYPD was violating the rules or the police saw the potential for terrorism wherever groups of Muslims gathered.

Sometimes that meant the rakers operated outside the city, in suburban towns on Long Island. There was even talk about scouring Baltimore and Los Angeles for hot spots, though neither materialized. In mid-2007 D'Ulisse sent Berdecia and his rakers to Newark, New Jersey, on the other side of the Hudson River, where former NYPD deputy commissioner Garry McCarthy was the police director. At police headquarters in Newark, Berdecia and Sergeant Tim Mehta told a lieutenant that they could provide a breakdown of the city's Muslim community. There was no evidence of a threat and no lead to follow up on. The Demographics Unit would simply spread out into the neighborhoods, explain who owns which businesses, identify mosques, and provide a law enforcement guide to the city's Muslims. Berdecia didn't know whether the Newark cops requested the report or whether they were simply allowing the NYPD to prepare it. He knew only that it was supposed to get done. Over the next several weeks, with a Newark detective as chaperone, Berdecia's team raked Newark. They photographed mosques and religious schools, spoke with workers at deli counters, and produced a sixty-five-page catalogue of places where police could expect to find Muslims. Dollar stores owned by Egyptians and Pakistanis were on the list, as were Afghan fried chicken joints and corner stores owned by black Muslims.[34] When Berdecia submitted the report to D'Ulisse, he said it had "no intelligence value" to the NYPD.

Berdecia's initial optimism and enthusiasm about the Demographics Unit gave way to a growing frustration. Nothing his team did ever led to an arrest or generated leads on terrorist plots. While the Debriefing Team was out talking to people, helping spot potential informants, and trying to glean information, the rakers were spending their days sipping tea in cafés. They never received specialized training, so their reports contained numerous errors. Dino's European Hair Style was put in a file because police noted that the owner was Albanian. But in reality, owner Sammy Eirovic was from Montenegro. Similarly, Sephardic Jews and Lebanese Christians were mistaken for Syrians.[35]

And because nobody ever trained the rakers on what exactly qualified as suspicious, they reported anything they heard, even political speech. One Muslim man made it into police files even though he *praised* President Bush's State of the Union address and said that people who criticized the US government didn't realize how good they have it. Two men of Pakistani ancestry were included for saying that the nation's policies had become increasingly anti-Muslim since 9/11. Muslims who criticized the US use of drones to launch missiles in Pakistan were also documented.[36]

Over time, the reports all began to look the same to Berdecia. The rakers were never given a specific lead to check out, and, no matter how detailed their reports, they never became criminal cases. It felt like gathering information for its own sake.

Sometimes, it felt worse.

Berdecia began to notice on expense reports that his rakers frequently visited the same businesses, like the Kabul Kabob House in Flushing, Queens, which was owned by a soft-spoken blond Persian named Shorah Dorudi, who'd fled Iran after the Islamic revolution in 1979. When Berdecia asked whether there was a problem there, whether there was a threat that should be reported up the chain of command, he was told they were routine follow-up visits. But a look at the reports showed nothing worth following up on. That's when Berdecia realized that, in the hunt for terrorists, his detectives gravitated toward the best food.[37]

Occasionally, Berdecia would see receipts for up to $40 at Middle Eastern sweetshops. The Demographics Unit had thousands of dollars to spend on meals and incidental expenses so police would look like ordinary customers—costs that are known as "cover concealment." But Berdecia argued that you could eavesdrop just as well over a $2 cup of coffee. Sometimes, the receipts showed, detectives were buying a bunch of pastries late in the afternoon before heading home.

If there were terrorist cells operating in New York, Berdecia wondered, why weren't they making cases? That's how they'd dismantled drug gangs in the Bronx. Gang members, like terrorists, were secretive, insular, and dangerous. Years earlier, when Berdecia's wife and newborn son had arrived home from the hospital, five officers guarded them because of gang threats.

Berdecia had talented detectives with invaluable language skills. It nagged at him to see them sitting around eating kebabs and buying pastries, hoping to stumble onto something. If it was worth writing up a report, then it was worth conducting an investigation. He was paying overtime so detectives could march in parades and take pictures, but they never generated a single lead, never pursued anyone, or built cases.

• • •

So in the fall of 2009, as Intel scoured its records for information on Najibullah Zazi and his friends, Berdecia was not surprised to find that the Demographics files had offered no early warning about the three men and no hint about what they were planning. It was not for lack of trying. The NYPD had been in Zazi's neighborhood restaurants, like the Kabul Kabob House. Police had a file on the YMCA near his old apartment because it doubled as a gym and a cheap place to stay. Detectives had visited his mosque, up the street from his family's apartment. They'd even secretly visited American Best Travel & Tours, the travel agency where Zazi bought tickets to Pakistan. The rakers took note of the agency's year-round travel packages for Muslims to make the holy pilgrimage to Mecca, Saudi Arabia. But that didn't offer much help finding the suspected terrorist at the ticket counter.

After years of raking, the NYPD knew where New York's Muslims were. They still didn't know where the terrorists were.

And they didn't know anything about Zazi, Medunjanin, or Ahmedzay. At this moment, when it mattered the most, the files told them nothing.

5

THE ACCIDENTAL TOURISTS

Late in the afternoon, Najibullah Zazi parked the red Impala in front of a run-down brick apartment building at 41-18 Parsons Boulevard in Flushing. The street was busy with cars and the sidewalks crowded with people, a typical day in Flushing. Zazi sat for a minute, peering through the windshield.

The FBI agents who tracked the Impala across Manhattan from the bridge had no idea what to expect next. One of the agents watching Zazi from inside an unmarked sedan radioed in on an encrypted frequency and made a note in the log. It was 4:32 p.m.

The agents saw Zarein Ahmedzay, whom they'd been watching for the past twenty-four hours, approach the car from the apartment building. Zazi got out, leaned into Ahmedzay, and said something out of earshot of the watching FBI agents. He motioned to Ahmedzay to follow him to the back of the car and popped open the trunk.

Ahmedzay looked around, picked something out of the trunk, and ran back inside the building with it.

• • •

Zazi and Ahmedzay were the sons of refugees, children who arrived in the United States in the great wave of Afghan migration during the

1980s and 1990s, precipitated by the Soviet war. They were born in different countries—Pakistan and Afghanistan—but ended up in the same neighborhood when their parents found comfort in the close-knit Afghan community of Queens. Originally settled by the Dutch, the borough has always been a patchwork of immigrant areas: German, Irish, Greek, and Italian. In the past three decades, Queens had become a kaleidoscope of nations, with immigrants from mainland China, the former Soviet Union, Latin America, and, increasingly, Central and Southeast Asia. Detach Queens from the four other boroughs that compose New York City, and it would rank among the largest city in the country, with a population of more than 2.2 million.

Along with the habits and folkways of their former homes, Queens residents have imported their likes and dislikes. In Astoria, across the East River from Manhattan, an Egyptian chef built a restaurant around his recipe for cow brains with caper sauce, making a delicacy of the offal usually discarded in American cooking. Hookah joints dot neighborhoods, drawing older Middle Eastern men and their American-reared sons to smoke flavored tobacco, or *shisha*. They watched the news on Al Jazeera or music videos from overseas, just as their European counterparts in adjacent neighborhoods might gather to watch satellite soccer broadcasts and drink Czech beer at a century-old Bohemian beer hall. At scattered cafés, they sip tea and play backgammon, chatting in their native tongues about their children, their jobs, or about politics and the corrupt governments that made a future in their homelands untenable.

The thread binding these diverse neighborhoods is the subway's No. 7 train, its elevated tracks making an elbow bend through northern Queens, tracing the rooftops of brownstones and bodegas marked with colorful graffiti. Among Middle Easterners and South Asians, the No. 7 is known as the "Orient Express," though it winds through considerably less romantic places than the legendary Paris-to-Istanbul train: Astoria, Woodside, Jackson Heights, Elmhurst, Corona. The last stop on the line is Flushing, a forty-five-minute trip from Grand Central Terminal in Manhattan, and the place where Zazi's family made its home.

The Zazis came to the United States because it offered something better than what they had in Afghanistan, one of the poorest countries in the world. Born in 1955, Najibullah Zazi's father, Mohammed Wali Zazi, endured a marginal early life in the capital, Kabul, a dusty city ringed by mountains. Soviet-style architecture, drab and gray, dominated the landscape.

The eldest of eleven brothers and sisters, Mohammed Zazi dropped out of school at sixteen to provide for the family. He found work driving a truck, an unforgiving job in a country where the roads were mostly unpaved and deadly. The trucking business offered few prospects for Mohammed. After an accident in which his truck was badly wrecked, he decided to look for opportunities beyond Afghanistan's fractious borders. Like thousands of his countrymen, Mohammed chose to go to what, in the oil-shock era of the 1970s, seemed like a Muslim promised land: Saudi Arabia. He left Kabul on the pretext of making the religious pilgrimage known as the hajj, and tried to make a living in construction. Over the next six years, he moved from city to city as the Saudi infrastructure grew, and sent what money he could back to his family. Conditions in his home country grew steadily worse. In 1979 the Soviets invaded Afghanistan to prop up the teetering Marxist government. The Red Army laid waste to the country as it battled the freedom fighters known as the mujahideen.

The war in Afghanistan created a humanitarian disaster, even for urban dwellers like the Zazis. No family was left unscathed. In a country of roughly fifteen million,[1] more than a million Afghans died. Many millions more became refugees as they fled the destruction wrought over nine years of conflict. Many headed two hundred miles east to Peshawar, a bustling city across the Pakistani border. It was a city of sprawling refugee camps, a place where the mujahideen bought weapons. Mohammed's parents and siblings joined the flood. Mohammed left Saudi Arabia and reunited with his family in one of Peshawar's camps, bringing with him enough money to find a wife. He married Sultan Bibi, his cousin, who had also fled Afghanistan's dangers and poverty.

Bibi gave birth to two children in the squalid conditions of their refugee camp. A daughter, Merwari, came first, followed by Najibullah, born August 10, 1985, a son to make a father proud.

• • •

Mohammed sought a path to North America, as so many other Afghans had done. Following an unsuccessful attempt to find a smuggler to sneak him to Canada, he went back to Saudi Arabia and applied for a visa to the United States. In 1990, after the weary and battered Soviets withdrew from Afghanistan, Mohammed, now thirty-five, flew to New York.

Flushing had an insulated and proud Afghan community numbering in the thousands long before Mohammed arrived. The neighborhood was a reflection of Afghanistan itself. There were Uzbeks, Tajiks, Hazaras—descendants of the fearsome Mongols—and Pashtuns like himself, members of the largest ethnic group in Afghanistan. Like most of the Afghans in Flushing, Mohammed prayed at Abu Bakr, a house that had been converted into a mosque. Established in 1987, the mosque was a central fixture of Flushing's "Little Afghanistan." It sat on a quiet street lined with leafy oaks and prosperous homes, and it was named after the Prophet Muhammad's father-in-law, who ruled after the Prophet's death in AD 632. While Abu Bakr anchored the Afghans to their faith, it was more than a place to pray the five times a day required by Islam. It was the focal point of the community, where immigrants could trade neighborhood gossip, mourn their dead, and discuss whatever recent disaster had swept over Afghanistan.

In the years before Mohammed came to the United States, the Afghans at Abu Bakr had rallied to the cause of the mujahideen fighting a holy war to oust the Soviets. Many of these men were deeply religious and believed that it was their duty as Muslims to expel the godless Soviets. With the Cold War still on, the mujahideen, considered guerrillas by the Red Army, were seen in America as allies in the battle against Communism. Television reporters trekked to the front lines in Pakistan to interview the men they glamorized. Members of Congress championed their cause, and the CIA secretly funneled hundreds of millions of dollars to them and supplied missiles to shoot down the Soviet helicopter gunships that strafed villages.

A sticker on the wall inside the popular Flushing Afghan-owned Kennedy Fried Chicken restaurant proclaimed, "I Love Afghanistan."[2] The owner, Abdul Karim, spoke openly in favor of the Islamic fighters and sent money home. "We are mujahideen," Karim said in 1988. "We wish to return, but it has to be a Muslim country and a new-fashioned government."[3] Around the corner, not far from Abu Bakr, a man named Imam Saifur Rehman Halimi, a member of an Islamic anti-Soviet organization called Hezb-i-Islami, opened the Afghan Mujahideen Information Bureau. At the time, Hezb-i-Islami's leader, Hekmatyar Gulbuddin, was an ally of the United States and on the CIA payroll. More than a decade later, the word *mujahideen* would take on a very different context in New York. And America would want former allies like Gulbuddin dead.

In 1989, with the war finally over, many in Flushing hoped their country would return to the relative prosperity it enjoyed in the decades prior. But some approached the future with wariness. They were concerned that the victorious Islamist factions would curtail freedoms and institute a harsh interpretation of Muslim law known as Sharia in a nation once known for its relative liberalism. "There will be no room for artists if the fundamentalists take over," Amanullah Haiderzad, the former dean of the College of Fine Arts at Kabul University, predicted at the time.[4]

The skeptics were right to be worried. In the vacuum left behind by the retreating Soviets, a ruinous civil war consumed the country. Warlords from the many tribes fought to take Kabul, which was still controlled by a pro-Soviet regime in 1992, leaving Uzbeks and Tajiks battling Pashtuns for power. Afghans were now dying at the hands of Afghans. The internecine fighting continued until Kabul had been destroyed. The schisms found their way to Flushing, where the growing community began replicating what was happening at home, fragmenting and splitting along tribal lines.

Mohammed Zazi, newly arrived but long used to the noise of expatriate politics, busied himself in carving out the abstemious life of an immigrant worker. For six years, he devoted himself to sending money to his wife and the children he didn't know, enough so they could move out of the refugee camps and into a house in Peshawar. He worked in a fast-food restaurant and was promoted to supervisor. But rather than open his own franchise like many other Afghans, he decided to become a taxi driver. His fares went to his children to go to school halfway around the world. "These years were very difficult for Mohammed," his wife would say many years later. "He was deprived from the joy of seeing his young kids, which is the joyous time of life for parents to watch their young kids grow."

In 1996 a group of fundamentalist Pashtun religious students known as the Taliban banded together to rid Afghanistan of violence. Their leader was a fearless peasant named Mullah Omar, who'd lost an eye fighting the Soviets. Omar was from the south of Afghanistan, near Kandahar, the country's second-largest city. With help from the Pakistani government, the Taliban succeeded in taking control of most of the country, except for a swath in the North controlled by the Tajik-dominated Northern Alliance. The Taliban brought peace to the country, but at a cost. Women could not go to school and were forced to wear full-length coverings known as burkas whenever they were in public. Music and kite flying, a popular Afghan pastime, were banned.

The Taliban also meted out harsh punishments for those who broke the law. Public beheadings at Kabul's Ghazi Stadium shocked the world.

That same year, Mohammed was granted asylum as a political refugee in the United States. Finally, he could apply for his family to join him in Flushing. Bibi, Merwari, and Najibullah boarded a plane bound for Queens. After Pakistan, it seemed like paradise. The family moved into a two-bedroom apartment. Najibullah, by then already eleven, enrolled in school and began learning English. But the family continued to struggle. In short order, Bibi gave birth to three more children, bringing the total to five. She and Mohammed took in a nephew, Amanullah, whose destitute parents remained in Pakistan. As the patriarch of the Flushing Zazis, Mohammed refused to apply for public assistance. He wasn't sick or handicapped. Those are the people who need food stamps, he'd tell his wife, adding that it was *haram*, forbidden by Islam, to take money you didn't need.

Instead, Mohammed drove the taxi six days a week, from eleven in the morning until one o'clock the following morning. He couldn't put together the thousands of dollars it would take to buy a taxi medallion, which would have allowed him to own a car instead of working for other people, but he still believed in the American dream that had brought him to Queens, and he reminded his children how fortunate they were to be in America instead of Afghanistan. He called the United States the greatest country in the world and told his children they should consider themselves Americans.

● ● ●

Najibullah Zazi embraced his new homeland as best as he could. But he struggled to learn English and wrestled with life in a foreign city. In 2000 he started as a freshman at Flushing High School. Built in 1875, the city's oldest public school was an imposing neo-Gothic landmark adorned with turrets and gargoyles. The building faced a commercial strip cluttered with Korean-language signs. In the halls of the school, Zazi found friends among those who had similar backgrounds. He bonded with other Muslim students—kids who, like him, had lived through war and displacement and were now faced with the battleground of American teenage life. Like Zazi, Zarein Ahmedzay had fled Afghanistan with his family. The two boys befriended each other immediately, and they also grew close to Adis Medunjanin, an ardent Muslim a year ahead of them who had escaped the Bosnian civil war in 1994 at age ten and whose family sought asylum in the United States.

When the school bell announced the end of the day, the three boys would walk the several blocks to pray at the new Abu Bakr, by then the largest Afghan mosque in the city. The original converted colonial-style house had been knocked down to make way for a mosque with an imposing marble facade capped by a blue-and-white diamond-patterned dome and a minaret that reached toward the urban sky. Zazi volunteered as a janitor and prayed there often, but he was also living a normal American teenage existence. With Ahmedzay and Medunjanin, Zazi would shoot hoops at a park down the street, and play pool and video games. Zazi loved his cell phone and computer, gadgets that were ubiquitous in Flushing's cheap electronic stores.

Then, at the beginning of Zazi's sophomore year, his world slipped off its axis. Flushing High was almost fifteen miles from ground zero in Lower Manhattan, but the crash of the al-Qaeda-piloted jetliners into the World Trade Center on September 11, 2001, reverberated throughout the Afghan community. Muslims—American citizens and immigrants alike—fell under intense suspicion simply because they were Muslims, requiring many to defend their allegiance to their adopted country in the newly declared War on Terror. The thousands of Afghans in Queens faced a doubly difficult reality: Their country had been used as a staging ground for al-Qaeda leader Osama bin Laden and his small army of terrorists to launch the devastating attacks on New York and

Washington, DC, and their homeland was now in the crosshairs of the US military.

One woman, Fatana Shirzad, a twenty-six-year-old who had left Afghanistan in 1993, told the *New York Times* how she felt: "When I saw this attack, I prayed, please make it not be Muslims. Because I knew. And I watched and I prayed, and I was very sorry."[5]

At Abu Bakr, ethnic tensions roiled the congregation. The mosque's soft-spoken and friendly imam, Mohammad Sherzad, was an educated Pashtun who despised the Taliban and accused them of committing atrocities against the insurgent Northern Alliance. But a contingent led by Imam Saifur Rehman Halimi, the former head of the Mujahideen Information Bureau, backed the Taliban, whose representatives had opened their own office the year before above a Taiwanese dental clinic on Flushing's Main Street. Halimi credited the Taliban with securing Afghanistan and ending the anarchy of the civil war. He wasn't convinced that bin Laden was behind the 9/11 attacks, and he believed bombing Afghanistan was a mistake. After Sherzad denounced the al-Qaeda attacks during services at the mosque, Halimi and his allies walked out and began to hold prayers outside. The split spilled into the newspapers. Sherzad complained that Halimi and his followers harassed him when he spoke out against the Taliban and bin Laden. They believed that bin Laden was a good Muslim.[6]

Mohammed Zazi backed Halimi. He and his son sided with the pro-Taliban faction praying in the parking lot. But, like others in the group, they appear to have been sympathetic to the Taliban, which was dominated by ethnic Pashtuns like them, not to al-Qaeda hijackers. "I don't know how people could do things like this. I'd never do anything like that," Najibullah Zazi told a friend later.[7] Like many in the Afghan community, he realized that people who had never given them a second thought were suddenly very interested in what they were doing. The police became a visible presence. Reporters were often around. In October the US invaded Afghanistan; pundits talked about bombing the country back to the Stone Age. In Flushing, Afghan immigrants began to subtly alter their behavior in public. Veiled women were reluctant to walk the streets. Mothers told their children to speak English and not Dari, one of Afghanistan's common dialects.

But as months and then years passed without incident, Zazi and the other Afghans went back to their daily routines. Restive and doing poorly in school, Zazi dropped out of Flushing High in 2003, his junior year. College wasn't in the cards, and he felt he could help his family most by earning money. He went to work stocking shelves in a Korean-owned grocery, packing a daily lunch of halal meat and rice. In 2005 Zazi decided to follow his older sister, Merwari, and her husband into the coffee cart business. Before the sun rose over New York, Zazi, now twenty, would trek to Brooklyn, load his cart with pastries, and tow it to Lower Manhattan, where he set up on Stone Street, eight blocks from ground zero. On his cart was a sign: "God Bless America."[8] His customers knew him, and he knew them, learning their tastes. When they approached, he had their morning favorites ready at hand.

But as time passed, customers noticed a change in the friendly Afghan coffee man. He tried to sell one of his customers a Koran, Islam's holy book. He lectured another about religion and happiness. He spoke less. The gentle, enterprising young immigrant seemed to be aging into a more severe and withdrawn adult.

Zazi wasn't alone. Already his friend Medunjanin had undergone a spiritual awakening in the ninth grade. He had prayed before a football game and scored a touchdown. The next game, he failed to pray and broke his arm. For Medunjanin, it was a sign that Allah was displeased with him, and he vowed not to fail again. He decided that he would teach his friends how to be good Muslims. Over the years, Medunjanin encouraged Zazi and Ahmedzay to dedicate their lives to Allah. By 2006, while Ahmedzay drove a cab and Zazi manned his coffee cart, Medunjanin worked as a security guard in Manhattan and studied economics at Queens College, where he became involved in the Muslim

Student Association. Medunjanin was active at Abu Bakr, holding short classes between prayers for the younger men, teaching them lessons from the Koran and proper Arabic. He explained the difference between spiritual and violent jihads.

All three were still living with their parents. Zazi had married a cousin, Marzia, in an arranged wedding in Peshawar in 2006. Ahmedzay was married and had a daughter living with his family in Afghanistan. The trio would still play hoops as they had when they were in high school; increasingly, though, they spent their time studying the Koran and other religious texts. Medunjanin introduced his friends to the sermons of Anwar al-Awlaki, a US citizen from Yemen and an influential al-Qaeda figure in his native land. A charismatic cleric, Awlaki had returned to Yemen from America, where he had lived in New Mexico, Southern California, and Virginia. He delivered inspiring sermons in English exhorting his followers to attack the United States. His diatribes were easy to find on the internet, and, in the view of American intelligence agencies, uniquely appealing to impressionable young men. Some of Awlaki's lectures dealt with becoming a martyr by fighting US forces in Afghanistan and Iraq. Others addressed such subjects as "The Hereafter" and "The Lives of the Prophets."

Zazi alone had a hundred hours of footage on his laptop and iPod. He also devoured lectures by Sheik Abdullah al-Feisel, a Jamaican-born imam who taught lessons with titles such as "Jihad, Aim and Objectives." Feisel said that suicide bombings were acceptable; they weren't considered suicide. Medunjanin agreed that was a good "war tactic."

Zazi and his friends listened to Awlaki's sermons almost every day. They also absorbed news about their parents' homeland. The American war in Afghanistan had demonstrably failed to improve the country. The Taliban, bolstered by hardened mujahideen fighters, was waging a relentless insurgency against US troops. For many Afghans, including those who had supported the invasion, the United States was now viewed as no better than the Russians or the British before them. Innocent civilians were dying in drone attacks and night raids, while the American-sponsored government foundered under the leadership of President Hamid Karzai. Zazi made regular trips to visit his wife in Peshawar, which the Taliban used as a base to wage war on the Americans in Afghanistan, recruiting fighters and raising money while Pakistani authorities looked the other way. What the young Afghan-American saw there only confirmed what he heard people say at home: The Americans were the source of Afghanistan's problems.

Together Zazi, Ahmedzay, and Medunjanin trawled the internet, collecting al-Qaeda videos of American forces being ambushed in Afghanistan and terrorists going on suicide missions. They grew beards. They kept up their American lives, but the propaganda was having its desired effect. The Taliban, they thought, were fighting for justice against American occupiers. It was up to them to do something about it.

• • •

In 2008 Medunjanin went on the hajj, the religious pilgrimage to Saudi Arabia. It was there that he learned, four years after they became public, about the photographs taken at the Abu Ghraib prison outside Baghdad by American military police as they abused and sexually humiliated their Iraqi captives. It only reinforced the sense of righteous injustice growing inside Medunjanin, who was looking for a purpose greater than guarding a fancy building in New York. When he returned to Flushing from Mecca, he talked about waging violent jihad. He challenged his Muslim friends to do something about US oppression. He thought they "didn't have the balls" to take on their adopted homeland. He imagined himself as a modern-day incarnation of rebel slave leader Nat Turner. Medunjanin refused to be a "house nigger."[9]

The three friends continued to pray at Abu Bakr, where Medunjanin wasn't shy about voicing his frustrations or inflammatory beliefs. They were an unlikely group of plotters: Medunjanin, doughy and book smart, the intellectual leader, a Bosnian who aspired to be a general in the Taliban army; Zazi, a polite but headstrong young man with a solid build and a disarmingly gentle expression, whose difficulty in school had left him insecure about his capabilities; and Ahmedzay, an avid conspiracy theorist who believed that Jews controlled a shadow government in the United States. In the spring of 2008, they gathered in the parking lot of Abu Bakr, out of earshot of anyone listening. After years of posturing, they had decided to turn their frustrations into action. "Allah doesn't like when you only talk about something and don't do it," Ahmedzay said, citing what he said was a verse from the Koran.

Standing outside the mosque, they made a pact: By summer's end, they would go to Afghanistan to fight with the Taliban against American forces. Medunjanin reminded his friends to be careful. Law enforcement was everywhere. He told them to avoid talking about their plans with anyone or putting anything in emails.

They decided to join the Taliban because the group seemed to offer the easiest route to the battlefield. Ahmedzay had heard there was a town called Zormat in eastern Afghanistan where a foreign fighter could find the Taliban at the madrassa, or religious school. The town was only thirty minutes from his wife's home. Both Zazi and Ahmedzay spoke fluent Pashto, and they could translate for Medunjanin, their Bosnian brother in arms. If anyone asked why they were planning to go to the region, Zazi and Ahmedzay had perfect cover stories: They both had family in Afghanistan, and wives whom they were going to visit. Medunjanin, they would say, was going to marry a cousin of Zazi's. To their minds, it was foolproof.

To finance their trip, Zazi turned to credit cards. He opened nearly twenty accounts in a space of months, with no intention of paying them back, and burned through about $50,000 on computers, cameras, batteries, and cash advances. Zazi, Ahmedzay, and Medunjanin went to a travel agency in Jackson Heights to buy their tickets, but instead of using Najib's credit cards, they paid in cash. They booked round-trip flights on Qatar Airways, changing in Doha, Qatar, even though it was more expensive. They didn't want the additional scrutiny that came with traveling on one-way tickets, but they had no intention of ever returning to America. Zazi and Ahmedzay got long-stay visas to Pakistan, but Balkan-born Medunjanin was granted only a monthlong stay. They decided to split responsibilities. Medunjanin was going to be in charge until they got to Pakistan. Then Zazi, after visiting his family there, would take over, and Ahmedzay would lead them through Afghanistan.

About two weeks before they were scheduled to fly to Pakistan, they told one person about their plan: another young Afghan born in New York named Zakir Khan, whom they knew at Abu Bakr. Khan had spent many hours with Medunjanin and the others. He had listened to their thoughts on jihad and expressed similar views. Medunjanin put Awlaki lectures on Khan's iPod. At the mosque, they cornered him and asked if he would be interested in joining them to fight in Afghanistan. Khan said he'd think about it. Rather than worrying he'd spill their secret, the trio encouraged Khan to talk to his family and friends about the idea.

Khan went home, where he helped take care of a little brother with physical and mental disabilities. When he returned to the mosque that same evening to talk to Zazi and Medunjanin, it was with disappointing news. He couldn't make the trip. The two responded angrily. Zazi showed Khan a verse from the Koran saying that it was his duty. Khan said he'd reconsider, and did discuss it with a family friend. But the next day, he ran into Medunjanin, Zazi, and Ahmedzay outside the mosque. Khan informed them of his decision. No.

• • •

On August 28 Zazi's father gave them a lift to Newark International Airport. There was nothing suspicious for security screeners to find in their bags, just some laptops. Customs officials asked all three separately why they were going to Pakistan They used the cover stories they had discussed. Medunjanin was carrying $3,000, money that he told customs agents would be the dowry in his marriage to Zazi's cousin. The trio made it through security, boarded, and settled in for the long flight to Doha and then on to Peshawar.

Peshawar is a sprawling frontier city, centuries old, that sits in a valley outside Pakistan's Federally Administered Tribal Areas, or FATA, the far-flung districts where tribal elders hold sway and remain somewhat autonomous from the Pakistani government. For decades, Peshawar has attracted Afghan refugees and Islamist radicals involved in pushing foreign troops—whether Soviet or American—out of nearby Afghanistan. Some 3.5 million people are believed to live in the city and the surrounding district, amid the constant noise of car horns and calls to prayer from numerous mosques. For the three American-raised Muslims, Peshawar's clogged maze of avenues, streets, and alleys, full of children dodging cars and donkeys, was alive in a way that Flushing had never been.

Zazi's family greeted them at the airport in Peshawar, trading hugs and kisses with Najib and his new friends. Then they drove their guests to the rented house of Zazi's uncle Lal Muhammad, fifteen minutes away, where the travelers spent the night. The next day, they split up, partly because Zazi wanted to spend time with his wife and family before heading on to Afghanistan. He urged Medunjanin and Ahmedzay to go ahead to Afghanistan without him.

They didn't get far. Zazi drove them to the bus station, where they rented a car. Ahmedzay was dressed in a traditional Pakistani garb called a *shalwar kameez,* which consists of a long shirt and pajama-like pants, while Medunjanin had on Western-style clothes. On their way out of town, they ran into a Pakistani police checkpoint, where they faced questions: Who are you? Where are you going? Ahmedzay replied in fluent Pashto that they were going to Khyber Agency, an area technically off-limits to foreigners, to see his family. Then Ahmedzay and Medunjanin pulled out their US passports. The police immediately suspected that the fair-skinned Medunjanin worked for the CIA and assumed that Ahmedzay was his translator. The officers ordered them into the back of a pickup. As the truck pulled away, Medunjanin started to chant from the Koran in Arabic. One officer grew curious, and asked Ahmedzay if Medunjanin was a Muslim. Ahmedzay answered yes. The sympathetic officer told Ahmedzay to tell the police chief they were visiting the area. At the station, they repeated what the officer told them to say, and the chief set them free. Ahmedzay called Zazi, who sent his uncle to fetch them.

The three were going to need help navigating their way across the border. Luckily, Zazi's cousin Amanullah had connections—and he owed Zazi's family a favor. In 1999 Mohammed Zazi had filled out paperwork claiming Amanullah as his own son, a lie that could have jeopardized the entire family's immigration status. He was close to Najibullah in age, and the two were like brothers during the years that Amanullah had spent with the Zazis in Flushing. But Amanullah struggled to adjust. He began smoking pot, his grades suffered, and he started getting into fights. In 2003 his uncle sent him back to Pakistan for six months to pull himself together. But Amanullah kept up his drug habit, and when he returned to Queens, he began drinking heavily and experimenting with cocaine. Fed up, Mohammed Zazi shipped him back to Pakistan in 2004. When Najibullah Zazi and his friends arrived in Peshawar, Amanullah was still doing drugs, but he knew an imam—someone with whom he'd once studied—who was the sort of person the young Americans were looking to meet.

The imam, it turned out, didn't know anyone from the Taliban. But he told Zazi and his friends that he had contacts with another anti-American mujahideen group. On Amanullah's reference, the imam introduced the three men to a Pakistani who was in his midtwenties and went by the name Ahmad. On the imam's recommendation, Ahmad agreed to take Zazi and his friends to a training compound in Waziristan, the tribal region in northwest Pakistan along the Afghan border that is a beehive of jihadist groups, including the only one with global brand recognition: al-Qaeda. Waziristan was nearly two hundred miles from Peshawar, and the trip would take two days on less-traveled roads. Medunjanin took the battery out of his BlackBerry, believing that the device contained a Global Positioning System that would allow him to be tracked.

It sounded even more thrilling than anything that the three could have imagined back in Queens. Zazi cut short his time with his family, and Ahmedzay postponed visiting his wife in Afghanistan. As they started their journey in a four-door gray Toyota, Ahmad instructed the three friends to begin using aliases. At the first police checkpoint they encountered, Zazi and the other Americans fell silent, fearing a repeat of what had happened to Medunjanin and Ahmedzay a few days earlier. Now, though, they had Ahmad to provide cover. He got out of the car and approached the checkpoint, speaking briefly with the police as Zazi watched nervously. The police walked toward to the car, moved to the back, and opened the trunk. Satisfied with their cursory search, the officers waved them on.

The hours passed. Zazi and Ahmedzay spoke in Urdu with Ahmad, leaving Medunjanin, usually the ringleader, frozen out of the conversation. Ahmad explained that there were many foreign fighters in his group. They believed in global jihad, he explained, not just fighting the Americans in Afghanistan.

Ahmedzay realized that Ahmad was not from any mujahideen outfit. They had landed themselves with a bona fide al-Qaeda operative. Every year, a new crop of American would-be jihadis flies to Pakistan or Afghanistan to try to join al-Qaeda. The organization, wary of infiltration by Western intelligence, maintained networks of screeners whose jobs were to weed through the eager young recruits, looking for moles. Ahmad, apparently, had decided that this motley little group—two Afghans, one by way of Peshawar, and a Bosnian, all thoroughly Americanized in Queens—were for real. For him, it meant bringing his superiors the prize that al-Qaeda most valued: assets who could move freely in the West, especially in America, without attracting the notice of intelligence and security services.

• • •

At the end of their second day on the road, the group reached Miram Shah, the town that had become al-Qaeda's de facto headquarters since the terrorist group fled Afghanistan. Perched high in the mountains southwest of Peshawar, it was originally built in 1905 by the British as a fort from which they could manage Waziristan. Today it is in one of Pakistan's Federally Administered Tribal Areas and is a frequent target for American drone strikes.

Ahmad deposited his charges at a guesthouse in a residential area, where they stayed for two days. There were about a half-dozen rooms surrounding a brick courtyard. The friends were comfortable as they waited to see what happened next. Soon a group of al-Qaeda operatives came to inspect the Americans. The first introduced himself as Ibrahim. He had a slight build, an olive complexion, and a beard. Zazi had no idea at the time that he was talking to Rashid Rauf. A dual citizen of Britain and Pakistan, Rauf had played a role in a failed 2006 plot to bring down as many as ten airliners over the Atlantic Ocean. In the wake of its disruption, he had been arrested by the Pakistanis but escaped to Waziristan. The other man who appeared with Rauf was a tall, slender black man who wore a paramilitary vest and carried an AK-47 slung over his back. He introduced himself as Abdul Hafeez, and the three Americans could tell that he was important.

Hafeez and Rauf watched these American strangers cautiously. Were they working for the CIA? Paranoia pulsed through the terrorist group. Over the years since the American invasion of Afghanistan, al-Qaeda's ranks had been thinned because of traitors who supplied information to the CIA. Then the drones came. These men weren't inclined to trust strangers.

They all sat on the floor of the ramshackle guesthouse and made small talk in English. Zazi, Ahmedzay, and Medunjanin said they were from New York. Hafeez inquired why the three had come to Pakistan. Zazi explained that they wanted to fight against the Americans in Afghanistan and kill as many as possible. He was careful to describe his countrymen as "the enemy." They had grown up hearing stories about their native land suffering under the scourge of foreign power, and they wanted to hasten the day when, once again, Afghanistan's oppressors were vanquished. Hafeez was impressed. It wasn't easy to make it here and find them, he said. These guys had guts and had already evaded US intelligence.

Before the meeting, Hafeez had already decided that these young men would not be wasted fighting the United States in Afghanistan. Pakistan had no lack of young men who could be served up as cannon fodder for the American howitzers and F-15 fighter jets. The men now sitting in front of Hafeez were unusual. They had American passports, they were not under suspicion by the US authorities, and they were apparently willing to die. Hafeez told the trio that he would like them to go back to America on a special mission. They had valuable assets, like their ability to speak English and blend in, Hafeez said. Zazi and the others knew what this meant. The three had been tapped to be suicide bombers.

Once Hafeez finished his pitch, Rauf recited a story about the Prophet Muhammad. "There was once a man who came to the Prophet from the opposing side and told him he wanted to help him, join his ranks. And the Prophet told him, 'You're just one man, and you don't really add to our numbers. You should go back and do something on the other side.' "[10] You should follow the words of the Prophet, Rauf concluded. Then Hafeez and Rauf asked the men if they had made their decision. Would they be suicide bombers? Startled, Zazi turned to his friends and, almost without thinking, replied, "No."

Hafeez responded with gentle persuasion. Think about it, he told them. He then asked the three New Yorkers to hand over their passports. Hafeez and Rauf left the house, leaving their impressionable young guests to mull over the situation. Carrying out a suicide bombing was the ultimate sacrifice, and Hafeez knew that he couldn't force them into taking on the role—not if he wanted whatever plans he'd laid for them to succeed. Hafeez had been down this path before with others. Hafeez and Rauf told the Americans they would come back.

Anxious and alone, the friends huddled at the house, unsure of what might happen next. They had told two representatives of al-Qaeda, the most feared terrorist group on earth, "No thanks." Who lives to tell that story? Al-Qaeda could behead them and bury their bodies, and nobody would ever know. But none of the three friends thought martyrdom by suicide sounded appealing, even though they had come all the way to Southwest Asia hoping to die fighting under a Taliban banner. This wasn't what they had signed up for when they talked big outside their mosque in Queens. So what if al-Qaeda thought they were cowards? They'd stick to their plan and go fight in Afghanistan, assuming that they made it out of there alive.

Four or five days passed without any contact from al-Qaeda, unsettling the trio. They waited and waited. They bickered and turned on Medunjanin, saying that his light skin was a burden and attracting unwanted attention. And he couldn't speak any of the local languages, either. With no word from Ahmad, the owner of the guesthouse told them to leave. He didn't want any trouble, and, clearly, these men were not from the area.

The three gathered their stuff and made contact with a shopkeeper in town, a man Ahmad had told them to seek out if there was trouble. The shopkeeper told them about a nearby hotel, where they spent the night. The next day, they returned to the shop. Finally, a pair of cars with tinted windows pulled up with Hafeez. They complained about his unexplained absence, about being kicked out of the house and having to find a place to stay. He brushed them off, saying that he had slept in worse places than a hotel. He took them back to the shop, where they were provided Pakistani identification cards with the names they had chosen. Ahmedzay would be Omar. Medunjanin would be Mohammed, and Zazi chose Salahuddin. Then, whatever their misgivings, they got in a car with Hafeez. Together the three young men continued their journey into the hinterlands with the mysterious man who held great sway in al-Qaeda.

Hafeez drove for hours, avoiding major highways, stopping for the night at an empty house. He told the friends not to tell anybody where they were really from. If someone asks, he said, Ahmedzay and Zazi are from Peshawar, and Medunjanin from Syria. He told them to use their fake names.

The next day, they reached their destination, a mud compound with twenty-foot-high walls. This was a terrorist training camp, one of the locations seldom seen by Americans who aren't drone pilots.

The three friends saw no other trainees, but they met a Pakistani who would teach them martial arts and a Canadian named Ferid Imam who handled weapons training. Over two weeks, they were taught to operate small arms. The weapon of choice was the Russian AK-47. Ferid taught them to take apart and clean the assault rifle, and how to assume the correct firing positions. They also handled another Russian weapon, the PK machine gun, which is commonly used in Afghanistan and is very effective in laying down suppressive fire for an ambush. The three fired rocket-propelled grenade launchers—exactly the kind of high-powered weapons they had dreamed of using when they first embarked on their journey. They developed an easy rapport with their instructor and settled into a routine, waking up before dawn to train but spending little time outside because of the increasing drone attacks. At night, they took turns handling guard duty.[11]

Zazi and his friends were in Pakistan at a pivotal moment in America's drone war. At the CIA, Director Michael Hayden persuaded President George W. Bush to increase the pace of attacks inside Pakistan. Drones became common sights above Miram Shah while Zazi was there. In early September, drones launched Hellfire missiles into a home in a village not far where Zazi was staying. The target was Jalaluddin Haqqani, a pro-Taliban insurgent leader who was once a paid CIA asset in the war against the Soviet Union.[12] Haqqani survived. Nearly two dozen others were killed, including his eight grandchildren, one of his two wives, his sister, and his sister-in-law.[13]

There were more attacks in September 2008 than in any month since the drone assault began in 2004. It was a turning point in the war against al-Qaeda: the moment when the drone went from being America's occasional weapon to its preferred method of hunting and killing. But there is a saying among the Pashtun people in Pakistan: "Kill one person, make ten enemies." The September drone campaign was a turning point for Zazi and his friends, too.

A few days after their arrival, another man appeared. He said his name was Hamad, and he had long hair, a slight paunch, dark skin, and a large nose. He also spoke with an American accent. Hamad's real name was Adnan el-Shukrijumah and he knew America better than almost anybody in al-Qaeda. He also spoke English better than anybody in the room, which surprised Zazi. Born in Saudi Arabia, Shukrijumah spent fifteen years in the United States, mostly in Florida, where he grew up and attended a community college in Miami. During the 1990s, he trained in al-Qaeda's camps in Afghanistan, and he left the United States in May 2001. American intelligence had been looking for him since 2003, but Shukrijumah had avoided both capture and death, and now used his knowledge of America to advise al-Qaeda on the best way to cripple its enemy.

Shukrijumah carried a laptop loaded with propaganda videos, which the three Americans watched when they weren't on guard duty or practicing their new weapons skills. The videos highlighted the September 11 attacks, ambushes on coalition forces in Afghanistan, the 2005 London subway and bus bombings, a 2008 suicide mission on the Danish Embassy in Islamabad, and assorted video testimonies by martyrs. They had already seen some of the videos, which were produced by the media arm of al-Qaeda. Shukrijumah pushed them to think harder about what they were seeing and how it related to what they were learning at the camp. He told them that mastering the explosives needed to build a bomb was easy.

When he had exhausted the videos, Shukrijumah pounced. He asked if the friends were ready to go back to the States and follow the path that Abdul Hafeez had suggested in Miram Shah. He promised all the glory and pleasure that a *shaheed*, or holy martyr, would receive in heaven. In private conversations, away from the solidarity of the group, he pressed each of them individually. But still the friends resisted.

Shukrijumah engaged them another way. Let's discuss potential targets, he said. What places should al-Qaeda attack? Shukrijumah volunteered that he thought Walmart, the world's largest retailer, would make an attractive target because it was a vital economic engine. The Americans began to throw out ideas. So would the New York Stock Exchange, Zazi said, near where he had once operated his coffee cart. As a taxi driver, Ahmedzay liked Times Square. There were many tourists there, he offered. The friends suggested the subway, which they argued was even more important than the one in London. They agreed it was the heart of New York City.[14]

The answers pleased Shukrijumah. They were engaged and thinking big. Shukrijumah said they could defeat the United States in Afghanistan by striking at home. That would put pressure on the government to pull out of Afghanistan. They would avenge the drone attacks. But Shukrijumah was running up against one of the toughest obstacles al-Qaeda has faced in planning strikes against the United States. Though America has a perception of al-Qaeda as a limitless army of holy warriors, the truth is that finding people willing to kill themselves for God was hard, particularly in the United States.

Zazi asked why Shukrijumah didn't send his own better-trained al-Qaeda operatives. Shukrijumah said it was too expensive and difficult to get past US security. "It's easy for you guys to go back and do the mission," Shukrijumah answered.[15]

Near the end of training, the three finally told Shukrijumah they would accept al-Qaeda's mission. Part of the reason they changed their minds: the drone attacks. Everywhere they looked, unmanned warplanes patrolled the skies. News reports showed a string of missile strikes and the screaming civilians left in its wake. That was the issue that finally broke their resolve. They would become suicide bombers.

• • •

When Abdul Hafeez reappeared and learned of their decision, he was pleased.[16] He told Zazi and Ahmedzay that they would complete the explosives training, while Medunjanin would return to the United States so he didn't violate the terms of his visa.

All three returned to Peshawar, taking a bus from Miram Shah. Ahmad met them and handed back their passports. On September 25 Medunjanin flew back to the United States. Ahmedzay then went to Afghanistan to see his wife and children. Zazi stayed in Peshawar with his family until November, when Barack Obama defeated John McCain in the 2008 US presidential election. Ahmad returned to take Zazi and Ahmedzay back for explosives training, but Ahmedzay didn't show. Zazi covered for his friend, telling Ahmad that there must have been a family emergency. The pair drove to Miram Shah and waited for Hafeez, who took them to a compound in South Waziristan, a five-hour drive away. It was different but built along similar lines, with high walls and spartan rooms. But here there was no Ferid Imam, with his assortment of guns. Instead, there were two men whose job it was to teach Zazi how to make a bomb.

Zazi studied safety and mixing procedures. Goggles and proper ventilation were necessary, he was told. He learned the parts of the bomb. He would have to master basic chemistry and figure out the mechanics of building a virtually undetectable TATP detonator and the main charge out of easily available ingredients: acetone, hydrogen peroxide, hydrochloric acid, and baking soda. The instructors walked Zazi through the steps. He kept a notebook and wrote it all down, suddenly a responsible student. His instructor said buying the components for the detonator was simple. The acetone could be found at a beauty supply store because it is used in nail polish remover, and large hardware stores would stock hydrochloric acid, used for cleaning pools, while hydrogen peroxide and baking soda were at any grocery.

After the TATP was ready, Zazi could start on the rest of the bomb. Buy a lightbulb, his teacher said, and break it so that the wires are visible. Then pack ground-up match heads inside. He would need batteries and wire to light the bulb. The visible wires would ignite the powder and set off the detonator. Last came the main charge. Zazi had several options, including hydrogen peroxide with flour; again, rudimentary, but effective. The final construction involved a two-liter plastic bottle, which would hold the detonator. He could carry it in a backpack, where he would place the main charge around the plastic bottle, and surround it with shrapnel, such as ball bearings. Zazi's instructors wanted him to have field experience, not classroom theory. As they supervised, he built and tested a TATP detonator inside the yard of the compound. It was a success. To be certain that the main charge worked, the student and his teachers drove about thirty miles from the compound to the top of a hill. They set a complete bomb under a rock and detonated it. One of the al-Qaeda members videotaped the explosion that followed.

One day Shukrijumah appeared and pressed Zazi to make a suicide video, the kind commonly released online after an attack. The young man struggled to find the right words for his video, so Shukrijumah wrote him a statement. Zazi read some verses from the Koran and said that this was payback for the atrocities America had committed in Iraq and Afghanistan. Shukrijumah said he'd keep the video in a safe place and release it after the mission was complete. Since 9/11, al-Qaeda had repeatedly tried and failed to carry out another attack inside America. Now these Americans were on the verge of doing just that.

By this time, Zazi was ready to leave the camp, figuring that his family probably worried about him. Abdul Hafeez said he could go but would need to teach his friends how to make the bomb. Hafeez then took him to Miram Shah and reminded him to stay in touch with Ahmad. Zazi boarded the bus to Peshawar with his bomb-making notes and pictures tucked in his bag.

Back in Peshawar, he found Ahmedzay waiting for him. Zazi asked why he had missed explosives training. There was a problem, Ahmedzay explained. He had told his wife about their first meeting with al-Qaeda, and when he told her he was going back for more training, she gave him an ultimatum: It's either al-Qaeda or his family. She threatened to kill herself and their daughter if Ahmedzay went back.

Zazi was undeterred. He empathized with his friend about his domestic troubles but promptly set about catching up Ahmedzay on what he had learned in Waziristan. Zazi copied his training notes into a new notebook and gave the old one to Ahmedzay, who was going back to Afghanistan to spend some more time with his family. Zazi then went to an internet café, scanned in his new notes, and saved them on a CD. He asked an employee to email him the contents of the CD so he could leave his notebook in Peshawar rather than risk being caught with it in his luggage on his way back to New York.

Before he left, Zazi created a new email address and gave it to Ahmad, his conduit to the al-Qaeda leaders who would guide his mission. Ahmad told Zazi not to discuss "bombs" in an email. When preparations were ready, Ahmad said, use a code word like *wedding*.

On January 15, 2009, Zazi flew home. Seven days later, Ahmedzay left Pakistan, too. Within days of returning to Queens, Zazi made his way through the winter cold to Abu Bakr. There he spotted his good friend Medunjanin. It has been four months since they had last seen each other, and they embraced warmly. Zazi explained what happened in Pakistan and how he trained to make bombs.

Abdul Hafeez sends you his greetings, Zazi said.

Hearing this name excited Medunjanin. While his friends remained in Southwest Asia, Medunjanin had been searching the internet for information about the mysterious al-Qaeda operatives who had recruited them.

Medunjanin eventually figured out that Hafeez was actually Saleh al-Somali, the man responsible for plotting al-Qaeda's terror attacks outside of Pakistan and Afghanistan. The CIA called him al-Qaeda's chief of external operations and he had a big bounty on his head. Few Americans had ever laid eyes on him. Back in New York, Don Borelli knew him only from the files the FBI kept on al-Qaeda's most senior leaders.

Al-Somali held one of the most important jobs in all of al-Qaeda, a position once held by 9/11 mastermind Khalid Sheikh Mohammed. It was up to him to execute Osama bin Laden's murderous vision. Though bin Laden was holed up in a compound in Abbottabad, Pakistan, without access to phones or the internet, he used his network of trusted couriers to send word to his subordinates demanding more attacks.

"We need to extend and develop our operations in America and not keep it limited to only blowing up airplanes," he wrote in one missive.[17]

In nearly a decade, bin Laden had been unable to orchestrate a follow-up to his terrorist masterwork. With three young men from New York, al-Somali might finally be able to give bin Laden what he wanted most.

Medunjanin had gone to Pakistan expecting to join a low-level Taliban brigade. Instead, he had touched what seemed to him like greatness. He had spent only a brief time with al-Somali but had developed intense feelings, a warmth he could describe only as love. He was devoted to al-Somali the way a soldier revered a beloved general. And he had no intention of letting him down.[18]

Zazi also told Medunjanin that he had decided to leave New York. His plan was move to a suburb of Denver, where his aunt and other relatives lived. Zazi was convinced that American law enforcement officials would eventually find out the trio had traveled to Pakistan on the same flight and then returned to the same neighborhood. If the friends split up, Zazi reasoned, it would appear as if they were going on with their lives. As the two parted, Zazi said they would see each other soon.

Zazi returned to New York in August 2009 to check on his coffee cart and to scout locations to buy hydrogen peroxide and acetone. While there, he met Ahmedzay, and the two spent a weekend at Bear Mountain State Park in upstate New York. Zazi said he was confident he could make three suicide vests. Zazi, Ahmedzay, and Medunjanin would die on the busy 3, 4, and 5 trains. The trio would strike during Ramadan next month.

The initial blast from a backpack bomb would kill anyone standing nearby, but the worst damage would come milliseconds later. The train would be permeated by speeding shrapnel: ball bearings, shards of metal from the subway car, plastic from shredded seats. Survivors would have to grope toward safety through billows of toxic smoke, past mangled bodies, and jagged debris in darkened tunnels.

The final step was for Ahmedzay and Medunjanin to tape their martyrdom videos. They would protest the presence of American troops in Iraq and Afghanistan. Medunjanin would look into the camera and tell viewers that he loved death more than they love life.

With the planning done, Zazi returned to Colorado for the last time.

• • •

A few weeks later, Zazi was back in his old neighborhood, exhausted after more than thirty hours on the road. He was also panicked from having been stopped on the bridge. When the police brought out the dog, Zazi had decided he'd jump off the George Washington if the cops found his explosives in the trunk.[19]

Sitting in the car, waiting for Ahmedzay to return from the apartment, Zazi felt he was being watched. But he had made it this far. Maybe he could still pull off the attack.

The jar he had instructed Ahmedzay to take and put somewhere safe was filled with acetone peroxide, the highly unstable chemical compound known as TATP. Even though TATP's instability was widely known, it remained an explosive of choice for al-Qaeda operatives because of its readily available ingredients. The kitchen-sink bomb had been used against subways and a bus in London in 2005. Hundreds died in those devastating attacks, a reminder that al-Qaeda still had the wherewithal to strike at the West.

The mixture was undetectable to most bomb-sniffing dogs, which sense powder explosives. Only dogs that undergo specialized training can recognize TATP. The dog on the bridge had not, so the explosives had been invisible. Maybe the cop on the bridge could have detected it if he'd been able to swab Zazi's trunk—as everyone at the FBI believed he'd done. But it was too late now. The FBI's plan of keeping a bomb out of New York had failed, and nobody knew it.

6

ZONE DEFENSE

Don Borelli arrived at the FBI's New York office in fall of 2005, a transfer from Dallas by way of Amman, Jordan. After a few months on a squad investigating a grab bag of cases, mostly civil rights abuses and child porn, he moved to CT-9: the Joint Terrorism Task Force squad dedicated to Iran and Hezbollah. It was a natural fit. As assistant legal attaché in Jordan, he'd frequently traveled to Syria and Lebanon. It was also a timely move. Borelli arrived on CT-9—a team of FBI agents, NYPD detectives, immigration agents, and more—months before war broke out between Israel and Hezbollah.

The assignment put Borelli in charge of one investigation that would color his view of Cohen. And though he didn't know it at the time, it provided a glimpse of a new strategy taking shape across the street at the NYPD Intelligence Division, one that secretly redefined policing and intelligence gathering in New York.

Hezbollah was infamous for truck bombings at the US Embassy and a US Marine barracks in Beirut in 1983, killing hundreds. It is heavily funded by Iran, does not recognize the right of Israel to exist, and opposes the influence of the United States and Israel on Lebanese affairs. Hezbollah is also a political party, a member of Lebanon's majority ruling coalition. It runs schools and health clinics and is extremely popular in Shiite-dominated southern Lebanon.

There are Hezbollah supporters and members in New York. Whether Hezbollah is using them to plan acts of terrorism, however, has been a subject of debate among policy makers and academics. Few people inside the US government knew more about the domestic Hezbollah threat than two CT-9 investigators, NYPD detective Wayne Parola and his partner, FBI agent John Sorge. Colleagues said the duo had a knack for making sources and "turning threats into friends." When analysts at CIA headquarters had questions about Hezbollah, they knew to call Parola or Sorge.

Based in no small part on that deep knowledge, many in the federal government had concluded that although Hezbollah was still a US-designated terrorist group, its presence in New York posed little immediate danger. And if one arose, Parola and Sorge would know. It wasn't a conclusion that the government liked to advertise, but investigators believed that Hezbollah members in New York functioned more as a criminal organization producing knockoff designer clothes and selling black market cigarettes. Some of that money got sent to Lebanon for families and the organization. But in the scheme of things, when compared with the funding from Iran's oil coffers, the money from counterfeit Nikes was a drop in the bucket. The FBI occasionally brought terror-financing cases against Hezbollah members. But for the most part, the government figured there was more to be gained by letting these Lebanese guys do their thing and letting Parola and Sorge do theirs.

When Borelli joined CT-9, investigators had their eye on a Lebanese man who'd entered the country a few years earlier from Brazil.[1] It appeared that he'd used a fake name and, thus, probably phony immigration papers. He'd settled in an apartment in the Bronx, selling counterfeit goods. The Joint Terrorism Task Force and Brazilian intelligence officials were working together trying to figure out the mystery man's identity. The Brazilians learned that he had ties to Hezbollah, having once helped the group buy equipment such as night-vision goggles.

Working with federal prosecutors, CT-9 began building a case against the man. They could probably get him on document fraud and supporting a terrorist group. But the plan was to turn him into a source and learn what he knew about Hezbollah. That intelligence was more valuable than a prison term. The FBI interviewed the Lebanese stranger several times, but delicately. Agents never mentioned terrorism or Hezbollah.

Across the street at Intel, Cohen, too, focused on Hezbollah. He had been interested since his CIA days and the string of deadly attacks in the 1980s. With Hezbollah and the Israel Defense Forces fighting in southern Lebanon, Cohen's focus intensified. Though some NYPD analysts shared the FBI's benign assessment of Hezbollah in New York, Cohen did not. In fact, one of his senior officers described him as fixated, a view that filtered through the ranks. Investigators were asked repeatedly what they had on Hezbollah. Supervisors told NYPD analysts to rewrite papers to punch up the militant group's significance, even when the analysts believed the importance was being overstated.[2]

In the NYPD's eyes, anyone from southern Lebanon could be a Hezbollah sympathizer.[3] The department's analytical documents made no distinction between Hezbollah supporters and Hezbollah members, a conflation that ignored the complexities of Lebanon and the difference between Hezbollah's political and militant roles. In 2006, with tensions between the United States and Iran mounting over Iranian nuclear enrichment, Cohen wanted his detectives to dig harder on Hezbollah activities. NYPD analysts believed that, if war broke out between the countries, Hezbollah supporters might stage an attack in New York.[4]

Cohen's distaste for the FBI's laissez-faire approach to Hezbollah was not new. In one tense meeting in 2003, members of the task force gathered in a fourteenth-floor conference room at One Police Plaza to update Cohen on a Hezbollah case. Agitated over the plodding investigation, Cohen quipped that his guys could do more in three weeks than the FBI could in years.[5] Parola, who'd helped investigate al-Qaeda's

1998 bombings at US embassies in Africa, piped up. As far as national security went, he said, the targets had done nothing wrong.

Well, get them to do something, Cohen shot back.

There are rules, Parola said. As part of the federal task force, he was bound by the attorney general's guidelines.

Your rules don't apply to us, Cohen replied.

There's a Constitution, Parola said.

The comment hung over the room. Detectives didn't talk to a deputy commissioner like that. Cohen waved his hand in the air, dismissing Parola's barb. The briefing continued.

Nevertheless, Borelli's boss, Joe Demarest, the special agent in charge for counterterrorism, made clear that his agents were to share information with Cohen and the Intelligence Division. That was fine by Borelli. Back in Dallas, he'd enjoyed good relationships with the locals. He was one of the first field office coordinators dedicated to planning responses to attacks by nuclear, chemical, or biological weapons. The job required him to work with police, firefighters, and hospitals. And in Jordan, he'd worked closely with the CIA station chief, Charlie Seidel, one of the agency's most respected officers, who had also served as Cohen's deputy in New York and took a major role in running operations.[6] Borelli didn't think twice about sending an investigator to brief the Intelligence Division on the mysterious stranger who'd arrived from Brazil.

The day after the briefing, Cohen's detectives drove to the Bronx and knocked on the Lebanese man's door. The cops pitched him: You should become an informant for the NYPD. Less than two days later, the man boarded a flight to São Paulo, Brazil, taking with him whatever information he had about Hezbollah. The FBI agent heading the investigation for the task force hit the roof. The NYPD had blown his case. Borelli had never seen anything like it. To this day, he won't discuss details of the case. But Borelli took it as a lesson: Cohen could not be trusted. To the FBI's top officials in New York, Cohen seemed more interested in making the big score than in keeping the city safe.

The bureau didn't understand the philosophical change that had occurred across the footbridge in NYPD Intel. Cohen wasn't preoccupied with outmaneuvering the FBI—although if that happened, too, then all the better. Rather, he had engineered a fundamental shift in strategy, one that in no way involved falling in line behind the FBI. Cohen would gladly take the FBI's intelligence, but that didn't mean he had to accept the bureau's conclusions about who was a threat and who wasn't. That's groupthink, the kind of blind allegiance to conventional wisdom that had created the biggest intelligence blind spot since Pearl Harbor.

Cohen rejected several offers by the FBI to put his people on the task force. Dustups like the one over Hezbollah happened, but he saw them as the natural result of a healthy tension between two intelligence agencies.

Emboldened by the new, lax Handschu rules, Cohen charted a new course. The FBI focused on spotting terrorists, and then putting agents on them to make cases. He hatched a bolder plan, one that preemptively investigated neighborhoods, ethnic groups, organizations, mosques, and businesses. The NYPD named it "zone defense,"[7] after the sports strategy in which a player guards a portion of the field rather than a specific man. To pull it off, the NYPD wanted to identify terrorists early. Not just before they launched an attack; that was a given. Cohen wanted to spot them before they picked targets, before they bought weapons, and, ideally, before a toxic ideology took root.

Cohen wanted to know whether you were going to be a terrorist before you knew yourself.

• • •

In 2007 the NYPD published *Radicalization in the West: The Homegrown Threat*, a ninety-page primer on how Muslims became terrorists. Drawing on case studies of terrorist plots in Madrid, London, Amsterdam, and elsewhere, it was a guide to spotting would-be terrorists. For the first time, here was a document that told authorities what warning signs to watch for.

The authors were two senior intelligence analysts, Mitchell Silber and Arvin Bhatt. Silber, an Ivy League–educated financial analyst and investment banker, became the public face of the report and would go on to lead Cohen's analytical unit. After the corporation Thomson Financial bought his company, Silber headed to Columbia University and earned his master's degree in international affairs in 2005. The NYPD was his first job in national security, and the breakout *Radicalization in the West* got noticed by the national media, scholars, and Congress.

It suggested that becoming a terrorist was a four-step process, from preradicalization and self-identification to indoctrination and, finally, "jihadization." Nascent terrorists are typically in an identity crisis, the NYPD said. Some might be angry over discrimination or racism. Others might be angered by the Palestinian-Israeli conflict or the plight of Muslims in war-torn countries. As they become more politically active and embrace fundamentalist interpretations of Islam, they are more likely to engage in what the NYPD called "extremist-like discussions" in cafés, gyms, halal butcher shops, student associations, and study groups.

Silber and Bhatt argued such troubling talk eventually leads to a spiritual mentor and a coterie of like-minded extremists. The budding terrorist withdraws from the mosque. His views harden and simplify: You are either a believer or a nonbeliever, and it is acceptable to use violence on nonbelievers. He and his friends discuss putting their views into action. Maybe they go overseas for terrorist training or try their hands at outdoor activities such as camping, paintball, or target shooting. They might make a suicide video or draft a will. At this stage, they can pick a target anytime.

Perhaps most frightening was what the NYPD described as the "candidates" for terrorism.

"Middle-class families and students appear to provide the most fertile ground for the seeds of radicalization," Silber and Bhatt wrote. "A range of socioeconomic and psychological factors have been associated with those who have chosen to radicalize to include the bored and/or frustrated, successful college students, the unemployed, the second and third generation, new immigrants, petty criminals, and prison parolees."

In short, the NYPD saw terrorists everywhere. The middle class and the unemployed. The aimless and the ambitious. Criminals and college students. Longtime American citizens and new arrivals. Anyone.

To Larry Sanchez, the analyst who came to the NYPD on loan from the CIA and stayed, *Radicalization in the West* was not merely an academic treatise. It was a map for law enforcement, one that the NYPD was already following. Zone defense was intended to spot would-be terrorists early in the four-step process. That meant police had to be in coffee shops, halal delis, gyms, bookstores, mosques, and student groups. They needed to know who was getting more religious and more politically active. They had to find the young men who felt that Muslims were discriminated against and those angered over the plight of the Palestinians.

They needed to think differently about activities protected by the Constitution.

"Let me try to answer it this way," Sanchez told Congress in 2007, when Senator Joe Lieberman of Connecticut asked how the NYPD identified terrorists before they attacked. "The key to it was first to understand it and to start appreciating what most people would say would be noncriminal, would be innocuous, looking at behaviors that could easily be argued in a Western democracy, particularly in the United States, to be protected by First and Fourth Amendment rights, but not to look at them in a vacuum, but to look across to them as potential precursors to terrorism."

• • •

127

In the 1970s, Police Commissioner Patrick Murphy made a similar argument as he tried to fend off Martin Stolar and his lefty lawyer friends in court. New York had endured bombings, kidnappings, shootings, and assassinations, all politically motivated. It would be foolish, Murphy said, for police to ignore the views that underpinned those attacks. It was the NYPD's responsibility, he continued, to keep close surveillance on "groups that because of their conduct or rhetoric may pose a threat to life, property, or government administration."[8]

The Handschu case curtailed the NYPD's ability to carry out such investigations. As soon as the new, post-9/11 rules took effect in 2003, the Intelligence Division again made political rhetoric a central motivator of its investigations.

The Demographics Unit was a start. The rakers catalogued places that the analysts believed could be "radicalization incubators." But knowing which coffee shops catered to devout Muslims wasn't enough. Cohen needed people living in the neighborhoods, checking in at the bookstores and buying goat meat at the butcher counter. What he needed was a roster of informants, people who could be what he called "listening posts."[9]

Recruiting informants became a priority for the Intelligence Division. Analysts scrutinized the city's long list of taxi-license holders, looking for Pakistanis and Afghans with criminal records or paperwork violations. Anything they could use as leverage. Detectives trawled central booking, identifying men from their countries of interest. Maybe they were there for drugs, maybe for drunken driving or jumping turnstiles. The detective would ask, "How'd you like to turn your life around?"[10] He'd get the charges reduced or dismissed, provide some walking-around money, and sign up a recruit for the war on terrorism.

Inside NYPD Intelligence, it didn't seem all that different from the way the police and FBI had dismantled the Mafia. Only now officers weren't infiltrating a criminal organization but a neighborhood. They were keeping tabs on whoever might be following the four steps of radicalization. Top NYPD officials regarded it as an innovative approach that set the department apart from its reactive FBI counterpart.

"NYPD Intelligence must be more proactive. It doesn't get gifts over the transom from CIA, so it digs around the city's hot spots," former NYPD deputy commissioner for counterterrorism Michael Sheehan wrote in his 2008 book, *Crush the Cell*, "NYPD takes a grassroots approach to finding sources and winds up covering areas the FBI ignores."[11]

The informant paperwork was kept in a small but busy third-floor office in Chelsea called the Sensitive Data Unit. As the informant ranks swelled, Cohen boasted to colleagues that he had an informant in every Yemeni market in New York. The goal, he told colleagues, was to have one inside every mosque within a 250-mile radius of the city.[12]

To accomplish his goals, Cohen got one of his detectives, Steve Pinkall, into the CIA's spy training school, the Farm, in Virginia. It was an unprecedented arrangement. The CIA trains officers to work in hostile environments, to make sources, to pass intelligence while under surveillance. The CIA trains its people to break the laws of foreign governments and to operate undetected in places where the Constitution doesn't apply. Pinkall ultimately failed to graduate.[13] But the NYPD bosses were still proud when he returned to work, trained in the ways of the CIA and ready to put them to use in New York.

The informants who served as listening posts didn't need CIA training. Their job was simply to keep eyes and ears open for literature and conversation. Informants reported periodically and were available to answer questions or identify photographs. When a CIA drone strike or a US military operation in Iraq or Afghanistan was in the news, Cohen would tell his detectives to take the pulse of the community—he called it "pulsing." The detectives called their informants: Who was angry? What protests were planned? What was being said at the coffee shops, on college campuses, or in the mosques?

Cohen lifted the strategy directly from the FBI's 1960s playbook. It was the bureau that coined the phrase "listening post" in 1967 as part of what it called its Ghetto Informant Program. FBI agents came up with the idea as a way to monitor black neighborhoods, which they saw as ripe for radicalization. Informants would report to the FBI on blacks planning civil disturbances and riots. Sometimes they'd just hang out. Other times, as the Church Committee discovered, the informants were "given specific assignments to attend public meetings of 'extremists' and to identify bookstores and others distributing 'extremist literature.' "

Now, beyond its informant network, the NYPD also relied on officers working undercover inside Muslim neighborhoods. Originally the Special Services Unit recruited them at the Police Academy, while they were still green and hadn't been programmed to look, talk, and act like cops. The cops created a cover story, usually one in which the new recruit fails out of the academy or decides the department isn't for him after all. But senior Intel officials worried that it was beginning to look suspicious that Muslim recruits were consistently failing. Better to recruit them after they applied to be cops but before they even arrived at the academy.

The undercover officers got fake names and were assigned NYPD handlers who would be their primary liaison to the department. Sometimes they were given specific targets. Often they were told to live their lives and report to their handler about what they heard and saw. Along with the informants and the Demographics Unit, the undercover officers helped the NYPD catalogue the city's mosques and Muslim student groups. Detectives scribbled license plate numbers in mosque parking lots and copied phone numbers from sign-up sheets for paintball trips. They attended study groups and went white-water rafting. And they reported to their handlers whatever rhetoric they heard in sermons or among worshippers milling about the mosque after prayer.[14]

Rhetoric was a hot topic in meetings at NYPD Intel. It came in a variety of flavors that were equally disconcerting to police: anti-American, anti-Israel, radical, extremist, and more. All made it into police files.

But Cohen's newly reinvented Intelligence Division faced a challenge similar to the one faced in the 1960s: How do you know what rhetoric to worry about? Encouraging someone to commit violence clearly crosses the line. But until then, when does political philosophy warrant criminal investigation?

Figures on all sides of the political spectrum have used violent language. In the 1960s, radical activist Abbie Hoffman declared, "The only way to support a revolution is to make your own." Decades later, Republican congresswoman Michele Bachmann issued a similar call in opposing a tax plan to reduce carbon emissions:

I want people in Minnesota armed and dangerous on this issue of the energy tax, because we need to fight back. Thomas Jefferson told us, "Having a revolution every now and then is a good thing." And the people—we the people—are going to have to fight back hard if we're not going to lose our country.

Similarly, at the University of California, Berkeley, in 1964, student leader Mario Savio implored left-wing activists to "put your bodies upon the gears and upon the wheels, upon the levers, upon all the apparatus" of the political machine. "You've got to make it stop." In upstate New York in the 1980s, antiabortion crusader Randall Terry inspired a right-wing cause with the simple command "If you believe abortion is murder, then act like it." One of the targets of those protests, Dr. Barnett Slepian, was murdered in his home in 1998 by an antiabortion fanatic.

During the 1960s and 1970s, rhetoric alone was enough to get a group investigated by the NYPD[15] or the FBI. Federal agents opened an investigation into the Socialist Workers Party, for instance, even though it had not espoused violence or revolution. It was based on politics. "The SWP is not just another socialist group but follows the revolutionary principles of Marx, Lenin, and Engels as interpreted by Leon Trotsky," the FBI wrote in opening its investigation.[16]

Under Cohen, Muslim rhetoric captured the division's attention. The new Handschu guidelines said that the NYPD could start investigating whenever there was a "possibility of unlawful activity." The department could retain any information as long as it related to "potential unlawful or terrorist activity." Those standards were so broad that analysts and investigators said they were meaningless. Where is there not a possibility of unlawful activity?

In a deposition taken by the Handschu lawyers, Thomas Galati, the commanding officer of the Intelligence Division, showed how broadly those rules were interpreted. Police could keep files on any conversation in Urdu, he said, because Pakistanis who spoke the language—there are more than fifteen million—qualified as a concern.[17]

The NYPD's zone defense considered rhetoric alone as a serious allegation of actual terrorism. In 2004, for example, the Terrorist Interdiction Unit created a watch list of twenty-six people. The document included dossiers on people suspected of donating money to al-Qaeda; a man believed to be an associate of an Algerian terrorist group; and two people who said they wanted to throw a Jew in front of a train.

And then there was Tariq Abdur Rashid, an assistant imam who made the list for his views on the wars in the Middle East. Police said Rashid repeatedly denounced US involvement overseas and condoned the death of American soldiers "trying to take over and occupy a land that they have no business being on." Rashid also said the United States is a puppet for the Jews.[18] Such views may be distasteful, unpatriotic, and anti-Semitic. They are not illegal.

Because an interest in Middle East politics was seen as an indicator of radicalization, NYPD detectives were interested in being wherever people gathered to watch Al Jazeera, the Arabic news channel. The NYPD's files on the Meena House Café in Brooklyn, for instance, noted that, "the Al Jazeera news network is shown here with all the local Arabic newspapers available for all." Similarly, police files declared the Bay Ridge International Café in Brooklyn a "traditional place for young people to gather. Al Jazeera is always on at this location."

Not airing Al Jazeera was also suspicious. At the Tea Room in Bay Ridge, police wrote, "The Al Jazeera news channel is prohibited inside this location because the owner feels it brings about extra scrutiny from law enforcement."

It was all part of the new strategy, outlined by Sanchez in his testimony before Congress, to investigate what police believed were the precursors to terrorism, even when they were legal.

"All you had was rhetoric," explained a former NYPD official who regularly attended meetings with Cohen and Sanchez. "If you had actual criminal activity, you'd have a case."

But NYPD Intel rarely made cases, much to the frustration of officers who didn't care for their new mission of just watching, following, and listening. There was a running joke: "This is Intel. We don't make cases. We make overtime."

• • •

If parsing political speech posed challenges for the NYPD, interpreting religious rhetoric was even more difficult. *Radicalization in the West* mentioned frequently the role of Muslim extremists and their speech in the process of creating terrorists. The NYPD's intelligence files often included, without elaboration, the fact that someone had engaged in extremist or radical rhetoric.

Exactly what qualified as radical rhetoric at the NYPD was a matter of debate. Galati, the commanding officer, said it was any "conversation which would be inciting somebody or encouraging somebody to commit an unlawful act."[19] He acknowledged that definition wasn't written down anywhere, leaving detectives, informants, and analysts to decide when religious speech should become part of a police file.

Such a decision is seldom clear-cut. Spiritual oratory, regardless of faith, can be fiery and passionate. If an imam says that the 9/11 hijackers were sent by Allah to get America's attention, is that radical Islamic rhetoric? When Bryan Fischer of the American Family Association religious group declared, "The jihadists on 9/11 were the agents of God's wrath in order to get our attention," was that radical Christian rhetoric?

In one document, the NYPD recorded the words of a Brooklyn imam: "Satan is with all people who do not accept Allah. Islam is the one and true religion." [20]

Seen through the lens of the NYPD's new preventive strategy, the words seemed to embody the indoctrination phase discussed in *Radicalization in the West*.

A theologian, on the other hand, might point out that the comment is a variation on the Catholic doctrine of *extra ecclesiam nulla salus* ("Outside the church there is no salvation") or the Protestant tenet of *solus Christus* ("Christ alone"). But Intel analysts and investigators, the ones deciding what went in police files, weren't sitting around discussing the universal theme of one true faith in monotheistic religions. They erred on the side of reporting the rhetoric.

From time to time, Stuart Parker, a city attorney assigned to the Intelligence Division, would tell people not to rely so heavily on adjectives such as *anti-American* and *extremist* in their files. [21] But that was a record-keeping issue. Once the Handschu rules allowed police to decide what religious views were suspicious, there was little discussion about whether they were qualified to judge. Or whether they should.

Rhetoric collection was driven in part by intense pressure on detectives to produce.

"If anything goes on in New York," Cohen told his officers, "it's your fault." [22]

If terrorists launched an attack, and it turned out they'd been radicalized inside a mosque and held meetings in a coffee shop, no cop wanted to be the last one to have visited there and reported nothing extraordinary. So they reported everything they saw.

"The living room contained a love seat and two futons," one official wrote in a report on how Moroccans assimilated into New York. "There was a small table as well as an entertainment center. There were two Korans. One on top of each speaker. On the wall, there was a 2006 calendar from the Beit El Masjid," a Brooklyn mosque.

Among Cohen's inner circle, nobody believed that all Muslims were terrorists. Even most Muslim extremists weren't terrorists. Neither were most people who opposed Israel's policies, criticized America, or railed against its use of drones. But recently it seemed most terrorists were Muslim. And all of them had been extremists. Among those, some had opposed Israel, disparaged America, or criticized drones. Zone defense meant watching the city's roughly seven hundred thousand Muslims to find the tiny few who might become terrorists.

Any trait shared among terrorists was seen as a possible indicator, even if that trait also applied to many innocent people. For instance, in 2009 Cohen started a program to monitor everybody in New York City who wanted a new name.[23] The initiative began after a Memphis man named Carlos Bledsoe killed one US Army private and wounded another in a drive-by shooting at a military recruiting station in Little Rock, Arkansas. Bledsoe was a recent convert to Islam and had taken the name Abdulhakim Mujahid Muhammad. A few months later, intelligence officials learned about David Headley, a Chicago man who'd helped the terrorist group Lashkar-e-Taiba plan a terrorist attack in India in 2008. Headley was born Daood Sayed Gilani and had changed his name to something more traditionally American so that he could travel without attracting suspicion.

The NYPD began reviewing court filings to see who was changing his or her name. Someone taking an Arabic name might be a recent convert and, like Bledsoe, might be angry and preparing to strike. Someone Americanizing his Arabic name might be the next Headley. Of course, most people who change their names are not terrorists. Taking a new Arabic name as part of a religious conversion is protected by the First Amendment. And in New York, immigrants have been taking new Americanized names since they first began stepping off the ferry from Ellis Island to Manhattan.

Once the NYPD had the names, analysts picked some—most often those that looked like they might be from Muslim countries—and ran what they called a "round robin" on them. Analysts performed background checks, looking at criminal records, travel history, business licenses, and immigration documents. The results were stored on a spreadsheet. Then, detectives from the Leads Unit would hit the streets to interview people about why they changed their names.

The Leads detectives had drilled their share of dry holes before. The unit was responsible for checking out every terrorist tip that came in, no matter how vague or preposterous. A sign in the unit read, "Deposit All Intel Division Bags of Shit Here." But the name-change program seemed like a new level of time wasting. They didn't find any radical converts. And those who abandoned their Arabic names for something more American all seemed to say the same thing: They were trying to blend in, but not for the reason that Cohen feared. They were simply tired of the discrimination that came with being Muslim in America.

"Let me guess," a detective would say when a colleague came back from a fruitless interview. "He was getting harassed."

Programs like this put the detectives and analysts in a tough spot. Everyone agreed that identifying a terrorist before he attacked was a good idea. And it *was* Muslims, not Catholics or Protestants, who'd hijacked the airplanes on 9/11. There were, without question, radical Islamic leaders espousing violence in the name of religion. Anwar al-Awlaki, the American-born cleric who'd been seen as a moderate when he preached in Virginia, went on to become al-Qaeda's chief propagandist. He inspired Western terrorists with his internet sermons:

To the Muslims in America, I have this to say: How can your conscience allow you to live in peaceful coexistence with a nation that is responsible for the tyranny and crimes committed against your own brothers and sisters?

And:

Don't consult with anybody in killing the Americans. Fighting the devil doesn't require consultation or prayers seeking divine guidance. They are the party of the devils.

So ignoring Islamic rhetoric—or anything that might be a warning sign—seemed foolhardy. But in the race to identify future terrorists, innocent religious and political speech was treated the same as legitimately threatening comments.

In late 2003 the NYPD received a tip that people were training for jihad in the basement of the Masjid al-Ikhwa, a Brooklyn storefront mosque with a congregation primarily of African Americans.[24] Over the next eight months, a pair of NYPD informants visited repeatedly, helping police compile dossiers on the imam, the teachers, and the man who collected donations during Friday prayers.

One teacher was especially worrisome. He had a history of violent crime and asked a police informant, "How many Jews do you think we could take out on a Saturday at Marcy and Bedford with an AK-47 in three minutes?"

As the informants informed, the catalogue of rhetoric grew. And the line about the AK-47 was given no more attention than general pronouncements about politics such as, "President Bush is behind it all and that Secretary of State Colin Powell has a deceiving tongue. Muslims throughout the world are being oppressed." The police files even noted that the imam declared—with total accuracy—"people are sent into the Mosque to spy on it and see what's going on."

By June 2004, the police hadn't found any jihadists in the basement. They hadn't made any case at all. But they had compiled two pages of rhetoric.

● ● ●

By using religious views and rhetoric as potential terrorist indicators, the NYPD was wading into a theological debate that began in the mid-seventh century: the schism between Sunnis and Shia.

When the Prophet Muhammad died in AD 632, he did not have a male heir, leaving open the question of who would follow him as Islam's leader. Most Muslims declared their support for the Prophet's father-in-law, Abu Bakr, who was chosen by a council of the Prophet's disciples. A small group believed that only God could choose the Prophet's successor and that Muhammad, acting on God's will, had appointed his son-in-law, Ali ibn Abi Talib.

Sunnis followed Abu Bakr. The Shia followed Ali.

At the NYPD, analysts were especially concerned with two strains of Sunni Islam that they saw as linked to terrorism: Wahhabism and Salafism. The mere existence of this analysis—trying to understand the complex theological and geopolitical underpinnings of terrorism—shows how rapidly Cohen and Sanchez had changed the NYPD to respond to the terrorist threat. Normally, such an inquiry would be left to scholars, think tanks, and, to some degree, analysts at the CIA and State Department.

Wahhabism and Salafism are puritanical movements, meaning their followers strictly follow Muhammad's word. True Islam, they believe, requires rigid adherence to the Koran, which is not subject to human interpretation. In post-9/11 America, the terms *Wahhabism* and *Salafism* are often used interchangeably, with *Wahhabism* used to describe Saudi Arabia's brand of Salafism.

Both Salafi and Wahhabi followers have launched terrorist attacks, including the 9/11 hijackings. And many scholars and politicians say the severe, unaccommodating, and intolerant strain of Islam actively inspires and encourages terrorists. But puritanical Islam is complicated. Scholars disagree, for instance, on whether Osama bin Laden really qualified as a Wahhabist, because he called for the overthrow of the Saudi government, which was backed by Wahhabist religious leaders.

Further complicating the analysis, there are three factions of Salafism that, while essentially identical in religious beliefs, disagree fundamentally on how to live them. Some believe in using politics to advance Salafist goals. Others believe that politics encourages deviancy, and that the only way to purify Islam is through peaceful study and prayer. When these purists speak of jihad, it is in the historic sense of a peaceful struggle to promote Islam. A third group, the minority, embraces violence and revolution, a tactic that has given rise to the modern interpretation of the word *jihad*.[25]

Mitchell Silber understood those distinctions, and in *Radicalization in the West*, he referred most often to the threat from the "jihadi-Salafi" ideology. In practice, however, the subtleties were often lost as police trawled for terrorists. Conversations overheard by undercover officers and paid informants, it turned out, were clumsy tools for determining the nuances of people's religious beliefs.

In public, Mayor Michael Bloomberg declared, "We don't stop to think about the religion. We stop to think about the threats and focus our efforts there." Whether he was in the dark about what was going on or whether he was lying, one thing is certain: He was wrong.

In secret, the term *Salafist* had become synonymous with "suspicious" at the NYPD. In a police presentation in 2006, for instance, Captain Steven D'Ulisse listed factors that could get someone labeled a "person of interest." Being involved in terrorism was one. A capacity for violence was another. And so was "ideological orientation (Salafi/Wahhabi)."[26] By mid-2006, the NYPD had identified twenty-four mosques in New York as having "a Salafi influence."[27]

The NYPD was particularly afraid of what it saw as the increasing popularity of Salafism on college campuses. Analysts worried because student groups were discussing the book *Kitab At-Tawheed* by Muhammad bin Abdul Wahhab, the father of Wahhabist thought.[28] The presence of Wahhab's books on college campuses was hardly unusual. Any serious study of modern Islamic history or Saudi politics includes his works, which are available in most libraries. But zone defense meant that the police needed to pay attention to places from which terrorists might emerge.

As they had done with political rhetoric, the NYPD investigated the many to find the few. The NYPD was looking for that tiny minority, and that meant looking at everyone in Muslim student groups. The police weren't going to wait for one angry young man to decide to become a terrorist, and then cross their fingers and hope they could spot him before he attacked. As Cohen told his officers, "Take a big net, throw it out, catch as many fish as you can, and see what we get." [29]

By late 2006, the NYPD had identified and investigated thirty-one Muslim student groups. Of those, it concluded that seven were Salafi and labeled them "of concern." [30]

In a presentation prepared for Police Commissioner Ray Kelly, NYPD analysts explained that Brooklyn College and Baruch College in Manhattan had "Tier One" student groups. Brooklyn College made the list for its "regular Salafi speakers, militant paintball trips." Baruch also was cited for having Salafi speakers, and the NYPD added that the "students are politically active and are radicalizing."

The Tier Two groups included Hunter College ("radicalization among students"), City College of New York ("Salafi website"), and St. John's University ("fund raising and speeches"). Queens College made the list for having a link to a member of Al-Muhajiroun, a banned Islamic extremist group based in Britain. LaGuardia Community College was listed because police said the Islamic Thinkers Society, an ultraconservative group that hoped the United States would someday be governed by Islamic law, wanted to revive the student group there.

The NYPD dispatched undercover officers and informants to spy on student groups. [31] Soon after that presentation, in November 2006, police also started a daily routine of monitoring the websites of Muslim groups at schools across the Northeast, including Columbia, Yale University, the University of Pennsylvania, and Syracuse University. Kelly received weekly reports telling him which lectures Muslim scholars attended, which professors spoke, and what they discussed.

"The talks elaborate on practical measures university students can take to ensure a balance and well rounded growth in both religious and academic matters in their time at school," Mahmood Ahmad, a detective with the Cyber Intelligence Unit, wrote in one report.[32]

Students who posted information about upcoming lectures were also documented.

"The message advertising this event was posted by a member of the Muslim Student Association at Buffalo who identifies herself as Adeela Khan," Ahmad wrote.

From time to time, the police would identify someone speaking to students whom they considered extremist, but they didn't find evidence that student groups were supporting or recruiting for terrorists.[33] The NYPD says it stopped its regular monitoring of student websites in May 2007.

The focus on student groups was a good example of Cohen's big-net strategy. Under the Handschu rules, the NYPD was allowed to gather intelligence from public websites. Inside Intel, the effort was seen as a logical and necessary preventative measure, even though the work—by informants, undercovers, the Demographics Unit, and cyber detectives—meant that many students who had no connection to terrorism were put into files.

The presence of police on college campuses listening in on religious and academic conversations may have harked back to surveillance during the 1960s, but to Cohen and his analysts, the only other option was to never know whether Salafist scholars might turn young men into suicide bombers. If the Handschu guidelines allowed it, and there was a chance that it could keep the city safe, the NYPD was going to try it.

• • •

At the federal level, these kinds of investigations are subject to a series of checks. The FBI and CIA have internal reviews to make sure that cases and covert-action programs are run correctly. Both are subject to inspector generals who investigate problems and see to it that the government is following the rules and the law. And everything is subject to scrutiny by the House of Representatives and the Senate, which control the budgets and can make every day a headache for the nation's agents and spies.

Once Cohen got the Handschu rules changed, the only real check on the NYPD's investigative authority was Cohen himself and a cadre of senior officers and lawyers that met monthly to authorize investigations involving political or religious activity. There was no inspector general, and the city council had shown no interest in demanding information from the Intelligence Division. The division had never undergone a city audit, and, while there were processes by which citizens and whistle-blowers could report police corruption, that didn't include a review of Intel's files and whether Cohen was using his authority appropriately. Kelly reassured the public that the internal Handschu review was more than enough.

The truth was, the standard for opening an investigation was so low that approval was easy. The whole process amounted to what a participant in the Handschu meetings called "a rubber stamp." And once an investigation was open, it could last for years, while its tentacles reached well outside terrorism and into the world of lawful activism, protest, and politics.

It was easy to open an investigation of political groups. Before dawn on March 6, 2008, security cameras captured the images of someone in a dark hooded sweatshirt riding a bicycle toward a military recruiting station in Times Square and then walking to the front door. Moments later, a bomb went off, damaging the front of the building. The attack, which didn't injure anyone, bore striking similarities to a bombing a year earlier at the Mexican Consulate and another three years earlier at the British Consulate. All three took place before sunrise, and, after each, a man was seen on his bike.

The Times Square bombing was immediately big news. Despite the hour, journalists were quick to report details as police cordoned off the scene and halted traffic. Everyone immediately noted the similarities among the three bicycle bombings. Within a few hours, police discovered a bike, a blue ten-speed made in the 1980s, abandoned not far from Times Square.

Within days, though, the case had gone cold. The prints on the bike had proven useless, and the bicycle was so old that there was no way to track its owner. Police released pictures of the bike, figuring that it might have been bought recently at a garage sale and hoping somebody might recognize it.

On March 27, Silber, who was now the director of intelligence analysis, and Captain Donald Powers filed a request with Cohen to open a preliminary investigation into an activist named Dennis Christopher Burke.[34] Because Burke was a member of political protest groups, the Handschu rules required Cohen to sign off on any investigation.

The evidence tying Burke to the bombing, though, was slim. It centered on a blog called *Bombs and Shields*, which posted news about protests around the world. The site was filled with what activists called protest porn: photos of burning buildings, overturned cars, and rioters clashing with police. The protests themselves involved a mishmash of causes. Some opposed police brutality, urban sprawl, or the military. Others were simply anarchist.

Bombs and Shields had been around for years, and an informant told police that—back in 2005, at least—Burke had been in charge of updating it. At 6:03 a.m. the day of the Times Square blast, *Bombs and Shields* posted an item about the explosion. It caught the attention of the NYPD.

"The less than 3 hour period between the bombing and *Bombs and Shields* posting on the bombing raises the possibility that Burke or someone else associated with *Bombs and Shields* had information concerning the Times Square Recruiting Station bombing prior to its occurrence," Silber and Powers wrote.

Police couldn't say for sure whether Burke was still updating the site. And the item that made police suspicious was merely a link to a Fox News article, a story that had been all over every news channel for hours. Yet it was enough for the NYPD.

Nothing else connected Burke to the recruiting center explosion. He had been arrested several times for protest-related crimes, but never for making bombs. Still, police linked him to two protest groups. The first was Time's Up, a New York nonprofit group that participates in monthly "Critical Mass" bike rides, loosely organized events in which hundreds of riders regularly clog the streets in what the NYPD considers an illegal form of protest. The second group was the Friends of Brad Will, a network of human rights advocates who opposed the war on drugs and sought to unearth the truth about the 2006 killing of independent journalist Bradley Will, who was shot dead by police in Mexico, where Will was covering a labor protest.

Based on those facts, Cohen approved an investigation not only into Burke but also his associates in Time's Up and the Friends of Brad Will. Under the new Handschu rules, police needed to show only that there was a "possibility of unlawful activity."

A month later, an undercover officer assigned to the case flew to Louisiana to attend the People's Summit New Orleans, a gathering of groups that shared an opposition to US economic policies and the trade agreements among the United States, Canada, and Mexico. The officer came to investigate the Friends of Brad Will. But while he was there, he gathered information about coming demonstrations in support of organized labor and prisoner rights. He took note of groups that opposed US immigration policy, labor laws, and racial profiling. All of this was summarized in a memo for Cohen dated April 25, 2008:[35]

"One workshop was led by Jordan Flaherty, former member of

the International Solidarity Movement Chapter in New York City. Mr. Flaherty is an editor and journalist of the *Left Turn* Magazine and was one of the main organizers of the conference. Mr. Flaherty held a discussion calling for the increase of the divestment campaign of Israel and mentioned two events related to Palestine."

In a matter of weeks, an investigation that had started with a blog linked to a Fox News article had metastasized to include broad intelligence gathering on liberal groups with no connection to Burke or the Times Square bombing.

Police similarly infiltrated demonstrations and collected information about antiwar groups planning protests and those who marched against police brutality. Cyber detectives monitored activist websites and copied the contents into police files, including one memo in 2008 for Kelly that reported the contents of a website about a group of women organizing a boycott to protest the police shooting of Sean Bell, an unarmed black man killed the morning before his wedding:

This boycott was set for May 11, 2008 (Mother's Day) there will be NO shopping for cards, flowers, clothing, shoes or dining out. Spend time with Mom at home, serve her dinner, or buy her flowers from a black-owned business. We can be effective if we unite in the name of our children.[36]

Police collected the phone numbers and email addresses from the website. One was for Agnes Johnson, a longtime activist based in the Bronx.

"We were women and mothers who said, 'We're going to hold our money in our pocketbooks,' " Johnson recalled years later. "That's all we called for."

At the NYPD, officials knew such programs would be controversial if they became public. But there was no suggestion that they were improper. Cohen had made it clear to Judge Haight back in 2002 what he intended to do, and Haight had approved. Activists and libertarians could argue that standards for opening an investigation and building police files on people were too low, but that matter had been settled.

It was like keeping track of people who spoke "anti-Shia rhetoric." Maybe they were professing their views on Islam. But maybe they were Salafists or, worse, jihadists. At the NYPD, the options were either to keep tabs on people or ignore them and take your chances.

One of those people, according to the NYPD, was a sixty-one-year-old Islamic scholar named Shabbir Hussain. In December 2008 the leaders of the Thayba Islamic Center in Brooklyn announced that Hussain would be one of several guest speakers at its annual conference commemorating the death of the seventh-century martyr Hussein ibn Ali. The NYPD took note because, according to its documents, the Thayba mosque had been "identified as Wahhabi."

So a few weeks before the conference, Detective Joseph Niebo filed paperwork to place Shabbir Hussain under ten-hours-a-day surveillance. Niebo knew a little about Hussain because, a year earlier, cops had stopped him in the Bronx to figure out his identity. At Intel, pulling over people to get their names was so common that Cohen actually had a unit, dubbed the "X Team," dedicated to that task.[37] On that particular Sunday, the Terrorist Interdiction Unit stopped Hussain. He cooperated and handed over his Pakistani passport, which the detectives photographed.

To get a surveillance team assigned, investigators had to justify the request, which meant including a synopsis of the case and the reason for suspicion. The justification Niebo filed for following Hussain was minimal. It said only that Hussain was speaking at the conference and added, "Subject speaks anti-Shia rhetoric."[38]

It should have been obvious that something didn't make sense. Hussein ibn Ali was the grandson of the Prophet Muhammad (not the nephew, as the NYPD documents said), and he's among the holiest martyrs in Shiite Islam. Shiites mourn his death each year on the holiday of Ashura. Wahhabists don't mourn on that day. Far from it. In addition to banning such ceremonies in Saudi Arabia, they've attacked Shiites who commemorate it

For all the investment the NYPD had made in trying to understand puritanical Islam, the obvious question went unasked: Why would a Wahhabist mosque hold a ceremony mourning Hussein ibn Ali?

As it turned out, Thayba Islamic Center was *not* Wahhabist. It was Barelvi, a Sunni sect known for its moderation and for speaking out against the ultraconservative policies of the Taliban. Far from being ideological allies, the Wahhabists have branded the Barelvis as heretics and, in Pakistan, have attacked their holy sites.

To a Muslim, mistaking a Barelvi mosque for a Wahhabist mosque would be like going to Northern Ireland and confusing a Protestant church with a Catholic church. Or like rummaging through the NYPD's spy files from the 1960s and finding that police mixed up Republican Barry Goldwater's campaign headquarters with a meeting spot for New Left radicals.

Such errors—and police confused Sunnis and Shiites more than once—mirrored those made by Demographics Unit detectives who mistook Montenegrins for Albanians, and Lebanese Christians for Syrian Muslims. And they raised a worrisome question about both programs: If there was ever a credible threat against New York, if al-Qaeda set a suicide bomb plot in motion inside the city, could the NYPD even rely on the information it had?

• • •

It is difficult to overstate the revolutionary nature of what Cohen and Sanchez had created: In a few short years, the NYPD—a force twice the size of the FBI—had gotten into the business of secretly assessing the religious and political views of US citizens, believed that it was not constrained by jurisdictional boundaries, and viewed activities protected by the First Amendment as precursors to terrorism.

Officially, the NYPD was following the same rules as the FBI. That's what Cohen assured Judge Haight, and the judge took Cohen at his word. If the NYPD was doing things differently, that's because Cohen was charting a new course, and the FBI was still stuck in its old, bureaucratic ways.

"If NYPD's programs were more innovative than FBI's, it was a direct result of Cohen's creative initiative," Michael Sheehan, the department's former deputy commissioner for counterterrorism, wrote in his book *Crush the Cell*.[39]

In truth, top officials at Intel understood that zone defense—the idea of monitoring beliefs to identify future criminals—was not something the FBI could square with federal law and its own rules. The bureau couldn't investigate activities covered by the Constitution as the NYPD did. The police considered that a flaw in the FBI's rules, not an indication that Cohen was crossing lines. Sanchez said as much to Congress in 2007:

"Part of our mission is to protect New York City citizens from becoming terrorists. The federal government doesn't have that mission, so automatically, by definition, their threshold is higher," he said. "So they're going to have a heck of a lot harder time having to deal with behaviors that run the gamut on First and Fourth Amendment rights and to be able to even look and scrutinize them without having even reached a standard of criminality that you need if your prime objective is, you're going to lock them up."

Agents wanted to know what Cohen was working on so they could prevent last-minute fiascos such as the one in 2008 when Abdel Hameed Shehadeh, the Palestinian from Staten Island whom the NYPD was monitoring, flew to Pakistan, and the FBI had no idea what was going on. And the FBI had capabilities that the NYPD did not, such as international wiretapping and nationwide subpoena power. It made more sense to cooperate from the beginning, the FBI argued.

When Mike Heimbach became the FBI's head of counterterrorism in 2008, he went to New York for a meeting at the NYPD.[40] He made his case that they needed to work together more closely. The FBI needed to know what Cohen knew. They needed to coordinate better.

Cohen was polite but firm. He wasn't going to simply turn over information to the FBI and trust the bureau to handle it. He knew that agents were frequently dismissive of Intel's reporting, so how could he be sure his information would be investigated correctly? Cohen said he wasn't trying to be confrontational, but, in all fairness, it was the FBI that had failed to connect the dots for years. And that failure had come crashing down on New York.

You didn't lose three thousand Americans, Cohen said. I did.

And now the FBI was asking the NYPD to fall in line again.

Cohen assured Heimbach that the NYPD wouldn't withhold information if it uncovered an imminent plot. But he wasn't going to go back to the days when the FBI took the lead and the NYPD was left to do little more than trust and hope.

Getting information from the NYPD had its risks, too. By accepting it, the FBI was affixing its seal of approval to the department's practices. When FBI inspectors came around to review case files, if they found information about protesters, religious sermons, and student groups, the agent who accepted the information would have to answer for it. It wouldn't matter that it had come from Cohen's investigators.

Once, the NYPD sent Don Borelli a report from a mosque saying that worshippers were bathing corpses and preparing them for burial in accordance with the Islamic ritual known as *ghusl*. Borelli didn't know what to do with the report. There was nothing criminal in there, no hint of anything nefarious. If he placed it in the FBI's files, he'd probably have to explain it someday. So he shredded it.

The FBI office in New York also had a standing policy against accepting files from the Demographics Unit. Larry Sanchez had shown one of the reports to a senior agent, who'd consulted with the FBI's lawyers. They decided that accepting it would violate their own rules designed to protect civil liberties. The Demographics Unit wasn't simply trying to know the neighborhoods, the FBI agents and lawyers concluded. It was running a widespread intelligence-gathering operation. The Demographics detectives, the FBI decided, were effectively operating as undercover officers, targeting businesses without cause and collecting information related to politics and religion.[41]

Cohen saw that kind of attitude as bureaucratic resistance, the kind of foot-dragging that had hurt the CIA so badly in the 1990s and contributed to the intelligence failures of 9/11. It reinforced the notion that the FBI wasn't interested in sharing information or working together. FBI agents wanted the NYPD to step aside and let them take charge.

To a large degree, Cohen was right.

When FBI agents griped about NYPD Intel, the complaints usually fell into one of three categories. Some took offense at tactics that they said violated civil rights. A second group focused on the fact that the NYPD could do things that the FBI couldn't. It wasn't clear whether these agents would be satisfied with the tactics if they were the ones using them. The third group took a more practical objection. The NYPD, they said, didn't have the basic ability to conduct international or nationwide counterterrorism investigations. By working alone, this third group of agents argued, Cohen made the nation more vulnerable.

The first complaint, about the civil liberties, was a moot point. The NYPD had briefed the FBI and the Justice Department about its programs. And though the briefings didn't get into the details of cases and tactics, they offered plenty of opportunities to explore the law. Attorney General Alberto Gonzales once left a meeting with the NYPD, turned to an aide, and said something to the effect of: "We could never do that." Justice Department officials at the meeting took that to mean that such controversial programs carried a political risk that New York was willing to take but Washington could not. Nobody took it as a suggestion to inquire about whether it was legal.[42]

Besides, while agents might wring their hands and complain about the constitutionality of the NYPD's tactics, the FBI remains the agency responsible for investigating civil rights abuses by police departments. Somebody could have opened an investigation.

There was little appetite for such a confrontation. FBI Director Robert Mueller had made it clear that he was not interested picking a fight with a politically connected police chief over how to fight terrorism in the city that had seen the worst of it. He fielded complaints from senior agents when the first NYPD officers arrived in their overseas postings and again when the NYPD's detective went to the CIA's training camp. Mueller let it slide. In cities like Portland, Oregon, the police refused to participate in the FBI's Joint Terrorism Task Force, so Mueller was willing to countenance a police department that was perhaps overengaged in the fight against terrorism.

Once, while Mueller visited the FBI office in Newark, agents asked him why the NYPD was allowed to operate unilaterally outside its borders, without coordinating with the Joint Terrorism Task Force. Mueller told the agents to stop complaining.[43]

So, when it was convenient, the FBI and the Justice Department were willing to overlook their concerns. When Cohen brought the FBI a nascent case in 2003 against a radical Islamic bookstore clerk in Brooklyn named Shahawar Matin Siraj, FBI agents in New York turned up their noses. Amy Jo Lyons, who preceded Borelli as assistant special agent in charge of the task force, told colleagues that the FBI shouldn't have anything to do with the case. Siraj was borderline mentally retarded and there was no evidence he was interested in terrorism until he met Cohen's informant, an unemployed Egyptian engineer named Osama Eldawoody. Eldawoody made about $100,000 keeping tabs on people and mosques for Cohen.

FBI and Justice Department officials who reviewed the case worried that Eldawoody seemed to be goading the bookstore clerk into a terrorist plot. Plus, it seemed to Lyons and others that the police were recording conversations selectively, taping and keeping the worst ones but leaving out those that might undermine the case.

Federal prosecutors in Manhattan reviewed the case and refused to bring charges.[44] Terrorism cases were hot items at the Justice Department, though, and prosecutors in Brooklyn were eager to land one. They reviewed the Siraj investigation and said they were interested. Cohen took his case to Brooklyn and never brought another one to Manhattan.

At the Justice Department in Washington, senior officials scrutinized the files. They agreed there were concerns about the reliability of the informant and the consistency of the recordings. But they determined that it was winnable.

And, in the end, they were right. Siraj and another man, James Elshafay, were arrested on charges of plotting to blow up the Herald Square subway station. The arrests were announced August 27, 2004, shortly before the opening of the Republican National Convention in New York, where President George W. Bush would be nominated for reelection.

Siraj argued entrapment but neither jurors nor a federal judge believed it. Though he never had a bomb, Siraj scouted the subway stop and sketched a rough map of the target.

"The crimes committed here were extremely serious," Judge Nina Gershon said while sentencing Siraj to thirty years in prison.

Kelly called the sentence a milestone in his efforts to safeguard New York City. Years later, however, the origins of the investigation remain in dispute. A reporter who interviewed Cohen soon after the arrest said a Brooklyn resident called a police tip line about Siraj.[45] Mitchell Silber, the former analyst, says the Demographics Unit identified the bookstore as a hot spot and that's what led police to Siraj.[46] Under oath, however, Assistant Chief Thomas Galati testified the Demographics Unit had generated no cases.

The Herald Square case gave the Justice Department deep insight into Cohen's new tactics. And though many FBI agents and even some NYPD Intel veterans still shake their heads dismissively at the case, it was a victory for the NYPD. Cohen's efforts had passed their first major test with the Justice Department, the FBI, a federal judge, and a jury.

So, typically, disputes between the NYPD and FBI never went beyond grousing on both sides of the footbridge in New York.

Cohen did share his best informant with the JTTF around 2008, with disastrous consequences.

His name was Ali Abdelaziz,[47] an Egyptian mixed martial arts expert. The NYPD recruited him in 2002 when he was a twenty-five-year-old sitting in a Colorado jail cell on charges of document forgery. Abdelaziz became an asset in the NYPD's long-running investigation into the Muslims of America, an extremist group based in rural Virginia. He was among Cohen's most important and best-paid informants, earning by his own account hundreds of thousands of dollars for his efforts.

Cohen wanted to share Abdelaziz, who was known in files as Confidential Informant 184, with the FBI so that he could work overseas. The bureau agreed to sponsor Abdelaziz and provide him with a special green card so he could enter and leave the United States. He worked in Trinidad and Tobago, Venezuela, and elsewhere. But the more that FBI agents worked with him, the more suspicious they grew. On April 8, 2008, at the FBI's demand, NYPD officials took Abdelaziz to the bureau's office downtown, where agent Michael Templeton strapped him to a polygraph machine.[48]

The questions started simply.

"Are you now in New York City?"

"Are you currently employed?"

"Is today Friday?"

When Templeton asked Abdelaziz if he intended to be honest with the FBI about whether he'd told anybody that he was a government agent, Abdelaziz said yes. The machine said otherwise.

Templeton seized on it. Polygraphers commonly use that question to spot double agents, people working as a spy for one agency but whose true loyalties lie with another. As he pressed Abdelaziz, the FBI agent began to believe that he had told people in Egypt about his secret life. Again and again, Abdelaziz denied it. The polygraph said he was lying. Templeton continued until, finally, Abdelaziz asked to use the bathroom.

Realizing that things were not going well, the NYPD officials in the room tried to smooth things over with Templeton. They offered him explanations for why Abdelaziz might have seemed deceitful. But when Abdelaziz returned from the bathroom, tension remained. As Templeton delved into Abdelaziz's past, the NYPD abruptly ended the test. It was an embarrassing moment. The department's prized informant was apparently lying. The FBI closed the file as "Deceptive with no admissions, interrupted and terminated by the NYPD." The FBI severed its relationship with Abdelaziz, and the government tried unsuccessfully to deport him.

That blowup occurred in private. While it led to eye rolling at the FBI over the reliability of Cohen's informants, it did not undermine the support that the NYPD's counterterrorism efforts enjoyed in New York.

The public didn't know about rakers. What it did know, however, was that nearly a decade had passed without another successful terrorist attack.

That was the yardstick by which Cohen wanted to be measured. In a 2005 deposition, a civil rights lawyer asked him how he knew his programs worked. Was he actually deterring terrorism? Was there some methodology to quantify that?

"I never bothered to look," Cohen said. "It doesn't exist as far as I could tell."

So how did he know what he did worked?

"They haven't attacked us."

The absence of a terrorist attack has been the silver-bullet argument for national security professionals for years. It has been used to prove the success of secret prisons, Guantánamo Bay, waterboarding, drones, and warrantless wiretapping. It is a flawed argument, the logical fallacy known as *post hoc ergo propter hoc* ("after this therefore because of this"). There have been no terrorist attacks since 9/11. Hence, whatever counterterrorism program being argued about must prevent terrorism.

From a political standpoint, though, it was nearly irrefutable.

Zazi and his friends jeopardized that argument. They'd become radically anti-American jihadists on the streets of Queens, within earshot of the NYPD's listening posts. Medunjanin had even been a vocal and respected member of the Muslim student group at Queens College while an undercover officer was also a member. It hadn't mattered. For all the files that the NYPD had on students, Salafists, protesters, and others with no ties to terrorism, these three men had slipped unnoticed through Cohen's zone defense.

7

OSTERMANN

DENVER
Thursday, September 10, 2009

Jim Davis, the special agent in charge of the FBI's Denver field office, was still not sure he had his man. The email about the marriage—the one that started this whole case running—had been sent from inside Zazi's parents' apartment. That much he knew for certain. But who could say for sure that Zazi had sent it? It had been sent from a Yahoo account. If Zazi had left himself logged in, anyone could have sat down at the computer and sent the email. Zazi left town in a hurry, and the FBI was trying to figure out what he was rushing toward. But, Davis wondered, what if Zazi wasn't running *to* something? What if he was fleeing something in Denver that he didn't want any part of? Or, even supposing that Zazi were part of a terrorist plot, what would be a better alibi than being 1,800 miles away when something blew up?

Though Zazi was in New York, the investigation was still being run in Colorado, where it had begun. Zazi's family blended in among the many Arabs and South Asians who'd settled in and around Denver. While Borelli and his team were chasing Zazi in New York, it was up to Davis to figure out whether anybody in Colorado was involved. He had his hands full.

From the beginning, Davis was suspicious of Mohammed Wali Zazi, the patriarch. In one email that the FBI had uncovered, the al-Qaeda figure asked Zazi how to contact someone named Mohammed. That actually referred to the fake name Adis Medunjanin had used in Pakistan, but the FBI assumed it meant Zazi's father. Mohammed Zazi was a limousine driver, which meant that he, too, had access to the Denver airport.

Separately, one of the detectives on the Denver Joint Terrorism Task Force, an Arapahoe County sheriff's deputy named Jackie Gee, had an informant who knew the family. The informant raised suspicions about Zazi's cousin Amanullah, a troubled young man with a history of drugs and anger. Amanullah was not happy in America, the informant said. Finally, when word spread from FBI headquarters that police had found no signs of explosives during their traffic stop on the George Washington Bridge, Davis became increasingly convinced that if something terrible were about to occur, it would be in Denver.

One event that very evening screamed target.

Two days earlier, Davis had scanned his appointments to figure out what he'd need to cancel as he focused on the Zazi investigation. That's when he had noticed that Governor Bill Ritter was taking part in a discussion about terrorism at the Denver Art Museum that Thursday. His guest would be Husain Haqqani, Pakistan's ambassador to the United States. That raised alarm bells for Davis. Haqqani represented a government that allowed US drones to fire missiles on al-Qaeda targets deeper and deeper into Pakistani territory. The Pakistani Taliban were also furious over the government's military crackdown on militants in northwest Pakistan. In 2008, Taliban snipers fired on Prime Minister Yousaf Raza Gilani's motorcade and pledged to keep attacking government leaders.

Now Haqqani was coming to Denver to speak about the changes in the world since 9/11. Other dignitaries would be at the museum: diplomats from consulates, representatives from the US military's Northern Command in Colorado Springs, Denver's mayor, and, of course, the governor.

The event was sponsored by the Center for Empowered Living and Learning,[1] a downtown museum that was dedicated to educating people about the threat of terrorism. It was an offshoot of the Mizel Museum, a gallery focused on Jewish history and culture.

Davis picked up the telephone and dialed the center's executive director, Melanie Pearlman. The two had met briefly but didn't know each other well.

Davis was polite but got right to the point.

"You have the ambassador of Pakistan in there on the tenth?" he asked. "I need to understand the details of the ambassador's security."

There wasn't much to understand, Pearlman said. Haqqani had a few events to attend before Thursday night's discussion. A small Denver police contingent would be escorting him. Security at the event itself was going to be light.

"Who's picking him up at the airport?"

It was the center's regular limo driver. A good man, reliable. He'd driven other dignitaries.

"What's his name?" Davis asked.

"Ahmed," Perlman replied.

"Let me get back to you."

Davis was soon sitting in the governor's office on the first floor of the state capitol. Jim Carpenter, Ritter's chief of staff, wasn't told what the meeting was about, but when the head of the state's FBI office says he needs a few minutes with the governor, you make time.

Ritter, a fifty-three-year-old Democrat, and Colorado's top law enforcement officers sat around the table.[2] Davis explained that there was someone in Aurora who'd been communicating with a known terrorist in Pakistan. The language suggested some kind of attack was in the works. Specifically, Davis said, a suicide bombing.

Though everyone in the room was cleared to receive classified information, Davis was circumspect. He didn't reveal the contents of the email. He didn't identify al-Somali, the al-Qaeda terrorist. He didn't even say there was an email.

If Ritter was nervous at all, nobody in the room noticed. After twelve years as Denver's district attorney, he was not easily unnerved. At the first reports of gunshots and explosions at Columbine High School in the Denver suburb of Littleton in 1999, he'd driven there and arrived while two teenage gunmen were still roaming the building, having slaughtered a dozen classmates and a teacher. He'd been through the difficult weeks of 1997, when skinheads unleashed a wave of shootings and beatings on Colorado's immigrants, minorities, and police. In 2007, his first year as governor, a deranged man walked into his office suite with a .357 Smith & Wesson and declared that he was there to take over the state government. State troopers shot him to death while Ritter was in the next room, interviewing a job applicant.

Back in 1995, Ritter had personally taken over the prosecution of a sixteen-year-old cop killer, leading a colleague to call him "a trial animal." Now the governor, clad in a suit and his trademark cowboy boots, was visibly trying to suppress his instincts to take over the briefing, to prod Davis for more information, and make sure they followed the right leads.

Davis assured the governor that the FBI had surveillance on the Zazi family. He was still concerned about the event with Haqqani, although, he added frankly, "I don't have anything to base this on." But somebody from Colorado emailing with al-Qaeda? With the Pakistani ambassador coming to town? On the eve of the 9/11 anniversary? It seemed too much to be coincidental.

They talked briefly about whether to cancel the event, but that seemed like an overreaction. Ritter had the same questions that Davis had asked Pearlman on the phone. Who was picking up Haqqani at the airport and who was in charge of his security? He didn't like the answers. Ritter put the Colorado State Patrol in charge of picking up the ambassador and providing security. Over at the CELL, Melanie Pearlman's phone soon began ringing with police wanting to discuss security plans. Investigators would need ten tickets to the speech for undercover officers. And Ahmed the limo driver was out.

• • •

The Denver Art Museum is a massive downtown complex stretching across two buildings connected by a footbridge. The newer of the two, a sleek, futuristic structure, cuts a jagged silhouette out of the city's skyline. Its exterior walls run at odd angles, none parallel, in a style inspired by the Rocky Mountains and geometric rock crystals. Its most noticeable feature is the nearly two-hundred-foot triangle jutting out like a ship's prow over three lanes of downtown traffic.

In a suite in an office park south of the city, Major Brenda Leffler and Captain Steve Garcia of the Colorado State Patrol stared at images of the museum. There was not much to say. The pictures, part of a blast analysis the state had previously conducted on the museum, spoke for themselves. A suicide bomb outside the museum would send a shock wave against the building, creating pockets of devastating pressure beneath its overhangs. The sharp angles would magnify the blast and accentuate the damage. One of the blast models reminded Garcia of the Alfred P. Murrah Federal Building in Oklahoma City, gutted and sagging after the 1995 bombing by Timothy McVeigh, a homegrown terrorist who opposed the US government.

The nine-hundred-square-foot office suite where Leffler and Garcia sat was called the Colorado Information Analysis Center, known in law enforcement circles by its acronym, pronounced "kayak." The CIAC was one of many analytical task forces, dubbed fusion centers, that sprang up around the country after 9/11. Backed by hundreds of millions of dollars in federal money and much more from state governments, the centers were intended to be clearinghouses for threats and terrorist intelligence. Members of Congress loved fusion centers because they meant money for their states. But it didn't take long to realize that, in most cities, the threat was not nearly enough to justify all the manpower, money, and equipment.

So in many states, the fusion center mission crept toward something broader. Like the NYPD, some centers began keeping tabs on rhetoric. In Missouri, the fusion center circulated a report warning authorities to be on the lookout for people espousing antigovernment, anti-immigration, or antiabortion views. In Texas, the center encouraged police to monitor Muslim lobbyists. No fusion center had lived up to the original mission to connect the dots and detect an actual terrorist plot. Still, the money flowed, as did warnings about Americans who protested against the war, favored gun rights, or supported Libertarian candidates. And those were only the reports that leaked out. Many more fusion center documents were shielded from public scrutiny on the grounds that they were too sensitive to release. And because Congress created a Byzantine system to pay for it all, nobody in Washington was sure how much was being spent on the centers or where the money went.[3]

Colorado went in a different direction. Leffler and Garcia wanted the CIAC to become a clearinghouse for information, but beyond terrorism. There were car-theft rings, meth labs, strings of robberies, and gangs to investigate—the kinds of problems that local sheriffs faced every day. Colorado has a substantial Muslim population, including large Libyan and Somali communities. CIAC never considered putting informants or plainclothes officers in mosques or student groups to find terrorists.

"I don't think that's a viable tactic," Leffler would say later. "Who's to say they're not meeting at a library? Or a child's school? Or a local community center? I think it's a flawed approach toward gathering information."

The CIAC took in information, ran it through its databases, and passed it to others. If a tip came in about terrorism, it would work it up and hand over the information to Steve Olson at the FBI. The relationship between the two agencies was rocky at first. FBI agents tended to talk down to the state troopers. And Garcia generated some angst at the bureau for saying that the Joint Terrorism Task Force was the investigative arm of the CIAC. But by 2009, Olson could count on the CIAC to quickly deliver leads that had been thoroughly analyzed. Things had improved so much that Garcia was among the first people outside the FBI that Olson told about Najibullah Zazi.

Leffler and Garcia looked through their databases. They had nothing suspicious on Zazi or his family.

• • •

As Jim Davis drove to the art museum Thursday night, he was struck by a morbid thought: "If something happens here, I hope I'm a casualty so I don't have to deal with what comes next."

There would be hearings, an investigation, finger-pointing. People would ask why the event was allowed to go on. It would be another intelligence failure, and on the eve of the 9/11 anniversary. Back then, in 2001, they hadn't pieced together enough details to see the complete picture of the imminent attack. Now everyone recognized the possibility—no, the growing likelihood. They'd shared the information, they'd responded correctly. None of that would matter if something happened.

Davis never wanted to fight terrorists. He grew up in Detroit, the son of a cop, and he wanted to be like his dad. His father knew that police work entailed patrol shifts, traffic duty, the midnight-to-eight. "Don't be a cop," he told his son. "Be an FBI agent." And that was that.

When Davis was about fourteen, he called the FBI field office in Detroit. He reached the complaints agent, the guy who takes cold calls. He wasn't interested in making chitchat with a teenager who said he wanted to be an FBI agent when he grew up. But before hanging up, the agent told Davis, "If you wanna be in the FBI, you gotta be an accountant or a lawyer." So Davis majored in accounting at Michigan State University. He got his CPA license. He didn't care at all about being an accountant. He wanted to join the FBI, and he did.

He worked violent Ku Klux Klan cases in Virginia. He worked fraud and corruption cases in Chicago with code names such as Sourmash, Hedgeclipper, and Silver Shovel. Before 9/11, the criminal investigative division was the bureau's premier assignment, the way toward promotions and great cases. But in the year following the attacks, one out of every four agents was pulled out of the criminal division. Davis was at headquarters in Washington then, as an assistant section chief in the fraud unit. But he felt like an executioner. He'd walk through the office, tap guys on the shoulder, and watch them walk out the door and into the war on terrorism.

Davis understood the realignment, but he wondered whether the surge outpaced the actual threat. There were crimes that weren't being investigated in the new FBI. A year after the attacks, when Davis got to Indiana as the assistant special agent in charge, he thought, "I don't know if there are terrorists here. But I know there are criminals." It didn't matter. Terrorism overshadowed everything.

It was ironic, then, that a tour in Baghdad, not a criminal case, had defined his career. It was 2003, and Davis had left Indianapolis to become the FBI's second-in-command in Iraq. Agents fingerprinted and photographed Iraqi detainees. They questioned prisoners and passed whatever they learned back to headquarters. Late one Saturday afternoon, word began spreading in the Baghdad Operations Center that the military had snatched someone important. Davis grabbed an FBI fingerprint specialist named David Shepard and headed out to meet a team of commandos from Delta Force, which led them to a house on a compound near the Baghdad airport.

The Delta guys allowed Davis and Shepard to talk to the prisoner.

He spoke English, the soldier said. But no chitchat. Get in and get out. They opened a door to a large, tiled room. There were more soldiers inside, seated around a small table on a raised platform. The room was otherwise empty except for a small bed, which is where Davis first saw Saddam Hussein.

Shepard could usually fingerprint and photograph a prisoner in about five minutes. He'd done thousands. But the Iraqi dictator's hands were slathered in moisturizing lotion to cure the dry, cracked skin that came from his time on the run, hiding in a camouflaged hole. Shepard couldn't get a good print. He tried baby wipes and alcohol swabs—even special wipes with cayenne pepper on them. Finally, Shepard began rubbing Saddam's fingers, trying to get more blood to his hands and improve the clarity of the fingerprints. It was a surreal scene: the young FBI agent massaging Saddam Hussein's hands.[4]

When the prints were done, they swabbed Saddam's cheek for DNA and took his mug shot. Davis then told him to face the wall for a profile shot. Saddam seemed genuinely upset.

"This is how you treat criminals," he protested.

"That's right," Shepard said. "Face the wall."

Davis took it all in. He was processing an infamous dictator in a war zone half a world away from home. And he thought, "All I ever wanted to do was work bank robberies."

• • •

As the hour for the Haqqani event drew near, and with the FBI still uncertain what, if anything, was being planned, police descended upon downtown Denver. Cops shut down roads around the museum. Snipers hid on rooftops. An FBI surveillance team camped outside Zazi's house in Aurora, and SWAT team members waited up the road. Garcia stationed a state trooper on the highway. Anybody who left Zazi's house and started toward Denver would quickly see blue lights in the rearview.

Despite those precautions, as Brenda Leffler and Steve Garcia from the Colorado State Patrol stood on the footbridge connecting the art museum's two buildings, they wondered privately whether that night would be the first time they'd have to use their guns.

The police kept Haqqani off the street as much as possible. He'd given interviews earlier in the night, and his security detail, rather than walk him around the corner to his next event, ushered him through a series of back rooms, up an elevator, across a rooftop garden, and down another elevator. Now he and the governor were at the footbridge, about to walk to the speech.

"Is everybody ready?" Ritter asked.

Leffler was surprised to detect a hint of nervousness in the governor's voice.

"Yes, Governor," she said. "Everybody's ready."

While Haqqani and Ritter spoke, Olson and Davis of the FBI decided to send the informant—the one that Jackie Gee from the sheriff's office had cultivated—into Zazi's apartment. It would be a social call. He'd talk to the family, get a sense of whether anyone was on edge, and have a look around. Short of having a video camera in the apartment, it was the next best thing.

Before arriving at the complex, the informant stopped up the street and met FBI agents and an ATF agent named Doug Lambert. He sat on the curb as Lambert walked his dog, Ostermann, around the informant. Like all bomb dogs, Ostermann, a four-year-old black Labrador retriever, was certified to detect bulk explosives. But Ostermann, named after famed NYPD bomb squad detective Glenn Ostermann, could also sniff out trace amounts of bomb-making materials and residue, including chemicals used to make peroxide explosives such as TATP. Ostermann's job was to make sure the informant was clean when he went into Zazi's apartment.

Olson called Davis at the art museum. The informant was in the apartment.

The art museum auditorium was packed with perhaps six hundred people. From a balcony, Davis and Garcia watched as the audience, bathed in blue houselights, settled in for a short film before the speech. It had been three days of nearly nonstop work, and both men were tired and edgy. Garcia reached for a white wooden chair nearby and sat down.

Just then an alarm went off. Police radios came to life. Garcia saw officers running. Something was going on. He sprang up. This was it.

But the officers weren't running to the stage or toward the governor. They weren't running down toward the crowd at all. They were running toward *him*.

The white chair was part of an exhibit, one that used chairs as a study of design trends over the years. When Garcia sat down, he'd triggered the museum's alarm. Security guards and jumpy police were heading his way.

"Stand down! Stand down!" he called out a bit sheepishly. "My bad."

The clamor on the balcony was lost on most of the crowd, drowned out by the film. Ritter took the stage to introduce Haqqani, who sat in a canvas director's chair to make remarks and field questions from a moderator. Haqqani told the audience that the United States and Pakistan were making progress in defeating al-Qaeda and its sympathizers.

"There has been no major attack in the United States since 9/11," he said. "We are able to find out about more planned attacks ahead of their execution than in the past."

Back on the balcony, by a small couch underneath a stairwell, Davis grabbed his cell phone, getting an update from Olson.

The informant had made it into and out of Zazi's apartment. He'd greeted Mohammed Wali Zazi with a hug. The apartment was nearly bare, with cushions and mats on the floor rather than couches and furniture. He'd sat and made small talk with the family. Nobody seemed jittery. No hint of anything sinister.

Once the informant left the apartment, the FBI put him back on the curb for Lambert and his dog to inspect. Lambert had never tried anything like this, using an informant as a human swab for bomb residue. He'd never even heard of it being done. But he'd seen dogs detect gunpowder on the sleeves of FBI agents long after they'd been to the firing range. In theory, this wasn't that different. "It's not a hundred percent," he'd told Davis and Olson. "But it's an indicator." To be cautious, he sat some FBI administrative employees on the curb next to the informant. If a dog is told to search one area alone, he's more likely to generate a false positive.

Ostermann circled the informant and smelled something for sure. The dog was drawn to the man's chest.[5] Perhaps he had picked up chemicals from hugging Mohammed Zazi, Olson and Davis surmised.

As Olson relayed the story, Davis couldn't help but respond with a rueful laugh. Then he turned to Garcia.

"This ain't good."

• • •

At FBI headquarters in Washington, Mike Heimbach, the FBI's top counterterrorism agent, wanted to know exactly what happened with the dog. He or his boss, Art Cummings, would have to brief the director.

Robert Mueller III, the sixth director in the history of the FBI, could be a fearsome man to brief. Everybody who's done it has a story, and it's always some variation of the red car:

An FBI briefer tells Mueller that agents are following a car.

"What color is it?" the director asks.

"Red," the agent replies. He'd seen that one coming.

"What shade of red?"

Politely put, Mueller was detail oriented. It was the former federal prosecutor in him. He liked to visualize things. Mueller would sit at his desk and listen intently. Sometimes he'd have his chair turned slightly, feet out to one side, shoulders angled a bit toward his briefer. Other times he'd lean in, elbows on his desk, hands clasped an inch or so beneath his chin. Experienced briefers could see it coming: prosecutor mode, machine-gun mode, blood-in-the-water mode, whatever you wanted to call it. One giveaway was when he'd cock his head to the left to ponder something. The briefing was over. It was about to become a conversation. Mueller had questions and there had better be answers.

Since 9/11, Washington has become a city of briefings. An infrastructure has sprung up to make sure that the nation's policy makers have every piece of information they want. There have always been briefings, of course, but now there are more, if only because there are more agencies and more people with security clearances. There are briefings at the Department of Homeland Security, the Office of the Director of National Intelligence, the National Counterterrorism Center, and the Transportation Security Administration—agencies that didn't exist before the attacks. Each day, the government churns out a small library of materials for the sessions. They have names such as briefing books, matrices, threat assessments, intelligence reports, and intelligence summaries. It would be impossible to digest them all, but they're all there, in case anyone wants to read them.

At the FBI, Mueller gets his daily briefing at seven in the morning. When a field office has an investigation that could make it onto the director's desk, an analyst in the field prepares a document for headquarters the evening before. If a case is that important, the office is almost certainly swamped, which means that the analyst must break away from a busy investigation and spend time explaining to headquarters what's already been done. On a terrorism case, the briefing document goes to the International Terrorism Operations Section, or ITOS, pronounced "eye-toss" in bureauspeak.

Information doesn't flow into ITOS. It floods. It gushes. Reports arrive from the CIA and the NSA, from satellites, soldiers, foreign intelligence agencies, and more. Back when Heimbach was an ITOS section chief, before his promotion to oversee all of counterterrorism, he took an eighteen-inch section of fire hose and mounted it to the office wall out at Liberty Crossing, the undisclosed location that is not a secret, hidden in plain sight near a northern Virginia shopping mall. The fire hose was a symbol of their shared experience drinking from the high-pressure intelligence spigot.

Each night before they go home, Heimbach and the other bosses review the documents so they know what the director might hear in the morning. If something isn't quite clear, or if there's a chance that Mueller might cock his head to the left, somebody will call the field office and ask for more information. Often that means more work for the analyst and more time away from the actual investigation.

That's for the morning meeting. There was a time when Mueller was getting a second briefing at four o'clock in the afternoon, too.

This was the stuff that drove Davis nuts. He was convinced that headquarters was often more focused on having the right answers for the next briefing than on making the right decisions for the investigation. If the briefing went bad, a supervisor was stuck standing there looking like an idiot in front of the director. If the investigation went bad, the field office would take the blame. Davis thought headquarters was cliquish and too removed from the reality that agents faced while making cases. He not only disliked headquarters, he cultivated an outsider's reputation.

Needless to say, Washington saw things differently. The agents and analysts at headquarters and out at Liberty Crossing were experts in their subjects. At any given time, the Counterterrorism Division had as many as 5,500 open cases, including legitimate terrorists, would-be jihadists, and the hapless idiots who try to buy plastic explosives or missile launchers from undercover agents.[6] The analysts knew how one investigation fit into another. People like Saleh al-Somali were not abstract ideas to them. That big case in the field, the one the analyst doesn't have time to brief? Maybe it's one piece of something stretching across five field offices. There's probably an international component to it, meaning the legal attachés in London or Pakistan might be involved. Maybe the White House wants to know the latest because it has policy implications. So brief it.

Heimbach could usually straddle that divide. He'd been a standout field agent and was sensitive to the implications of demands from head-quarters. He and Davis were old friends, so Davis didn't get upset when Heimbach wanted to know more about the dog and the informant. Ostermann seemed to be validating the FBI's suspicion that there were explosives in Zazi's apartment or had been at one point. There had been no sign of a bomb in the rental car on the George Washington Bridge, so it could still be in Colorado. The Zazi family had easy access to the Denver airport. If there had been explosives in the house, Heimbach wanted to be sure that Zazi hadn't loaded them into one of the cars parked outside.

Zazi and his parents lived in an apartment on the top floor of one of the many identical three-story buildings in Saddle Ridge Village, a gated community set in earthy greens and tans that, like the others nearby, had sprung up during the nationwide building boom in recent years. The apartment manager had given the FBI a remote control for the gate, making surveillance easy. Cars were always coming and going, winding through the maze of parking lots and access roads. Nobody noticed someone sitting in his car for a while. The agents took turns, in different cars from different vantage points. There was only one en-trance to the apartment, and it was easy to keep watch.

With Saddle Ridge Village's many buildings, no resident could have known all his neighbors. So when ATF agent Doug Lambert dressed in street clothes and walked Ostermann the black Lab around the Zazi family's cars parked outside, anyone peeking out his window would have seen a man taking his dog for an evening stroll. He and Ostermann had never done a surreptitious search. The parking lot was nearly empty as Lambert worked his way around Mohammed Zazi's white airport shuttle van and whispered to Ostermann, "Seek."

Olson called Davis again. The cars at Saddle Ridge were clean. Ostermann didn't smell a thing. The event at the art museum was winding down. It had gone off perfectly—except for the white chair. The security was tight but unobtrusive, and if there had ever been a threat, it didn't materialize.

Thanks to Ostermann, the FBI was more convinced than ever that there was an al-Qaeda bomb maker at work. The art museum event had been their best guess as to the target. Now they had no idea.

8

MOSQUES

While the NYPD and FBI worked together on the Joint Terrorism Task Force to figure out what Zazi was up to, Cohen and his team at the Intelligence Division were going their own way.

Early Thursday morning, September 10, hours before Zazi crossed the George Washington Bridge, Cohen and his top lieutenants gathered downtown in his office on the eleventh floor of One Police Plaza for their regular seven fifteen morning meeting. As the men took turns updating Cohen about operations and fresh intelligence, the conversation shifted to Zazi and what the division should do. The FBI led the investigation, but Intel had the kind of granular information about New York's Muslims that the bureau hadn't been able to collect, whether by choice or by regulation. The NYPD was going to work its sources and find out what it could.

Deputy Inspector Paul Ciorra, a balding, stout former soldier, asked whether one of his detectives could show pictures of Zazi and his friends to an informant in Queens. Cohen agreed.[1] Nobody at the table, including Assistant Chief Thomas Galati or Cohen's closest aides, raised objections. And nobody suggested checking with Borelli or even with Jim Shea, the NYPD's chief on the JTTF. It was understood that this was going to be a unilateral operation.

Daniel Sirakovsky, a former Bronx narcotics detective, had been moved to the Intelligence Division after 9/11 and had spent years developing sources in the Muslim community. He didn't recognize any photographs of Zazi, Ahmedzay, Medunjanin, or Zazi's cousin Amanullah, but he had an informant who might.

Sirakovsky knew an Afghan imam in Flushing named Ahmad Wais Afzali. A native of Kabul, Afzali had followed the familiar path of refugees from the Afghan capital to Queens, arriving in 1981 as a ten-year-old in flight from the Soviet invasion. He'd gotten his green card but never finished high school. Afzali had been married and then divorced after pleading guilty to attempted sexual abuse with an ex-girlfriend. He maintained that the sex was consensual and received probation, but the experience deepened his commitment to studying Islam. In 1993 he joined his parents in Virginia, where they had opened a pizzeria. Afzali enrolled in a Koranic Arabic course at an Islamic institute in Fairfax, Virginia, a suburb of Washington, and earned money as a housepainter and plasterer. Three years later, he returned to Flushing, where he continued his Islamic studies, and by 1999, he was an imam and an assistant to the president at Abu Bakr—the same mosque where Zazi and his friends had spent time; where they began plotting their transformation into terrorists.

Sirakovsky met Afzali in 2008 at 26 Federal Plaza, the Manhattan building that houses a federal immigration court. Afzali was embroiled in a five-year fight to avoid deportation after the sex charge. The US Board of Immigration Appeals ruled that Afzali could stay in the country, but officials hadn't yet returned his confiscated Afghan passport and US green card.

Sirakovsky began meeting Afzali at a mortuary in Woodside, Queens, where he was now working as a funeral director. Soon Afzali invited the detective to his home on Parsons Avenue not far from Flushing. He lived there with his wife, Fatimah Rahim, in a three-story building that his parents had bought with the money they'd made selling their pizza parlor. Afzali was at ease around cops. He'd gone out of his way to establish a relationship with patrol officers in the nearby 109th Precinct.

Afzali was happy to tell Sirakovsky what he knew about the local Muslim community. He wanted to be a peacemaker and saw his work with the NYPD as a way of bridging the gap between his immigrant community and his adopted American home.[2] He answered questions about people who attended Abu Bakr and other mosques. His work at the funeral parlor made him especially valuable because he visited more than a dozen mosques regularly and talked to leaders and congregants. He knew the personalities and conflicts that animated the community.

In NYPD jargon, Afzali was labeled a "cooperative," rather than an informant, because he didn't take money. Unlike many informants with whom the Intelligence Division's detectives worked, Afzali maintained a comfortable lifestyle, thanks to his parents' success. He leased a new cream-colored Jaguar XF and decorated his apartment with expensive mirrors, marble floors, and off-white leather couches that matched the color of the car.[3] On a glass wall in the living room was a sticker with a quote from the Koran: "Enter here in peace and contentment."

Afzali's wife was a linguistics student at nearby Queens College. When Sirakovsky stopped by—sometimes as often as once or twice a week—she would make the men tea and disappear to do her schoolwork in the bedroom. Rahim was American born, from a mixed Puerto Rican and African American background, and she was deeply suspicious of Afzali's arrangement with Sirakovsky. Her father was an imam, and she had grown up in a rough part of Brooklyn, where the NYPD was the enemy. She worried that her husband was naive. "You don't know their motives," she would tell him. Afzali said not to worry. Sirakovsky wanted to know only about people in the mosques. Afzali thought he was the one with the leverage in the relationship. He had the information. And he didn't need the NYPD's money.[4]

That changed when Afzali asked Sirakovsky for help in getting back his green card and passport. When the documents arrived, the dynamic shifted: Afzali now owed the NYPD a favor.

With orders coming directly from Cohen for the Intelligence Division to pump sources for information—any information—on Zazi, Sirakovsky called in this favor. Thursday, September 10, 2009, was Afzali's thirty-eighth birthday. Sirakovsky asked Afzali about Zazi and his friends over the phone, but Afzali wasn't sure he knew them.[5] He said he needed to see the faces. Later that day, at Afzali's home, Sirakovsky showed the imam three printed photographs and another on his cell phone. Afzali immediately recognized Zazi, Medunjanin, and Ahmedzay. He told the detective a little about their families and childhoods, where they worked, where they hung out. He had known them from his time working at Abu Bakr, when the three were still in high school. He also remembered running into Medunjanin and Zazi a few years later, maybe in 2007. By then, he told the detective, they had full beards and were praying in the front row. He didn't have much more to offer.[6] The detective thanked him and asked Afzali to find out as much as possible about Zazi and his friends. Where were they praying? When? And most importantly, what were they up to?[7] Afzali said he understood and showed Sirakovsky to the door.

•   •   •

A few miles away, the surveillance team watched Zarein Ahmedzay reappear from his apartment, where his friend Zazi waited in the late-afternoon sunlight. He had been out of sight for only a few minutes when he slipped into the red Impala with Zazi. The JTTF radios burst to life: He's rolling. There were six cars, driven by members of the task force's surveillance squad, all in civilian clothes, ready to follow. They didn't know if the pair in the car were about to attempt mass terror or drive around the block.

In the car, Zazi told Ahmedzay about the police stop in Denver and the car search on the George Washington Bridge. It was like the police were waiting for him there. And he had a feeling he was being followed. Every time he turned, it seemed, the same cars were behind him. But he couldn't be sure. He was wiped out from the cross-country drive; maybe he was seeing things. How could anyone know what he was up to? He'd been careful. Zazi drove aimlessly around his old neighborhood, peering anxiously into his mirrors.

With an FBI plane still circling out of sight, Zazi and Ahmedzay pulled into the Muslim Center of New York, a large mosque and school not far from Zazi's old apartment. The mosque had a dome decorated with the Muslim declaration of faith: "There is no deity except Allah. Muhammad is the messenger of Allah." It was about five o'clock during Ramadan, and the mosque was busy with worshippers convening for the third of five daily prayers. Zazi parked in the back, out of view of the FBI agents, and got out carrying a plastic shopping bag. He and Ahmedzay then entered the mosque, disappearing into the crowd. Like that, they were gone.

The surveillance radios crackled. Nobody had eyes on the targets. Back in Chelsea at the Joint Terrorism Task Force, a supervisor told Don Borelli that Zazi and Ahmedzay had entered a mosque. Like churches and synagogues, mosques were protected by the First Amendment. Things had gotten complicated for the FBI.

"Okay," Borelli said. "Do what you can do."

He knew the FBI's tortured history with mosques since 9/11. After the attacks, the bureau realized it had no relationship with Muslim communities, and agents struggled to figure out what they wanted it to be. The FBI's first response—rounding up Muslims and holding them in secret without charges or access to lawyers—did not get the relationship off to a good start.

Agents showed up at mosques, handed out business cards, and tried to build relationships with worshippers. But all trust would be lost when there'd be a raid like the one in Queens in 2002, when FBI agents stormed a mosque looking for guns and rocket launchers but left empty-handed. In 2006 they marched into a building in Pittsburgh to arrest a felon on an outstanding warrant. The agents were surprised to discover it was a mosque.

"Our place of worship was ransacked," its director complained. "Doors were kicked in, and a storage closet turned upside down. The FBI left no list of what was taken." [8]

And then there were sting operations, in which the FBI used agents or informants to pose as terrorists and offer to sell plastic explosives or some other deadly weapon to Muslims. Agents said the targets had put themselves in that situation, and that the FBI had no choice but to see whether the men were talking tough or really wanted to commit terrorism. Muslims saw it as entrapment. Inside the mosques, worshippers sensed that the FBI wasn't interested in being friends so much as it wanted to gather intelligence, make you an informant, maybe offer to sell you a Stinger missile.

The FBI can send informants into a mosque to follow suspects and report criminal activity but not when it's simply speech protected under the Constitution. In training sessions, FBI agents were asked whether they could sit outside a mosque as part of an investigation and collect license plate numbers of people in attendance. The answer was no.

If an FBI office wants to investigate an entire mosque, church, or synagogue, agents are required to inform their superiors at headquarters and the Justice Department. [9] Approval requires clearing a high legal bar, designed in part to make sure that prosecutors can bring charges without facing constitutional objections from defense lawyers. FBI guidelines demand that agents seeking to target houses of worship for investigation be able to explain clearly how the religious institution itself poses a serious criminal or national security threat. [10] The FBI could conceivably investigate a mosque as a possible terrorist organization, but the rules were designed to make it difficult.

Since 9/11, the FBI hadn't opened a single investigation targeting a mosque as a terrorist enterprise—not even in New York. [11]

"We don't target mosques," said Brad Deardorff, a supervisory special agent of the FBI in Houston. "We do collect domestic intelligence. But mosques are buildings. Mosques don't conspire. Mosques don't blow things up."[12]

The FBI's rocky relationship with American Muslims and their mosques had been the subject of congressional inquiry. Reporters and civil rights groups had used public-records requests to unearth training materials that offended Muslims, and documents that showed the FBI blurring the lines between outreach and spying. And the Justice Department's inspector general had weighed in. Luckily for Cohen, Intel was not burdened by such problems. He didn't have to worry about an angry lawmaker or a nosy inspector demanding he reveal his secrets. And the NYPD had made it unwritten policy to deny requests for public information.[13]

To Cohen, it had been obvious that police should have eyes and ears wherever Muslims might be radicalized or where people might even be plotting terror. It was his job to know what the enemy was doing, and because Islamic terrorism presented the primary threat to New York, Muslim houses of worship were naturally the top targets.

As far as Cohen was concerned, churches, synagogues, and mosques were fair game. They were quasi-public spaces where any citizen could go. Why shouldn't his officers or proxies be allowed to go inside too?

It wasn't the first time that law enforcement officials had faced the thorny issue of criminals who also attended religious institutions. Mob bosses had been churchgoers. Members of the Irish Republican Army had occasionally gathered at St. Patrick's Cathedral, the Fifth Avenue seat of New York's Catholic archdiocese. In those cases, the FBI hadn't followed. It picked up the trail after the suspects had left the churches.

To run the NYPD's intelligence operations as Cohen and Kelly believed necessary, Cohen needed a formal way to target mosques themselves. He told Judge Haight that in the war on terror, mosques and Islamic organizations would be used "to shield the work of terrorists from law enforcement scrutiny by taking advantage of restrictions on

the investigation of First Amendment activity." NYPD lawyers pro-
posed a new case category called a terrorism enterprise investigation.
It would allow officers to investigate political or religious organizations whenever the "facts or circumstances reasonably indicate" that
the groups were made up of two or more people involved in plotting
terrorism or other violent crime.[14]

"A mosque is different than a church or a temple," a former senior
NYPD official involved in the effort explained. "It plays a bigger role in
society and its day-to-day activities. They pray five times a day. They're
there all the time. If something bad is going to happen, they're going
to hear about it in the mosques. It's not as sinister as it sounds. We're
just going into mosques. We just want to know what they're saying."

To police, there are many benefits to investigating a mosque as
a criminal enterprise. If you're targeting only two people who pray
there, the rules say you can collect intelligence related only to those
two people. If the whole mosque is the target, however, then everyone
who attends prayer services is a potential suspect. Sermons, ordinarily
protected by the First Amendment, could be monitored and recorded.

The proposal was modeled on federal organized crime statutes and
the lenient guidelines that US Attorney General John Ashcroft had
written for the FBI after 9/11. Civil rights groups were furious, saying
those rules would open the door to government spying on domestic
groups when there was no suspicion of wrongdoing. The change to the
NYPD's rules attracted less attention.

In his April 2003 decision relaxing the Handschu guidelines, Judge
Charles Haight wrote that the focus of a terrorism enterprise investigation "may be less precise than that directed against more conventional
types of unlawful conduct." The investigations themselves, he went
on, might look different from traditional probes. "There may be no
completed offense to provide a framework for the investigation," the
judge wrote. "It often requires the fitting together of bits and pieces of
information, many meaningless by themselves, to determine whether a

pattern of unlawful activity exists. For this reason, such investigations are broader and less discriminate than usual." [15]

"As a consequence," the judge added, "these investigations may continue for several years."

Haight had seemingly given Cohen the same authority as the FBI to investigate mosques as terrorist organizations. Unlike the FBI, Cohen would actually do it.

The judge's ruling gave Cohen wide latitude to interpret the new rules. What qualified as reasonable indication? Cohen, who was neither a lawyer nor a cop, retained the sole authority to decide. The only oversight came from within the NYPD, from people who weren't going to buck Cohen or his boss, Kelly. The five district attorneys in the boroughs didn't have the authority to tell Cohen or Kelly what they could or could not investigate. Neither did the federal government.

Even before Haight issued his decision, Cohen began lining up targets. As soon as he had the judge's green light, he moved, opening investigations like an air traffic controller clearing jets off a stacked runway. In the first eight months under the new rules, the Intelligence Division opened at least fifteen secret terrorism enterprise investigations. At least ten targeted mosques. [16]

It was an unprecedented moment in the history of American law enforcement. The NYPD regarded houses of worship—and everyone who prayed there—as possible criminal organizations.

The first target of a terrorism enterprise investigation was a Brooklyn house of worship, the Masjid At-Taqwa in Brooklyn. The imam, Siraj Wahhaj, had been included on a three-and-a-half-page list of suspected accomplices in the 1993 bombing of the World Trade Center. The NYPD determined that Wahhaj promoted a political ideology that was "moderately radical and anti-American." [17] But the department expanded the investigation to include an unassuming storefront in downtown Brooklyn, the Zam Zam Stop & Shop Store, which sold Islamic books alongside incense and shea-butter bath products. The shop's Sudanese owner was involved with the mosque. He had no criminal history, but the NYPD put him on an internal watch list based on vague assertions that he had made anti-American statements and might have given charitable donations to a terrorist organization—assertions that never became criminal cases.

The Intelligence Division also began investigating the Masjid al-Falah mosque in Corona, Queens, which served as the US headquarters of the Tablighi Jamaat (Group for Preaching), an eighty-five-year-old movement that relies on missionaries to spread the word of the Prophet Muhammad. They were Islam's version of evangelicals. Tablighi Jamaat is supposed to be apolitical, but its many converts include John Walker Lindh, the infamous American Taliban captured as an enemy combatant in 2001 by US troops in Afghanistan.[18] The Intelligence Division opened its terrorism enterprise investigation into the group on April 18, 2003, two weeks after Judge Haight's order came down. It was clear why Cohen's team found Tablighi Jamaat worrisome: While the State Department had never declared it a terrorist organization, federal law enforcement believed that al-Qaeda used the group as a recruiting pool. According to the NYPD document authorizing the investigation, "al-Qaeda and affiliated groups are suspected of using Tablighi Jamaat membership as cover while traveling in order to appear as legitimate visitors."

But as far as the FBI was concerned, being affiliated with Tablighi Jamaat didn't necessarily mean a person was a terrorist. Investigators had nothing to indicate that the organization was a front for al-Qaeda in the way that the Mafia had once operated restaurants and social clubs in New York as wholly owned criminal subsidiaries. From the perspective of federal law enforcement, Tablighi Jamaat was more like the Ku Klux Klan, an organization formed to promote a set of beliefs—beliefs that, however distasteful, were protected by the US Constitution. The goal of the KKK wasn't to enable or conceal the criminal activities of its members. FBI agents didn't investigate the KKK. They'd tried that during the 1960s, and the Church Committee skewered them for it. Now agents investigated only those KKK members who put their hate into violent action.

Cohen interpreted the judge's revised Handschu guidelines more broadly. As long as there was a reasonable indication that people associated with the mosque were part of a terrorist group, then he was free to send investigators to take a closer look at the institution as a whole.

Al Marwa Center, a nonprofit that operated a trio of New York mosques, was another early target. According to NYPD files, investigators suspected a link between Al Marwa and the Muslim Brotherhood, the Egyptian Islamist group that long advocated violence in the name of establishing Sharia law. Rather than focusing solely on Al Marwa or on people suspected of advocating violence, Cohen's investigators used undercover officers and informants to watch the organization's mosques. The NYPD even had undercover officers with access to Al Madinah, an Islamic grade school in Brooklyn that al Marwa had established.[19]

• • •

In August 2003 Cohen requested a meeting with top FBI officials at the Joint Terrorism Task Force, then housed in Lower Manhattan, not far from city hall and One Police Plaza. Cohen brought Michael Sheehan, the NYPD's deputy commissioner for counterterrorism. Sheehan, a West Point graduate and a former Green Beret, had served on the National Security Council staff for both Presidents George H. W. Bush and Bill Clinton. He retired from the army in 1997 as a colonel and later worked in the State Department and the United Nations, where he built an impressive résumé combating terrorism overseas. Like Cohen, he had little experience with domestic criminal prosecutions.

Cohen and Sheehan sat across from Joseph Billy Jr., the FBI's special agent in charge for terrorism in the New York field office, and Amy Jo Lyons, his deputy. Billy had been the on-scene commander after al-Qaeda attacked the US Embassy in Tanzania in 1998. Lyons, who started her career working organized crime, had been in New York when al-Qaeda struck in 2001 and, in the aftermath, had been in charge of the 9/11 command center. She'd also spent six months managing the investigation of Zacharias Moussaoui, the so-called twentieth hijacker in the 9/11 attacks. Both Billy and Lyons were dedicated to making sure that terrorists didn't succeed in hitting New York again, not only because it was where they worked but also because they would be the ones hauled before Congress if anything happened.

Cohen and Sheehan explained to Billy and Lyons that they were concerned about Masjid Al-Farooq, one of the most infamous mosques in New York. It occupied a converted six-story factory on a stretch of Atlantic Avenue in Brooklyn lined with Middle Eastern restaurants, bakeries, and spice stores. To Cohen, it was a potential terrorist breeding ground, where invited preachers raged against the United States, the Bush administration's war on terror, and against Israel. It had a long history of extremist connections. Omar Abdel Rahman, the blind Egyptian sheik who was convicted of plotting to blow up New York City landmarks, once preached briefly at Al-Farooq.[20] Congregants there blamed the Jews for 9/11.[21]

Cohen's team had opened a terrorism enterprise investigation into Al-Farooq in 2003 and begun sending informants to monitor activities there. The NYPD believed that the mosque's imam, Abdul Zindani, was recruiting young men for jihad. Zindani had no criminal history, but police believed that he had al-Qaeda ties. Informants reported that both the mosque's treasurer and his wife had solicited money for weapons for jihad in Iraq. In total, the NYPD placed seven people associated with Al-Farooq on an internal watch list.[22] The list included Zindani, the treasurer, and the treasurer's wife.

The FBI knew Al-Farooq well. Prosecutors had mentioned the mosque that same year in their case against a Yemeni cleric and his aide accused of raising more than $20 million for al-Qaeda and Hamas, a

US-designated Palestinian terrorist organization. According to the Justice Department, the cleric, Sheik Mohammed Ali Hassan al-Moayad, had confided to an FBI informant that he had friends in New York who'd raised money for jihad at Al-Farooq.[23] The details were sketchy. It wasn't clear how much had been raised or when, or whether the donors knew where the money was going. Mosque members told reporters later that they thought the money was to help the poor. But the indictment put Al-Farooq on the map in the worst possible way. Police Commissioner Kelly told reporters that al-Qaeda operatives "did their fund-raising right here in our own backyard in Brooklyn."[24]

Now an informant had recently told the NYPD about a secret meeting in which an imam at another mosque delivered $30,000 to one of Al-Farooq's leaders. The source of the money was believed to be Masjid al-Ikhwa, the mosque that the NYPD later suspected of harboring jihadists in the basement.[25]

Cohen and Sheehan wanted the FBI to bug Al-Farooq.[26]

It was imperative, the NYPD men said, that they be able to listen to conversations. Cohen and Sheehan wanted all the rooms, including the prayer hall, wired. That would mean eavesdropping on everybody in the mosque. Sheehan asked whether they could get a classified warrant from the intelligence court in Washington, which authorizes the government to monitor Americans believed to be working for terrorist groups or foreign governments.

FBI agent Lyons said that was impossible. Even considering the case against the Yemeni cleric, the FBI didn't have probable cause to bug the mosque. The evidence was too murky, and they couldn't go to a judge without specifics. They had no hard evidence tying anyone in the mosque to a terrorist group. Even if they did, they wouldn't be able to use that to justify listening to everyone. There were rules, the FBI said.

We don't go into mosques and wire them up, Lyons told them.

Outside the door, as agents prepared for a retirement party, they could hear raised voices from inside the meeting. At one point, Cohen stormed out of the room. He returned after his temper cooled, but the meeting was over.[27]

In the end, despite the allegations and concerns about Al-Farooq, the Justice Department's case against the Yemeni cleric al-Moayad fell apart. At trial, prosecutors never even tried to establish that Al-Farooq had played a role in financing terrorism.[28] When the FBI's informant testified, he didn't mention Al-Farooq. The mosque never came up in secret videotapes with the cleric, either. Prosecutors won a conviction and seventy-five-year sentence but an appeals court threw out the case three years later. The court cited a number of problems with the informant's story.[29] For example, it turned out that the informant had written his notes for the FBI only after agents agreed to pay him—"a significant motive to fabricate," in the view of the appellate court.

The Justice Department salvaged its case by cutting a deal in which al-Moayad and his aide were allowed to go free if they admitted helping Hamas—not al-Qaeda. Though Attorney General John Ashcroft once publicly accused Al-Farooq of raising money for al-Qaeda, the government could never establish that Al-Farooq or its members were involved in terrorism.

And nobody in the NYPD's secret files on Al-Farooq was ever charged in connection with Cohen's lengthy investigation.

• • •

The FBI's refusal to bug Al-Farooq was a minor setback. Cohen turned instead to his legions of informants and undercovers. To manage the monumental task of infiltrating the mosques, Cohen tapped Larry Sanchez, his terrorism consultant on loan from the CIA. Just as the NYPD borrowed the original idea of listening posts from the FBI's 1960s playbook, Sanchez borrowed freely from the CIA.

Early in the Bush administration's war on terror, the CIA had tried a number of tactics to infiltrate al-Qaeda and give America an early warning on terrorism. One approach involved paying informants to visit mosques overseas and report on what they heard. Was the imam preaching violence? Was the ideology radical? Were fanatical factions of the congregation breaking away? The informants became informally known as "mosque crawlers."

It didn't take long for CIA officials to realize the effort was a waste of time and money. The mosque crawlers never produced valuable intelligence. The CIA scrapped the idea and focused its efforts elsewhere. But Cohen and Sanchez picked up where the CIA left off and duplicated the effort in New York.

A good crawler was one who made the rounds, visiting several mosques and listening closely to what people were saying. The best crawlers filed hundreds of reports, and not just on radical or violent talk. Cohen wanted his network of informants and undercover officers to take note of what Muslims in the tristate area were saying or doing, no matter how innocuous.

The NYPD's web of cops and crawlers slowly amassed a great deal of information, not only in the city but also on Long Island, in suburban Westchester County, and across the state line in New Jersey. They reported on the ethnicities and national origins of those who prayed. They wrote down the names of those who sat on the governing councils, or *shuras*. Informants snapped pictures and collected license plate numbers of congregants as they arrived. Police mounted cameras on light poles and aimed them at mosques. When a new imam was hired, the NYPD used a pole camera to identify him.[30] Plainclothes detectives working for the Demographics Unit mapped and photographed mosques for their files. The NYPD had its informants go into the mosques and collect lists of people attending classes, including cell phone numbers and email addresses.[31]

Still, Cohen wasn't content with the information from the field. He had the analyst's instinct to gather as much data as he could to understand where his enemy lurked. He launched an initiative to exploit

I-94s, the immigration forms that foreign nationals filled out when they visited the United States, to find people for questioning. Through contacts at US Customs and Border Protection, officers in the Intel Division obtained the forms and then tracked down the people who filled them out. These foreigners and their families were asked a series of questions, including, "What mosques might a visitor attend if he wanted to lie low during his time New York?" The detectives would pass the answers to the informant builders at the Terrorism Interdiction Unit.[32]

All this information went into the police reports that were supposed to help Cohen's analysts figure out which mosques and imams needed closer monitoring. By 2004, approximately two years after Sanchez came aboard, the division had produced an intelligence packet identifying eight former and current imams as radical religious leaders. Another list catalogued forty "mosques of concern"—including several with congregations composed largely of African American converts, many of whom had petty criminal records but no demonstrable connections to terrorism.[33]

"Just about any mosque can be a mosque of concern," said a former official involved in the program.

Eventually Cohen got his bugs. Instead of hiding them inside walls, he hid them on people. Because the FBI wouldn't play ball, he armed his undercover officers and informants with recording devices, careful to use them only at the mosques under investigation. The NYPD had a variety of devices available, with commercial names such as the F-Bird and the Eagle. They could hide a microphone inside a wristwatch or the small electronic key fob used to unlock car doors. The devices allowed NYPD informants to secretly record sermons and conversations.[34]

And just as their investigation into Time's Up and the Friends of Brad Will allowed the NYPD to collect information about other liberal groups that planned to protest the government, terrorism enterprise investigations allowed the police to collect information otherwise protected by the First Amendment.

After a Danish newspaper published cartoons lampooning the Prophet Muhammad in late 2005 and early 2006, protests erupted around the globe. Scores died in Africa and the Middle East. In Denmark, a Somali man armed with an ax broke into the home of the cartoonist, who hid in a panic room and was unharmed.

At the Bronx Muslim Center, however, Sheik Hamud al-Silwi gave a long sermon exhorting followers to use their American right to protest peacefully:

We have to do something about it, but not what those people are doing back home. They are burning and destroying stuff, and they should know that the Prophet does not want something like that to happen. We should follow the Prophet in the best way we can, boycott anything that was made in Denmark, don't buy or sell anything that has to do with them. We should send letters to our legal organizations and explain how we feel and demand that they do something about it.[35]

Al-Silwi's comments were reported, verbatim, in police files. Normally, a call to protest and boycott would be off-limits because it related to First Amendment activity, not a crime. But al-Silwi was the target of an investigation, which meant that the NYPD considered his sermons fair game, even when they were peaceful political comments.

Responding to the Danish cartoon controversy, police prepared a report for Police Commissioner Kelly in February 2006, a document that provided a window into the NYPD's collection efforts. Informants slipped into at least five mosques to listen to remarks about the cartoons.[36] Nothing in the report pointed to any incipient violence in New York City.

In some instances, the conversations catalogued had nothing to do with terrorism or violence at all. In October 2006, after New York Yankees pitcher Cory Lidle crashed his single-engine plane into a residential tower on Manhattan's Upper East Side during a flying lesson, investigators determined almost immediately that it was an accident.

Yet the NYPD's informant machine kept humming along. At the Brooklyn Islamic Center, a confidential informant "noted chatter among the regulars expressing relief and thanks to God that the crash was only an accident and not an act of terrorism." [37]

"The worshippers made remarks to the effect that 'it better be an accident; we don't need any more heat,' " an undercover officer reported from the Al-Tawheed Islamic Center in Jersey City, New Jersey. [38]

"In summary," the NYPD's analysts concluded, "there is no known chatter indicating either happiness over the crash, regret that it was not a terrorist attack, or interest in carrying out an attack by similar method." [39]

•   •   •

By 2006, the intelligence community had al-Qaeda on its heels. The CIA had rounded up dozens of its operatives and sent them to secret prisons around the world. There had been attacks in London and Madrid, but none in the United States. In New York, the NYPD regularly trumpeted its role in keeping America safe in a stream of news stories and television interviews. "We have brought on board some of the best young minds in this country to help us analyze intelligence," Kelly told TV talk show host Charlie Rose. "We have a lot of, as I say, energetic young people who maybe want to have a career in the world of intelligence but have come to the NYPD because that's where the action is."

Cohen was happy to take credit. "Our job is to raise the bar and make it more difficult, if not impossible," Cohen told the CBS news program *60 Minutes*. "That's what we certainly try to do. I like to think that we've had some success."

In a lengthy internal PowerPoint presentation entitled "Intelligence Division—Strategic Posture 2006," the NYPD laid out its accomplishments. The department had catalogued more than 250 mosques as to their ethnic makeup, leadership, and group affiliations in the metro area. The presentation showed that the department had a source in many of them—either a confidential informant or an undercover officer. Though no investigation resulted in charges against a mosque for being a terrorist organization, the list of mosques of concern kept growing: from 40 to 53 in two years. Cohen could actually measure his success in the war on terror.

The NYPD had also expanded the number of people under investigation. Cohen's analysts had identified 138 "persons of interest" in New York City. A person of interest was "an individual with threat potential based on their position at a particular location, links to an organization, overseas links, and/or criminal history."

Evidence of current criminal activity wasn't listed as a factor.

The list included imams who were prominent in civic activities. Some had decried terrorism. Others, such as Sheikh Reda Shata, had stood shoulder to shoulder with the NYPD and Mayor Michael Bloomberg to show support for the police in their counterterrorism efforts.

Shata was the imam at the Islamic Society of Bay Ridge, one of the mosques that the NYPD had been investigating as a terrorism enterprise since 2003. It's not clear what more Shata could have done to avoid suspicion. He invited NYPD officers from the local precinct for breakfast and threw going-away parties when they transferred. He had breakfast and dinner with Bloomberg at Gracie Mansion, the mayor's official residence, and he invited FBI agents into his mosque to speak with congregants.[40]

"I have been impressed with his desire, as he's expressed it to me, to do good and do right," Charles Frahm, the FBI's top counterterrorism agent in the city, told the *New York Times* for its Pulitzer Prize–winning series on Shata's life in America.

Born and raised in Egypt, Shata was educated at Al-Azhar University in Cairo, a center of Islamic learning. He taught Islamic law in Saudi

Arabia and worked as an imam in Stuttgart, Germany. After 9/11, when someone defiled his mosque with feces and graffiti,[41] he decided it was time to leave. When the job at the Islamic Society of Bay Ridge opened, with its hundreds of worshippers, he jumped at the opportunity.

Shata arrived in New York in 2002, about the same time that Cohen was hired to transform the NYPD Intelligence Division. It didn't take long for the NYPD to hear about the new Egyptian imam at the mosque, which had a large Palestinian membership. He quickly fell under suspicion, and his name was among those the police considered part of the city's "radical leadership." The secret NYPD files noted his education at Al-Azhar and his birth date but wrongly described him as Palestinian.[42]

The Special Services Unit assigned an undercover officer, and the Terrorist Interdiction Unit sent a confidential informant to spy on Shata and his mosque, even as he met with Kelly and conducted cultural-sensitivity training at the Sixty-eighth Precinct in Brooklyn in 2006.[43]

The same year that the *Times* held up Shata as an example of how one imam learned to "find ways to reconcile Muslim tradition with American life,"[44] hints of the NYPD's extensive spying were trickling out.

Shahawar Matin Siraj, the twenty-three-year-old Pakistani immigrant accused of plotting to blow up the Herald Square subway station, had gone to trial, forcing the NYPD to reveal some investigative methods. An informant testified that he'd attended 575 prayer services at the Bay Ridge mosque.[45] His handler generated hundreds of reports, many of them based on daily visits there.[46] An undercover officer, testifying under a fake name, said that his job was to be a "walking camera" among the Muslims.

Covering the trial, the *New York Times* wrote that NYPD documents unearthed at trial "suggest that there could be as many as two dozen such investigations, but it could not be learned whether any others bore fruit."[47] What reporters didn't realize was that the mosques themselves were the targets, and the NYPD had decided that houses of worship might be terrorism enterprises. In a city where routine police reports aren't public and where NYPD press officers hand out summaries of cases they consider newsworthy, the police made it hard for journalists to dig deeper into the secret programs they'd glimpsed.

"Beyond the detective's testimony, police officials yesterday would not discuss the scope of the program and provided no details about its structure, its guidelines, or its successes or failures," the *Times* wrote. "Several officials, however, suggested it was in its early stages." [48]

Through it all, Shata was unaware that he was under suspicion, though he thought the NYPD was shadowing a board member at his mosque. [49] The surveillance continued after Shata left Bay Ridge to become the imam of Masjid Al-Aman, or "mosque of peace," which was flourishing on six acres in Middletown, New Jersey. [50] In December 2008, after Shata performed the hajj, the spiritual pilgrimage to Mecca in Saudi Arabia, an NYPD informant drove him home from the airport. The informant told his Intelligence Division handlers that he had "nothing significant to report." [51] Years later, when Shata learned that the NYPD was spying on him, he was devastated, believing that he'd been targeted for no other reason than his religious affiliation.

"This is very sad," he said, looking at his name in the NYPD files. "What is your feeling if you see this about people you trusted?" [52]

Shata's case wasn't the only one in which the NYPD and FBI diverged in thinking and tactics. Both agencies were interested in a twenty-six-year-old Islamic teacher named Mohammad Elshinawy. He taught at several New York mosques, including the Al-Ansar Center, a windowless Sunni center that opened in 2008 in southern Brooklyn and was attended by young Arabs and South Asians.

The FBI learned that Elshinawy might have been involved in recruiting people to wage violent jihad overseas, prompting agents to investigate him. The case remained open for many months but was eventually closed without charges being brought against Elshinawy. Federal investigators never bothered trying to get permission to infiltrate Al-Ansar. "Nobody had any information the mosque was engaged in terrorism activities," a former law enforcement official recalled.

Cohen and his commanding officer, Assistant Chief Thomas Galati, were not convinced. As one former law enforcement official recalled, Cohen and Galati thought that Al-Ansar could be the next Finsbury Park Mosque in London. The imam there was convicted of soliciting murder and inciting racial hatred, and was widely believed to be encouraging his followers to wage violent jihad.[53]

Short, bearded, bespectacled, and fluent in Arabic, Elshinawy was a Salafist whose father was an unindicted coconspirator in the 1993 World Trade Center attacks.[54]

"Elshinawy is a young spiritual leader that lectures and gives speeches at dozens of venues, mostly in the NY area. His views are hardcore Salafi ones. His following is generally young (10 years to 25 yrs)," a 2008 surveillance request stated. "He has orchestrated camping trips and paintball trips in the past."

According to the document, detectives in the Terrorist Interdiction Unit considered the imam a threat because "he is so highly regarded by so many young and impressionable individuals."

In other words, Elshinawy was a puritanical Muslim with a platform. He had the oratorical power to radicalize other Muslims, even if he had never been involved with terrorism. Other Muslims who had been radicalized had attended his lectures, reinforcing the NYPD's suspicion.

"There have been clusters of individuals who are being investigated by other units of this division who have made overt attempts to go and get Jihadi type of training from overseas," police wrote. "Some of the members of these clusters have stated that they regard Elshinawy as their spiritual leader."[55]

Meanwhile, Cohen's informants were keeping tabs on the mosque's members. One report noted that members of Al-Ansar were fixing up the basement and turning it into a gym. "They also want to start Jiujitsu classes in Al-Ansar," according to the report.[56]

As far as the NYPD was concerned, no part of Elshinawy's life was out of bounds. In March 2008 a police informant attended a gathering for the imam before he left for Egypt on a six-week trip to find a bride. When Elshinawy returned, US immigration officers stopped him at the airport. According to NYPD documents, Elshinawy refused to answer questions beyond saying that he had been visiting family. He wouldn't even empty his pockets. In addition, the report noted, "he was clean shaven upon his arrival. Very unusual for him, and we don't know why at this point." [57]

Cohen's people wasted no time following up. Within days of Elshinawy's arrival, two NYPD informants monitored his lecture at the Brooklyn Islamic Center. It turned out that the airport story was a false alarm. In a follow-up report from one of the informants, an NYPD lieutenant reported to Cohen, "He is not clean shaven, so that info we got was wrong . . . but everything seems normal with him." [58]

By October, as Elshinawy prepared for his wedding to the woman he'd found in Egypt, the NYPD prepared a full-scale surveillance operation for the ceremony at the center, which was the target of its own terrorism enterprise investigation. [59] The plan included wiring up an informant to record the wedding and placing a camera in a parked car nearby and pointing it at the mosque entrance. The NYPD could record everyone who came and went. Before the wedding, a lieutenant with the Terrorist Interdiction Unit submitted the details to Cohen as part of the written daily summary of Intelligence Division activities.

"We have nothing on the lucky bride at this time but hopefully will learn about her at the service," the lieutenant wrote. [60]

The NYPD continued to keep an eye on Elshinawy and his students for years, sometimes using an informant named Shamiur Rahman, a nineteen-year-old American of Bangladeshi descent who grew up in Queens. He had been arrested on marijuana possession and cut a deal to work as an informant. The NYPD Intel detectives also submitted a separate request to the surveillance specialists in the Technical Operations Unit, known for its distinctive logo depicting a pair of eyes peeking out of a garbage can with a camera.

Rahman took pictures of the sign-up sheet listing those who attended Elshinawy's classes, and then sent them to his NYPD contact, a detective named Stephen Hoban. Rahman communicated with Hoban by text message. He'd send the detective his daily plans, including which mosque he planned to visit or if he was going to attend a prayer session, a class, or a rally.

"Okay, let me know who is there," Hoban would respond.

Wherever Rahman went, Hoban was especially interested in names and pictures.[61] Rahman would send photos of people who led prayers at the mosques—including, in one case, a Muslim NYPD officer.[62] He even took pictures of the bags of rice, canned beans, and boxes of Cheerios being delivered to needy Muslims.

"I need pictures from the rally," Hoban wrote. "And I need to know who is there."

"Can you text me the names of who was at the rally today?"

"Did you take pictures?"

"Get pictures."

For all his success in blanketing the community, by 2009, Cohen had little to show in the way of arrests or prosecutions other than the Herald Square case. What mattered, though, was that there had been no terrorist attacks. In the same way that the NYPD's CompStat computer system of mapping crimes had prioritized reducing crime rates over arrests or convictions during the late 1990s, the Intelligence Division prioritized a 100 percent success rate in avoiding attacks.

When investigations don't have to lead to arrests and prosecution, they can linger for years. There was little incentive to close investigations on mosques, because without the investigations, collecting information about sermons, boycotts, and protests would be against the rules. Shutting down a case would shut off one of the major intelligence pipelines flowing out of Muslim neighborhoods. By Cohen's reading of the new Handschu rules, the standard for renewing an investigation was low. And because Cohen didn't have to make arrests, he didn't have to justify keeping cases open with no end in sight.

As a former colleague observed, "Who was going to tell Cohen no?"

On May 12, 2009, four months before Zazi set off alarms, Cohen and his top deputies and lawyers gathered to approve and renew investigations. Larry Sanchez was there, as were Deputy Inspector Paul Ciorra, analytics chief Mitch Silber, and Stu Parker, the Intelligence Division's attorney. Two lawyers working for the city, Thomas Doepfner and Andrew Schaffer, were also in the room. The agenda included a slew of requests to renew some of the terrorism enterprise investigations that had been going on since 2003.

The Brooklyn Islamic Center, Al-Farooq, the Islamic Society of Bay Ridge, and Masjid Al-Falah had all been under investigation for six years. All were approved for another extension.

There was nothing on the agenda about a trio of angry young men from Queens and a plot to bomb the subways during Ramadan.

9

THE AMERICAN WHO BRINGS GOOD NEWS

Zazi and Ahmedzay didn't stick around long at the Muslim Center of New York. Zazi was infecting Ahmedzay with anxiety, escalating his paranoia about who might be watching. Neither knew that Borelli's agents were outside, waiting for them to emerge, but before they left the mosque, they ditched Zazi's bomb-making components that he had carried in his bag. They dumped the hydrochloric acid down the toilet and threw Zazi's goggles and Christmas tree lights in the bathroom trash. A scale and a calculator, needed to measure the bomb-making ingredients, remained in his suitcase in the car. He'd need to discard those later.

The plan was off, at least for now. Their goal was staying out of prison.

Zazi dropped off his friend at his apartment. By that time, Flushing was dotted with task force surveillance cars. Ahmedzay went upstairs. Fear washed over him. He couldn't shake it. Damn being a martyr. If the FBI was really onto them, he was the one who had the most to lose. He had the jar of explosives in his closet. He'd look like the mastermind.

Ahmedzay hurried to his bedroom, threw open the closet door, and grabbed the jar that Zazi had brought from Denver. He went to the bathroom, dumped it into the toilet, and flushed. There was residue in the basin, so Ahmedzay scraped at it with a piece of cardboard, picking up the rest of the powder.

He figured that he should burn the cardboard to destroy any trace of the chemical. He struck a match. *Pop!* The TATP ignited, unleashing a burst of bluish light. Ahmedzay's head jerked back. Even knowing that the powder was designed to make a bomb, he hadn't expected it to be so explosive.

The burst of light only confirmed Ahmedzay's deepening conviction, the one he had originally felt in Pakistan: They were in way over their heads.

Ahmedzay stepped back into his bedroom and grabbed his computer. With a few keystrokes, he pulled up the videos and lectures about jihad stored on his hard drive—all representing hours and hours he had spent thinking about waging war on America. He erased them. Then he hunkered down, not daring to leave the house the rest of the night.

Zazi, meanwhile, headed to Abu Bakr, his childhood mosque, which was full with Ramadan worshippers. Men prayed on the first and second floors while the women held prayers in the basement. Zazi spotted Medunjanin in the crowd and maneuvered his way next to him. He pulled out his cell phone and quickly tapped out a text: The plan is off.

He didn't send it. Rather, he showed it to Medunjanin, who responded calmly, "I love you. I love for the sake of God."

Escape was now the priority. Zazi had to get out of New York before the shadows following him closed in.

They split up. Zazi decided it would be too suspicious to return to Ahmedzay's house, and he didn't want to put Medunjanin at further risk. Still, he needed somewhere to spend the night. As prayers ended, he noticed an Afghan immigrant named Naiz Khan, a high school pal from the neighborhood. They'd shot pool and played video games together as teens. Zazi said he was in town for the night and needed a place to stay. Khan gladly offered to share his apartment. It was on Forty-first Avenue, he said, up the street.

It looked to the FBI as though Zazi might be headed back to Ahmedzay's house after leaving Abu Bakr. But he surprised the agents by parking his car on the street and unloading his luggage. Bag in hand, he walked to a seven-story apartment building at 144-67 Forty-first Avenue, pressed the buzzer, and disappeared. This address wasn't associated with any of Zazi's relatives. He hadn't called anyone there. Nor had he sent any emails or text messages indicating that he was spending the night there.

That was just the beginning of Borelli's problems. An email was making its way around the FBI that night, and each time it was forwarded, more people got concerned. It summarized the traffic stop on the George Washington Bridge, and one line in particular jumped out at everyone. The cop on the bridge had noted a large water jug on the floor of Zazi's car. That was all he'd written. Had he inspected the jug? Was anyone even sure it was water?

Mike Heimbach, the FBI's head of counterterrorism, didn't get the email. Instead, he received a phone call from Jim McJunkin, the deputy assistant director working out at the undisclosed location in northern Virginia. The two were old friends, both Pennsylvania natives who'd started as cops—McJunkin as a state trooper, Heimbach as an officer in the Rust Belt town of Pottstown. Heimbach was in his office on the fifth floor of FBI headquarters, overlooking Pennsylvania Avenue, when McJunkin broke the news.

"How the fuck does that happen?" Heimbach thought. They'd repeatedly discussed the importance of the car search.

Down the hall from the director, Art Cummings had a similar response.

"Are you fucking kidding me?"

"I know," Heimbach said. "You can't make this up."

But nobody was more upset than Brenda Heck, the ITOS section chief for domestic operations. In the chain of command, there were Cummings and Heimbach at headquarters and McJunkin at Liberty

Crossing in northern Virginia. Heck came next. She had been on special assignment for the FBI in London in 2006, when authorities there unraveled a plot to detonate liquid explosives aboard transatlantic flights, so she was unnerved by the thought of an al-Qaeda operative driving into New York with a jug full of liquid.

Borelli had read the email. Not long after, he got a call from Bill Sweeney from the Counterterrorism Division. Sweeney worked for Heck, who had a reputation for driving her people hard. "I don't give a shit what you think," she'd snap. "I need to know what you know." Sweeney was on the hook to get answers, but Borelli didn't have any. Zazi's whole plot seemed based on some kind of chemical mixture. With a big bottle of liquid in his car, somebody should have done something.

"Talk to New Jersey," Borelli said, frustrated. They'd been in charge of the traffic stop.

Sweeney said they were already questioning the cop on the bridge to figure out exactly what he'd seen. Could he describe the jug? Could he draw it? Was it really a jug? Or was it more like a bottle that someone would buy to take to the gym or wash down a sandwich at the deli? Did it look like Zazi had been drinking out of it? In any event, now the water jug was in New York, and it had to be addressed. At that moment, Borelli was preoccupied with the apartment building at 144-67 Forty-first Avenue. This address wasn't linked to any of Zazi's known associates. It wasn't in any of the biographical workups. The FBI had been operating under the assumption that if Zazi was part of a terrorist cell, the other members were Ahmedzay and Medunjanin. Neither had ties to this building.

When the surveillance team located Zazi in an apartment on the fifth floor, and it looked as though he wasn't coming out anytime soon, Borelli told the surveillance team to send someone to peer inside the car. "Take a walk by," he said. "See if we can find this bottle." The car was empty. The surveillance guys had gotten a good look at Zazi when he'd parked. He hadn't taken a jug with him into the apartment. Whatever the officer had seen on the bridge that afternoon, it wasn't here.

Meanwhile, Borelli received more information. Five people lived at the apartment, all believed to be Pakistani or Afghans. It looked as though some, maybe all, were cabbies. It looked to the FBI like a flophouse.

The FBI watched Zazi's ATM card purchases and listened to his phone calls as they happened. So they knew immediately when, from inside the apartment, Zazi bought a plane ticket back to Denver for Saturday, September 12. It made no sense. Why would he drive all the way across the country, stay for a day, and then buy a ticket home? Was the plane the target? Or was he planning to make a fast exit from the city after tomorrow?

Zazi didn't appear again that night. He hid the scale and calculator in a closet, distancing himself from the last of his bomb-making materials. For the agents in the field, there was no more work to do. It was now up to the analysts to figure out everything they could about the five men living in the apartment. To the agents in the command center, that flophouse appeared to be a sleeper cell. Especially when the FBI determined that one of the men, Naiz Khan, had flown back from Pakistan the same day as Zazi on January 15, 2009, on a separate flight.

• • •

Despite the common misperception, 9/11 was not a failure of intelligence collection. All the signs of an impending attack had been there. The system was blinking red. Al-Qaeda's plan succeeded because the United States did not understand what it was seeing. It was a failure of analysis.

Before 9/11, the FBI's analytical ranks were a mess. The bureau had been designed to build criminal cases, not to predict attacks. Agents in Boston, Chicago, and Seattle might be working cases involving the same terrorist group. Nobody was in charge of combing the information and finding common threads. And nobody was reading CIA cables and NSA reports and seeing how they related to the FBI's own investigations. While the CIA's analysts were trying to predict trends and assess risks, the FBI's analysts were there to help the agents build cases—what's known as tactical analysis. There was nobody to conduct *strategic analysis*, to help the bureau understand all that it had collected.

The analytical corps was a ragtag group, many of them former secretaries and support staff who were still responsible for emptying trash and answering phones. There was no formal training—which wasn't surprising, because everyone knew that analysis was a dead-end job. There was no way up from the analytical ranks into senior management, which meant that agents with no analytical experience were in charge of supervising analysts.

The FBI had never completed a comprehensive analysis of the threat of international terrorism. Nobody saw the value in a written, structured report on the nation's vulnerabilities. FBI agents relied on their experience and their guts to tell them what the threat was.[1] Even had they conducted such an analysis, it's not clear how much it would've mattered. Back then, two out of every three analysts were not qualified to do their own jobs.[2]

In the eight years since the attacks, the CIA had dispatched more spies around the world, the FBI had put more agents on the streets, and the NSA was listening to more phone calls and reading more emails than ever before. By 2009, the once-decentralized FBI had become one in which headquarters oversaw all terrorism investigations. The analytical corps had more than doubled. A new generation of graduates from top-flight universities arrived eager to serve after 9/11. They joined the holdovers from the pre-9/11 era, analysts who found a niche and managed to thrive in the new FBI.

The first analysis of Zazi's travel records—the work that told the FBI that he had likely traveled with Medunjanin and Ahmedzay—had been carried out in Colorado under the supervision of an analyst named Laura Brady.[3] She had started as a secretary and on 9/11 was one of the few analysts with terrorism experience. Until then her focus was domestic attacks by animal rights groups, homegrown radicals, and right-wing extremists. She'd worked the 1998 ecoterrorism investigation into the firebombing of the Vail Ski Resort.

Albert Banke had been in the FBI's New York office for more than two decades. He'd started as a mechanic, fixing the bureau's cars. Then, in the days when analysts came from all corners, Banke landed on the analytical desk. As it turned out, he had a talent for analyzing phone records. During the 1990s, when the FBI was taking on the Mafia, Banke used its members' calls to paint a picture of a criminal organization.

A lifelong New Yorker, he sometimes carried a shop rag in his back pocket, as if to underscore his blue-collar roots. Banke and his team papered the command center walls with easel paper, using Zazi's and Ahmedzay's phone records to create a timeline of their relationships.

There were analysts at FBI headquarters in Washington working the Zazi case, too. In the early stages of the investigation, one of them had named the operation. Unlike CIA officers, whose operations receive randomly generated code names, FBI officials can label their cases whatever they wish. That led to puns like the marriage-fraud case "Knot So Fast" and the cigarette-trafficking probe "Secondhand Smoke." The Washington analyst picked High Rise because Denver was the Mile High City.[4]

The FBI can collect a staggering amount of information and, in terrorism cases, get it quickly. With an address, agents can obtain a list of everyone who lives there. With names, they can ferret out credit scores, financial histories, and account information at every bank and investment firm. That sort of information had always been available with a grand jury subpoena from the Justice Department. The 9/11 attacks, however, prompted Congress to pass the USA Patriot Act, which made it available with a different subpoena, called a national security letter.

As the name suggests, these were simply letters from the FBI ordering companies to provide information about its customers. Before 9/11, that power was limited to counterintelligence cases in which the

FBI was investigating people connected with foreign governments—basically, spies. The Patriot Act widely expanded its scope. No longer limited to banks, the bureau could now get information from pawnbrokers, casinos, travel agencies, dealers in precious jewels, car dealerships, title companies, or, as a final catch-all, any other business "whose cash transactions have a high degree of usefulness in criminal tax or regulatory matters."[5]

The FBI can get this information without the tedious review of Justice Department lawyers or a grand jury.

One of the first things the FBI did when investigating Zazi was to obtain a national security letter for his phone records and those of his friends and family. Once, an analyst like Banke might have had to retype these records to get them into Telephone Applications, the FBI's proprietary database. Now they usually drop in neatly.

The owners of known phone numbers automatically show up. Because the FBI has so many records in its system, there are countless known phone numbers. That helps the analysts spot calls to terrorists but ignore the Friday night order to Sal's Pizza—unless, that is, Sal's Pizza has come up in another national security investigation. If that's the case, the analysts will see an alert that there might be something more going on in the pizza shop.

The FBI can map financial transactions, looking for unusual wire transfers and signs of money laundering. Taken with the phone data, that can help the FBI visualize connections and create "communities of interest."

A national security letter will get only records. To listen to a call or read an email inside the United States, the Justice Department must obtain a warrant from the Foreign Intelligence Surveillance Court, a highly classified panel in Washington that rarely allows information to become public. To get a warrant, the Justice Department needs only to show that the target of the surveillance is an agent of a foreign power, which can mean a country, a state-controlled entity such as a foreign airline or a news outlet, or an international terrorist group. The warrants are authorized under the Foreign Intelligence Surveillance Act, and they've become known in the FBI simply as FISAs.

A FISA wiretap allows the bureau to listen to calls in real time. The conversations were fed into the FBI's computers, allowing agents and analysts anywhere in the country to listen. For emails, however, a FISA warrant is like turning on a spigot. In an instant, every email sent, received, or archived comes pouring into the FBI's computers. That can mean thousands, even tens of thousands of old messages. The government's software can group them by subject, sender, keywords, or where they were sent and received. The software can detect patterns and unusual behavior to help decipher the trove of data.

The FBI office in Denver handled the FISAs on Zazi and his family. Medunjanin and Ahmedzay were done in New York. All the data were saved on a shared computer drive so analysts in Colorado, New York, and Washington could see it.

That's merely a sliver of the data to which the FBI has access in the post-9/11 world. The FBI, CIA, NSA, and others operate on computer platforms that don't talk to one another. That was a problem until a Silicon Valley start-up called Palantir Technologies pulled off what *Bloomberg Businessweek* called "one of the great computer science feats" of the post-9/11 era. Palantir figured out that the government's computers didn't need to talk to each other. They just needed to talk to Palantir.

Software from the privately held Silicon Valley company grabs data from around the government. It can quickly alert an FBI analyst that a single phone number among thousands in a case was used to call a number linked to someone in a second case who sent an email to someone identified as a terrorist financier in a third case. It can collate airline reservations, border crossings, passport applications, suspicious financial transactions, and emails. It's why many in the FBI regard it as the biggest change in analytical software since 9/11.[6]

It was an analytical revolution. And it took almost no time for the FBI to start abusing its new powers.

When the FBI needs toll records, it calls the phone company. But after 9/11, agents were collecting so many that the FBI decided it made more sense to pay phone companies to place workers inside the FBI, alongside agents. AT&T, MCI, and Verizon employees became an arm of the government. They got FBI email addresses and FBI computers, and went to FBI happy hours and going-away parties. If the bureau needed phone records, agents could turn to the AT&T representative, hand over a national security letter, and get the data almost immediately.

The FBI then came up with an even faster way. In a pinch, rather than have to get approval for national security letters, the agents would give the phone companies documents known as "exigent letters," which said, essentially, "This is an emergency. We're working on getting you a subpoena or a national security letter, but give us the records in the meantime." Even though it was never formally approved by the FBI and clearly violated Justice Department rules and federal law, the practice became commonplace.

Nobody was really sure what qualified as an exigent circumstance. Some thought it was a major case; others, a life-and-death situation. Still others thought it was any case in which the FBI brass clamored for information. The bureau collected information on thousands of phone records belonging to Americans that way.

When signing boilerplate exigent letters became too cumbersome, the agents used sticky notes, scrap paper, or phone calls to demand records. They were essentially IOUs: "Give us the phone records. We'll get you the legal justification later." Frequently, that justification never came. When a company employee raised concerns, an intelligence analyst responded that it was "not practical" to provide legal justification every time.[7]

FBI agents and analysts could also walk over to the phone company's desk for what was called a "sneak and peek" at the company's computers.

Congress fumed when the Justice Department's inspector general revealed what had happened. The exigent letter scandal forced FBI director Robert Mueller and the bureau's top lawyers to testify on Capitol Hill. The FBI's cozy relationship with the phone companies ended.

By 2009, the FBI had tightened restrictions on national security letters. Exigent circumstances letters were out. If the FBI wanted something immediately, faster than the normal turnaround that came with a national security letter, a supervisor had to certify, with his name, that there was an imminent threat of death or serious physical injury.

The national security letter scandal highlighted the difference between the NYPD and the FBI. Both inherited sweeping new powers after 9/11, and both pushed the boundaries of those powers. But the FBI had an inspector general and Congress looking over its shoulder. Cohen had freed himself from the shackles of oversight. Nobody outside the department was reviewing his operations.

In the Zazi case, Don Borelli was signing "imminent threat of death" letters as fast as people could put them in front of him. Before then, he had signed one, maybe two. Everybody in the flophouse was a suspect, because in the morning, the inhabitants would probably scatter. The FBI already had twenty-four-hour surveillance on Zazi, Medunjanin, and Ahmedzay. Adding five more people to the surveillance plan would require more manpower than the FBI could handle. Cohen, however, had his own surveillance team, each decked out with $20,000 spy kits: GPS equipment, infrared flashlights, small digital video cameras, and still cameras that looked like what a tourist might carry. Intel's surveillance team even had a real yellow cab, complete with an authentic taxi medallion registered under a fake name. Nobody gave a second look at a cabbie parked outside, waiting for his fare to arrive.

When the sun rose on September 11, 2009, teams from the FBI and Intel would be on the streets working together.

. . .

At the FBI, Borelli settled in for his second-straight night on his office couch. Downstairs, supervisors kept vigil in the command center. His agents and analysts—all members of CT-4, the counterterrorism squad responsible for Afghanistan and Pakistan—kept working down the hall, behind the vault door.

Borelli kept replaying in his head a similar case of a US citizen who had managed to get to Pakistan and somehow do the presumed impossible of making contact with al-Qaeda's operational chief and training to be a bomber on American soil.

In late 2007 and early 2008, the National Security Agency, which intercepts massive amounts of emails and phone conversations from around the world every day, began hearing chatter from Pakistan about an American jihadist. People were talking about an "Ameriki" from where the "Twin Towers" had fallen; a man who had lost a toe. The CIA began working its sources on the ground. The information was funneled to headquarters in Langley, Virginia, where analysts at the agency's Counterterrorism Center began piecing together the fragments into a coherent story. Within a few weeks, the CIA had determined that an American had indeed joined the jihadist ranks in Pakistan. The challenge was to find him.[8]

The intelligence was quickly passed to the task force in New York. Its analysts pored over travel records, using databases that show when people passed through customs. The Pakistani government helped by providing records on Americans who arrived there. The result was a massive set of data and other clues that analysts plumbed for weeks. By March, the FBI and CIA were certain they had their man: Bryant Neal Vinas, a former Catholic altar boy from Medford, Long Island. Travel records showed that he had flown to Pakistan. And he'd sent emails from Peshawar to a girlfriend in Cuba. In New York, detectives and agents started investigating associates of Vinas, including an Afghan American named Ahmad Zarinni, trying to figure out who might have helped him contact al-Qaeda.

Scrawny and impressionable, Vinas was born in Queens to an Argentine mother and a Peruvian father, Juan, an engineer who moved his family to the middle-class suburbs on Long Island. At his father's behest, Vinas took an active role in the church, and would read Scripture during Sunday Mass.[9]

When he was fourteen, his father had an affair, and his parents split, upending his world. Vinas grew his hair long and started listening to rap music. At eighteen, his mother kicked him out of her house.[10]

After the planes crashed into the Twin Towers in September 2001, Vinas, still living on his own, decided to join the US Army. But the marching and yelling of boot camp overwhelmed him, and he cracked. Three weeks after enlisting, he left Fort Jackson, South Carolina, with a general discharge. He had never even fired a weapon. Back home on Long Island, Vinas took up boxing with a Muslim friend, a turning point in his life. The friend loaned him an English translation of the Koran. Desperate to be part of something meaningful, Vinas devoured the book in two days.[11]

By January 2004, he was reciting the *shahada*, the Muslim profession of faith, at the Masjid Al-Falah in Corona, Queens, one of the mosques that the NYPD was monitoring. The mosque was affiliated with Tablighi Jamaat.

Vinas's focus moved toward becoming a serious boxer, and he spent the next few years evading US travel restrictions to Cuba, famous for churning out great fighters. When boxing didn't work out, he turned again to Islam, with a renewed purpose. He embraced the religion with such unusual intensity that his friends began to notice. He began learning Arabic and visiting Islamic websites while attending a mosque in Selden, Long Island, near his mother's house in Medford. There, he befriended Zarinni, who observed a strict interpretation of Islam.

For Vinas, Zarinni was a bridge to another world: a darker one warped by anti-Semitism and anti-Americanism. Zarinni introduced him to a group called the Islamic Thinkers Society, which was based in Queens and had ties to a militant group in Britain. In 2005 it posted on the internet a video of a demonstration it held in New York, with its members ripping apart an American flag after what turned out to be a false story about a Koran having been desecrated at the Guantánamo Bay prison. The video, according to the group, was intended to "expose the agenda of the Crusaders and Zionists and their war on Islam which many still do not see today." [12] The following year, the society held a rally outside the Israeli Consulate in Manhattan to proclaim that Islam would "dominate the world" and to call for the destruction of Israel. The protesters taunted authorities: "We know many government services are watching us, such as the FBI, CIA, Mossad, Homeland Security." [13]

They were close. Somebody was watching them, but it was the NYPD. Well before Vinas appeared in this hotbed of radicalism, the Islamic Thinkers Society had come to the attention of the Intelligence Division. Cohen and others around him believed that the society was the next platform for jihad for disaffected Muslims. "In a sense, they're almost bug lights for aspiring jihadists," Mitchell Silber, the Intelligence Division's top analyst, would say later about the group. "They've got an anti-Western, antidemocratic, anti-US, pro-al-Qaeda message." [14] In 2003 Cohen used his authority under the Handschu guidelines to target the organization with a terrorism enterprise investigation that dragged on for years. As part of the probe, Cohen's Intelligence Division fanned out wherever society members gathered, publicly or privately, to eavesdrop and take clandestine pictures. When the group held its weekly meetings or proselytized in Queens, the NYPD was observing. Cohen's detectives and analysts kept intelligence files and noted that Zarinni and others had attended the Selden mosque and society-run lectures at Stony Brook University in 2006. [15]

Under the influence of his new friends, Vinas started dressing in Arab-style garb, and his sentiments became more bellicose. [16] He told a friend that he loved Osama bin Laden and hated Israel. The US occupation of Afghanistan and Iraq enraged him, and he told people he yearned to go to Pakistan to train and then head across the border to Afghanistan, where he could kill American soldiers. It didn't seem so far-fetched: Vinas had managed to sneak into Cuba twice; surely he could make it to Pakistan's lawless borderlands. A way was out there, and eventually he found it.

He read a book titled *Inside the Jihad: My Life with Al Qaeda*, by Omar Nasiri, a Belgian man of Moroccan descent who claimed he had been a spy for Western intelligence services and described infiltrating Afghanistan's training camps after traveling to Pakistan. The book captivated Vinas, who saw it as a road map to a great adventure. He soaked up the details, and by March 2007, he had come to the conclusion that he would do the same. He was going to be part of something important.

On September 10, 2007, Vinas boarded a plane to Pakistan, buying a round-trip ticket to cloak his intentions. He told his family he was going to study Islam and Arabic. Before he left, his best friend asked, "When are you coming back?"

"I'm not coming back," Vinas responded. "I will call you in your dreams." [17]

The day after Vinas flew to Pakistan, on the anniversary of the 9/11 attacks, Police Commissioner Kelly published an op-ed in the *New York Post* boasting about the "groundbreaking analysis" that Cohen's team had developed to enable the NYPD to spot homegrown terrorists. [18] Fran Townsend, President Bush's homeland security advisor, told NBC News on that evening's broadcast that the NYPD set the "gold standard" and was "incredibly effective" in fighting domestic terrorism. [19] But Cohen and the rest of the NYPD's new intelligence apparatus didn't have a clue about the skinny kid from Long Island named Vinas, despite his conversation at Al-Falah Mosque and his involvement with the Islamic Thinkers Society, which were both still under surveillance. For all the NYPD's efforts, it was no better off than anyone else in the American intelligence community.

After a brief layover in Abu Dhabi, Vinas landed on September 12 and passed through customs in Lahore, the second-largest city in Pakistan and a commercial center. He chose his destination carefully, avoiding landing in Peshawar, a known hive of jihadist activity. Authorities, he surmised, wouldn't think much about his going to Lahore. With the aid of a friend's family, he quickly found a place to stay and got to work trying to make contact with militants. His first couple attempts failed, but then Vinas got lucky. He asked members of an Afghan family living on the same street if they could help him find someone willing to take him across the border to fight the Americans, and it turned out they had a cousin who knew people. Like Zazi a year later, Vinas had managed to do with no training and no real connections what most of the American intelligence community assumed took special relationships.

From Lahore, his neighbors' cousin drove Vinas to Peshawar, where he met a man named Shah Sahb. Vinas traveled with Shah's jihadist group to the Mohmand Agency, a district along the Afghan border north of Peshawar. From there Vinas crossed the border with Shah and about twenty others to attack a US base. The men split into two teams. One conducted a small-weapons attack on the installation. The other, Vinas's group, climbed a mountain and waited to strike with mortars. But circling US warplanes made the operation too risky, and they aborted the attack. Disappointed, Vinas returned to Pakistan, but he was promptly offered another opportunity by Shah's gang: Would he become a suicide bomber? Vinas agreed, mainly because blowing himself up seemed like the easiest path to glory. He was told to go to Peshawar and await further instructions—time during which his doubts began to crowd in. He decided he didn't know enough about Islam to become a martyr for it.

Vinas stayed in Peshawar into the early months of 2008, recovering from frostbite that required the little toe on his right foot to be amputated. From there he sent the emails from a cybercafe that attracted the notice of the NSA. But in March Vinas stopped emailing, confusing CIA and FBI analysts. What happened? Why did he disappear? Had he been killed? Or had he gone dark for operational reasons?

Vinas had met a Kuwaiti who introduced him to an old Tunisian man named Haji Sabir. In turn, Sabir referred him to al-Qaeda, and he was quickly taken to Waziristan, where he was assigned to a camp outside Miram Shah for basic training. Just as he'd disliked the many rules and restrictions of boot camp in South Carolina, Vinas found the terrorist lifestyle didn't suit him. Trainers were strict and yelled at the rookie jihadist like Fort Jackson's drill sergeants. They routinely meted out punishments, forcing Vinas and his comrades to do extra push-ups or to pull guard duty. The day was regimented: Morning prayer. Exercise. Wash. Breakfast. Class. Prayer. Lunch. Break. Class. Prayer. Break. Class. Prayer. Dinner. Free time. Prayer. Bedtime or guard duty.

Far away from home, though, he managed to stick it out. In training courses, Vinas familiarized himself with a variety of weapons and learned how to strip and clean an AK-47. There was a basic explosives course that covered wiring and fuses. Another one delved into the art of the suicide vest. Vinas learned how to assemble the components of the bomb using ball bearings, explosive material, and some glue. The instructors demonstrated how to detonate C-3 and C-4 plastic explosive. On the last day of class, the students got to fire the weapons and throw grenades.[20]

An al-Qaeda leader, Sheikh Nasrulah, visited the class to talk about suicide operations. He told the students they could volunteer but warned that those who signed up would need to be patient. The sheik explained that patience was the most important quality al-Qaeda looked for in a volunteer. He said the 1998 embassy bombings in Kenya and Tanzania had taken approximately nine months to plan and execute.

Vinas listened and kept training. In July, after more than four months in the mountains, he started his final course, on projectile weapons theory. He learned how to set up and fire rockets and mortars, and two weeks later he completed al-Qaeda's basic training. Vinas, the US Army dropout, had become an al-Qaeda soldier. He was told to move to another town and wait for deployment orders. He and a friend, a Belgian citizen, listened to BBC broadcasts of the 2008 Beijing summer Olympics to pass the time. In September Vinas was among a group of fighters who received instructions from Mustafa Abu al-Yazid, al-Qaeda's top military commander in Pakistan and Afghanistan. They departed for a town near the border of Afghanistan and linked up with another outfit led by Abu Yahya al-Libi, a Libyan who eventually rose to the number two spot in al-Qaeda. The fighters prepared to mount an attack against US Forward Operating Base Tillman, in Afghanistan. The outpost was named after Pat Tillman, the former football safety for the Arizona Cardinals who joined the US Army and was killed by friendly fire near the base in 2004.

Using a spotter, the fighters climbed the side of a mountain and launched four missiles at the base from the Pakistani side of the border. They missed their mark, but if al-Qaeda had any doubts remaining about Vinas, that day erased them. He wasn't a spy. He was an eager infantryman.

A world away, in Vinas's hometown, New Yorkers were preparing to commemorate the seventh anniversary of the September 11, 2001, attacks. Kelly told the Associated Press that his department's counter-terrorism operations had been transformed. "We can put in a lot of measures, a lot of procedures, and brag about what we're doing," he said. "But preventing another attack—that's the ultimate standard. So far, so good."[21] The investigators on CT-4, the squad handling the Vinas case, had no idea where he was. Borelli thought he might have been killed in a training accident or drone strike. There were plenty of ways to die in Waziristan.

The Vinas case could have been the NYPD's moment to shine. Cohen had been keeping tabs on the Islamic Thinkers Society since 2003, yet he hadn't been able to spot Vinas. But he knew plenty about the Islamic Thinkers. So while the FBI worked desperately to figure out whether someone in New York had helped Vinas gain entrée to al-Qaeda, Cohen was running a secret parallel investigation. The case, dubbed Operation Witches Brew, targeted Vinas's friend Zarinni.[22] Cohen had an informant in the inner circle of the Islamic Thinkers

Society. But he didn't tell the FBI, which was separately investigating one of the group's top members.

Neither the FBI nor the NYPD knew at that time that Vinas was connected to Islamic Thinkers. But, as usual, the dueling investigations caused intense friction. That came to a head in March, when the society member whom the FBI was investigating threw his computer hard drive into the Passaic River in Paterson, New Jersey. One of the NYPD's informants was in the car at the time, but Cohen didn't tell the FBI for weeks. When the bureau's dive team recovered the drive, it was useless.

On April 18 Lauren Anderson, the acting special agent in charge of terrorism in New York, went to Cohen's office to smooth over the tensions and learn more about the NYPD's informant. Cohen told her it was the "policy of the NYPD not to reveal asset information to any outside law enforcement agency." [23] In this case, Cohen went on, he had decided to make an exception because of the national security concerns. He then lectured Anderson, who had spent most of her career investigating terrorism and handling sensitive espionage cases, about how to handle sources. He said he would agree to share information about the Witches Brew investigation, but that "any such possible disclosure of a highly sensitive NYPD Intelligence Division asset must be treated with the utmost discretion." [24] He then demanded that Anderson create a subgroup of agents—"a very small internal compartment"— who would be the only ones privy to whatever information he agreed to share from his Intelligence Division. After Anderson had agreed to all Cohen's conditions, he handed her a file with the latest intelligence that his team had collected on Zarinni. There was nothing in the file that helped the hunt for Vinas.

Vinas, sitting in Pakistan, never imagined that he was the target of a major US manhunt. Neither, apparently, did his al-Qaeda commanders, who, freshly convinced of his commitment to their cause after the attempted raid on the Tillman base, tapped him as a kind of operations consultant. He was, after all, an American passport holder intimately familiar with their targets in New York. Vinas, it turned out, had a lot to tell his al-Qaeda bosses. He had a near photographic memory and an eye for detail. He told al-Qaeda's operatives about a choke point on the Long Island Rail Road, which connects the suburbs of Long Island to New York City and carries nearly three hundred thousand commuters daily. He drew a diagram so his commanders could understand what he meant when he explained where he thought a well-placed bomb could inflict maximum casualties on passengers.

Vinas quickly became something of a celebrity. He took meetings with al-Qaeda's top leaders, who came to Waziristan to speak with the scrappy American kid from New York. Vinas met several times with al-Libi, a close associate of Osama bin Laden's. He mingled with Atiyah Abd al-Rahman, who the following year would launch a devastating attack on a US base in Afghanistan, killing five CIA officers and two contractors.[25] Vinas even appeared wearing a mask in a propaganda video with al-Libi.

One evening he dined with Saleh al-Somali, the head of worldwide operations, who unbeknownst to Vinas was also overseeing the training of another American, Najibullah Zazi, and his two friends who had slipped out of New York and into al-Qaeda's shadow world. As far as Vinas was concerned, all that mattered was that, for once, he was valued, and he was a success. His new friends gave him a nickname: Bashir al-Ameriki, "the American who brings good news."

By November, with winter approaching, the fighting season in Afghanistan was coming to a close. Al-Qaeda, along with the Taliban, would regroup in the spring after the snow melted and recommence operations against the Americans. Tired from the months of training, Vinas was looking forward to leaving Waziristan and returning to Peshawar. He had a friend there who said he could stay with him and even offered to help Vinas find a wife. On November 13 he bought a ticket for a bus—known locally as a "flying coach"—in Miram Shah and settled in for the long journey back to Peshawar. At a checkpoint, one of many that ringed the city, Pakistani police stopped the bus. Vinas stood out. Who was the white guy coming from the lawless tribal areas in a bus filled with dark faces? Vinas panicked and tried to stab a Pakistani police officer, hoping to create confusion and make a quick escape. It didn't work. The police beat him up and took him into custody, notifying the US Consulate in Peshawar that they had arrested an American. The FBI legal attaché at the US Embassy soon received word about Vinas and alerted Borelli's team in New York.

When Borelli, now the assistant special agent in charge of counterterrorism, heard the news, his first thought wasn't about what possible threats might be looming. All he could think was, "Holy shit, he's not dead."

The day after the FBI arrested Vinas, he was secretly indicted in Brooklyn federal court. In the cramped offices of the FBI's Counterterrorism Division in Washington, Jim McJunkin and Michael Heimbach devised a strategy for getting Vinas home without al-Qaeda's leaders realizing that their prize was in American custody. If the terrorist group figured it out, it would change or abort whatever plans it might have told Vinas about. The FBI was going to be responsible for asking Vinas questions, but its CIA partners had specific information they wanted: Where was the last place you trained? Where did you stay? Which al-Qaeda leaders did you see? Where did you meet them? Ideally, the CIA could use the informant to launch immediate drone strikes against their top targets.

Vinas remained in Pakistani custody for several days. He was then moved to a military base in Rawalpindi, the home of Pakistan's intelligence services, where they questioned him before handing him over to US custody. From Rawalpindi, Vinas was flown to the US-run prison at Bagram Air Base, north of Kabul in Afghanistan. When he arrived, he was met by Jeffrey Knox, an ambitious federal prosecutor from Brooklyn, who was there in case Vinas wanted to cut a deal. Almost immediately, Vinas was read his Miranda rights.

Within less than a week of his arrest in the western mountains of Pakistan, Vinas was aboard the FBI's Gulfstream 5 at John F. Kennedy International Airport in Queens. On the tarmac, Borelli and several heavily armed FBI agents stood in the cold and watched as Vinas came off the plane. It had been almost a year since US intelligence had learned about the American jihadist, and now they had him.

Once he was on US soil, Vinas was treated like any other high-risk criminal suspect. He was taken to the Brooklyn detention center and given a lawyer. The next day, the lawyer told Knox, who was handling the case, that Vinas might be willing to offer something prosecutors wanted in exchange for lenience: information about the threat to the Long Island Rail Road. On November 22, a Saturday—when federal courts are typically closed—Vinas appeared before a judge for a special hearing. That Tuesday, the FBI and Department of Homeland Security put out an alert about a possible threat to New York's transit system. In late November and December, American drones pummeled North Waziristan, where Vinas had trained and lived. One of those killed was the Saudi trainer, a top al-Qaeda bomb maker, who taught the explosives course that Vinas had taken. Vinas's information was precise.[26]

In January 2009 Vinas pleaded guilty to terrorism charges in secret proceedings. FBI agents continued to interview him, and he talked freely. As he had found in his last months with al-Qaeda, his knowledge made him important. He had the respect of the FBI.

For Jim McJunkin, Vinas's cooperation was a victory in a war in which some argued the FBI had little value. McJunkin held out hope that Osama bin Laden, who was under indictment for the 1998 embassy bombings in Africa, would someday be captured and prosecuted in New York, just like Vinas. Even during war, McJunkin once told his agents, the FBI was in the business of building cases that lead to trials. "Never forget that," he reminded them.

Vinas also proved that the worst fears of the US intelligence community were real. For years, the assumption had been that an al-Qaeda sympathizer had to know someone to get into al-Qaeda. There was, intelligence analysts believed, an organized method for screening recruits and funneling them to Waziristan. When FBI agents looked at "radicalizers" in American mosques, they looked for that pipeline. It was reassuring to imagine that a would-be terrorist couldn't wind up in an al-Qaeda camp simply by showing up in Peshawar one afternoon.

Vinas disproved that theory. Anybody with enough resolve and luck, it turned out, could make his way into al-Qaeda's embrace. Vinas's capture turned out to be one of the greatest successes in the war on terror. But his case served as a reminder to Borelli and his colleagues that other Americans could easily go down the same path without anyone in the intelligence apparatus noticing. Vinas told investigators that nobody in New York helped him with plans to wage jihad.[27] His old friend Zarinni didn't have any ties to al-Qaeda. All those guys in New York, he said, they were all talk.[28] All it took, Vinas told them with a hint of pride, was the guts to get on a plane and go.

The fear that had been nagging Borelli for a year now was, What if somebody managed to make it to Pakistan for training and then returned to the US unnoticed? Everything he'd seen suggested that's exactly what he faced with Zazi and his friends. He closed his eyes on the couch for a bit, but he did not sleep well.

10

IN THE WIND

NEW YORK
Friday, September 11, 2009

The morning of September 11, 2009, dawned gray and rainy, the opposite of the clear blue sky the hijacked jets had torn through in 2001. Just as every year since, workers had spent days preparing ground zero, still a construction site, to welcome hundreds of mourners for the reading of the names of the almost three thousand people killed in the attacks. The list of dignitaries due to appear at the service included Mayor Michael Bloomberg, Secretary of Homeland Security Janet Napolitano, and Vice President Joe Biden, who would lay flowers and read a short poem, "Wild Geese," by the American writer Mary Oliver.

Security was tight, but only a select few, if any, of the NYPD officers responsible for securing Lower Manhattan were aware of Zazi, or that some of their counterparts had spent the night in Chelsea trying to figure out whether his sudden appearance in New York had anything to do with the memorial service. The task force office was alive with investigators trying to puzzle out Zazi's plans, combing records for clues and taking in reports from surveillance teams tailing fifteen identified associates of the young Afghan.

Shortly after 6:00 a.m., the FBI intercepted a phone call from Zazi, who was still in his friend Khan's apartment, to the man renting his coffee cart. Zazi said he was heading downtown to check on the business. The two men talked about the security and agreed that taking the subway would be easier than driving.

Borelli huddled with Ari Papadacos, the supervisor helping run the command center. They still needed Zazi to disclose more of his plan, but they couldn't let him carry a bomb onto the subway. They decided that if he was seen leaving the apartment with a backpack or bag, they would stop him. If not, they would continue to follow.

At about 6:50 a.m., a little more than an hour before the memorial ceremonies were to begin, Zazi walked out of Khan's building with his computer bag and suitcase. He put them in the rented Impala, and headed toward the subway station empty-handed. He was in jeans and a long-sleeve blue shirt, no backpack—nothing that looked as if he were carrying a bomb. In Chelsea, Borelli and Papadacos told the surveillance team to keep up its guard. They still didn't know whom Zazi was going to meet or who else might be involved with his plan. Don't stop him, they ordered. Let's see where he goes.

About 7:15, Zazi stepped on the 7 train heading into midtown Manhattan. Within a half hour, he was at Grand Central Terminal, where he climbed the stairs to transfer to the express 4 train, along with hundreds of commuters heading downtown. Fifteen minutes later, he popped out of the Bowling Green stop in the heart of New York's Financial District, not far from the famous bronze statue of Wall Street's charging bull. Zazi walked to the intersection of Stone Street and Broadway, a fifteen-minute walk from where the Twin Towers crumbled. Nervous FBI agents watched for almost an hour as Zazi hung around talking to the man running his coffee cart and joking with former customers.

Blocks away, about 8:45 a.m., Mayor Michael Bloomberg spoke after a moment of silence, paying tribute to the thousands who had died, including rescue workers:

Just as our hearts return to those we lost, we also remember all those who spontaneously rushed forward to help, however and whomever they could. Their compassion and selfless acts are etched in our city's history.

Zazi left about 9:15 a.m., heading back the way he came. For the twenty-four-year-old, the expedition was nothing more than a ruse. If anyone questioned what he was doing in New York, Zazi wanted to be able to say that he came to check on his coffee cart. Now he could.

He descended into the Bowling Green subway station, this time hopping the 5 train to Grand Central. Once he arrived, Zazi hustled up the stairs, cutting his way through the crowds. He stepped behind a pillar and, in the bustle, the surveillance team didn't notice him darting down the stairs and onto a 7 train to Queens.

Panicked, the surveillance team canvassed the dim, low-ceilinged station for Zazi. Had he gone back to Queens? Had he jumped on a train the other direction? The entrance to the Times Square shuttle was down a long corridor. Had they missed seeing him go in that direction? Or was he out of the subway altogether and heading upstairs into Grand Central's vaulted central hall?

There are certainties in the surveillance business: You will either lose your target, or you will get made. Get too close, and you'll be blown. Stay too far back to avoid detection, and the target will get away.

Zazi, as the professionals say, was in the wind. Gone.

• • •

In Denver, Mohammed Zazi's phone rang. Ahmad Wais Afzali, the imam from Abu Bakr, was calling. The two men didn't know each other well, and it was still early in the morning in Colorado. The imam spoke quickly: He needed to get in touch with Mohammed's son right away. The young man was in trouble. The police had come around asking questions. They had showed him photographs of Najibullah Zazi and his cousin Amanullah, as well as Ahmedzay, and Medunjanin.

Mohammed Zazi was stunned. He hung up and called his son.

Najibullah Zazi was already back in Flushing at the popular Cyber Land internet café on Northern Boulevard near Flushing High School, killing time before his 2:50 p.m. flight from LaGuardia to Denver. "Peace be upon you," he answered in Pashto after he saw his father's number come up on his phone. It was about 11:40 a.m.

"How are you, my son?" Mohammed asked.

"I am well," his son replied.

His father told him about the phone call with Imam Afzali.

"He said they brought pictures of these four people, asking, 'What kind of people are they? What do they do?' " Mohammed explained.

"Okay," Najibullah replied.

"What's going on anyway? What did you all do?" Mohammad asked.

"We haven't done anything," Najibullah insisted.

Mohammed advised his son to speak with a lawyer or to seek Afzali's advice.

Najibullah's phone beeped. Imam Afzali was calling on the other line.

"Peace be upon you," he told his father by way of good-bye and then picked up Afzali's call. The two exchanged formal greetings in English, and the imam asked how things were going in Colorado.

"Colorado is a beautiful state," Zazi responded, a much better place than New York to raise a family.

"Full of headache," Afzali agreed. "Big-city problems."

Afzali got to the point. He needed cell phone numbers for Medunjanin and Ahmedzay.

In Denver, agents were listening to the call, courtesy of the secret warrant they had obtained days before.

"You're in New York now?" Afzali asked.

"Yeah, I'm in New York."

"I would like to have a meeting with you," Afzali said. "I was exposed to something yesterday from the authorities. And they came to ask me about your characters. They asked me about you guys."

Afzali asked when Zazi and the others had last traveled to Pakistan, and why. They talked about Zazi's marriage and Ahmedzay's two daughters. The imam asked whether Zazi was going to Friday prayers. Perhaps they could meet there.

"I have a flight to catch. I am going back to Colorado. I have business."

Afzali said be careful.

"Go home, be with your father and mother, praise be to God, do your job, keep your head down, mind your own business," he said.

"You know," Afzali continued, "don't get involved in Afghanistan garbage and Iraq garbage. That's my advice for you. You're an American."

Zazi understood. "I always supported the Ameri—I mean, the thing is, I always tell people I'm, you know, the US is the best," he said.

Afzali ignored Zazi's nattering: "Listen, our phone call is being monitored.

"Even if you feel that US is not the best," he continued, "we have no business Islamically; we have no business with those people." He told Zazi not to be like the Salafists. "This is not the right path or attitude."

Afzali said he would try to convince the authorities that Zazi and his friends were good people. "I pray for you," he said.

"May God grant you goodness," Zazi replied and then hung up.

Now he knew that the ghosts following him since the stop on the George Washington Bridge the day before were real.

While that call was going on, Borelli and Papadacos were at the FBI command center across town in Chelsea. They were on a video-conference with colleagues and Justice Department lawyers. Jim Shea, a deputy chief in charge of the NYPD detectives on the task force, was seated at the table. And in a moment of comity, the FBI invited Paul Ciorra, one of David Cohen's top deputies, to join the call.

The computer screen was divided into small boxes, each containing the video feed from another office. With headquarters leading the session, each group took turns reviewing the day's events. Downtown, the 9/11 memorial ceremony was in hour three, though the key public figures had made their appearances and left. Zazi was at large, and the task force still didn't know his intentions.

Jim Davis, the special agent in charge in Denver, abruptly interrupted the overview. He had news: Someone had called Zazi and tipped him off about the investigation. The tipster was in New York, and his name was Ahmad Afzali. No one at the command center conference table recognized the name. FBI headquarters demanded to hear from each office whether anyone there knew Afzali, the man who had just blown their case.

As one office after another reported knowing nothing, Paul Ciorra, sitting next to Shea, typed feverishly on his BlackBerry. Then his face turned ashen.

"That's my source," he announced to those at the command center. The room fell silent.

The meeting finished quickly, and most of the participants scattered. The phone in Chelsea had been muted, so it didn't broadcast Ciorra's confession. For now, only those in the room knew what had happened. Shea, an ex-Marine, stood up and faced Ciorra.

Shea was furious. Cohen should have talked to the task force so they could decide together whether Afzali was trustworthy.

"This is rookie 101 shit!" Shea shouted. "This was totally fucking irresponsible! How could you do that? Any entry-level detective knows you can't do that kind of shit. You've jeopardized this whole thing!"[1]

Ciorra didn't say anything about Cohen's signing off on Intel's decision to approach Afzali. Instead, he absorbed Shea's outrage without rebuttal. The FBI officials in the room stayed out of the fight; they were mad, too, but they didn't want to get between two cops. Borelli felt bad for Ciorra, who he thought was a stand-up guy. It took courage to admit that Afzali was working for the Intelligence Division. A lesser man would have walked out of that room without saying a word.

Jim McJunkin, the head of FBI terrorism operations, thought FBI leadership should confront Cohen. A year earlier, after Cohen tried to let a would-be jihadist into Pakistan for training, McJunkin had given the order to turn him around, avoiding a potential international incident. Cohen was steamed; but in a meeting with FBI colleagues in New York, the hot-tempered McJunkin let it be known that if Cohen had a problem with the decision, they could settle it in an alley.

McJunkin told friends that the NYPD treated the FBI like "the fat kid at the end of the lunch table." Cohen easily bullied the FBI because it never fought back.

When Art Cummings, the head of all FBI national security, learned about the Afzali phone call, he too was livid. Cummings reviewed the wreckage in a phone call with Joe Demarest, the head of the FBI's office in New York. The case was compromised, and Shea and Ciorra were on the verge of brawling.

"We are having fistfights in the squad area over this," Demarest said.

In Robert Mueller's office on the seventh floor of FBI headquarters in Washington, Cummings told the director what happened. They were burned, he said. The investigation was compromised. Mueller was furious, but only for a moment.

"What's done is done," he responded. "Get the operation back on track."

Cummings dialed David Cohen in New York. Cohen didn't try to obfuscate. "We fucked that up," he said. "I'm going to deal with it." FBI officials didn't have to wonder long who would take the fall. Within days, Ciorra, a major in the Army National Guard who had earned a Bronze Star during a deployment in Iraq, was transferred to the department's Highway Patrol.

The blowup was the culmination of years of friction between the New York Joint Terrorism Task Force and Cohen's Intelligence Division. There had been plenty of instances of what the FBI perceived as recklessness: the approach of the Hezbollah operative in 2006; the fiasco with the hard drive in the Passaic River; Cohen's trying to let Abdel

Shehadeh fly to Pakistan for jihadist training. Once, Intel had recruited a source inside the building that housed the Iranian Mission to the United Nations. Counterintelligence is the responsibility of the FBI, and the stunt could have imperiled a sensitive operation. The bureau was so enraged that the Justice Department considered charging Cohen or someone from his unit with obstruction of justice.[2]

Some episodes had been comic, such as the NYPD's amateurish safe house near Rutgers University. This time, the task force believed that the department might have blown the biggest terrorism case in the United States since 9/11. For the FBI agents and the police officers on the task force, it was irrefutable evidence that Cohen was more liability than partner. His army of informants had failed to spot the threat posed by three terrorists from Queens. Now one of those same informants had proven more loyal to his friends than to law enforcement.

But Borelli and the rest of the task force had more pressing things to think about than who was at fault: They had to find Zazi.

• • •

By 1:00 p.m., the surveillance teams still hadn't tracked him down. They knew he was in Queens, thanks to data from his cell phone, but they couldn't pinpoint his location. The investigators were fairly confident that Zazi's plan, whatever it had been, was disrupted, but they wanted to gather enough evidence to bring charges before he could regroup or, worse, flee.

One thing they knew for sure was that Zazi's red Impala was still outside the apartment where he'd spent the night, and his computer bag was in the car. The laptop represented the FBI's best chance for unraveling his plan and figuring out who else was involved. They knew Zazi had a flight to Denver booked from LaGuardia Airport at 2:50 p.m. Borelli was desperate to get the computer before Zazi returned for the car and headed for the airport. They needed to tow that car.

When FBI officials gathered on another videoconference to discuss it, however, there was reluctance to tow the Impala. With Zazi in the wind, it was a risk. What if he walked around the corner toward the car as police were hooking it to the wrecker? The car was parked legally. How would they explain that? They had no idea what Zazi had been up to in the hours since the surveillance team had last seen him at Grand Central. FBI agents don't like unknowns, and this case was producing new ones at a rapid clip.

Davis and Steve Olson in Denver pushed for towing the car. Countless vehicles were towed every day in New York, they argued. What was the big deal?

Borelli agreed.

"We're doing it," Borelli said. "We're doing it. We're getting the car." Nobody objected.

Borelli turned to Ray Johnson, an NYPD sergeant on the task force.

"Tow the car," he said. "Get one of your wreckers, tow the car, get it out of there."

Just before 2:00 p.m., a police tow truck pulled up, hooked the car, and drove it to an FBI hangar at LaGuardia. When the agents were finished searching, the police would return it to Zazi, saying that it had been stolen and recovered. A judge's secret warrant authorized the search.

Zazi missed the tow truck by minutes. He left the internet café and walked back toward where he had parked at Thirty-eighth Street and Parsons Boulevard. When he found the Impala missing, he called Hertz. A customer service agent named Rhonda called him back. "Have you reported it to the police yet?" she asked Zazi.

"No, I haven't," he replied.

Rhonda told him to file a police report and call back with a case number.

"Okay, no problem," Zazi said. "Thanks, I appreciate it."

In a panic, Zazi immediately called Afzali, who was still busy trying to help the NYPD. When his phone rang, Afzali was with Zazi's brother in arms, Adis Medunjanin, pushing him for answers to the questions his police handler had asked.

Zazi was certain that the police had his car. He didn't know what to do.

"Hertz told me to call the 911, but if I call the 911 and I know the car is in their hands—" Zazi began.

"How do you know that?" Afzali asked.

"Because they've been watching it for the last two hours," Zazi said, stumbling over his words. "I mean, it looks like they've been watching me."

"That's fine. That's fine. Let them watch you as much as they want," Afzali said, reassuringly. "That's their job. But you still call 911."

"Should I call 911?" Zazi repeated.

"Yes," the imam advised. "Say your car is missing. You're only speculating, right? You don't know that. Do you have evidence they took your car?"

"No, I don't have evidence," Zazi conceded.

"Exactly. So how do you know they took your car away from you?"

Zazi fretted about whether to go back to where the car had been parked, so close to Khan's apartment. Afzali told him to go to the exact spot, call the police, and file a report.

"*Salaam alaikum*," they told each other, and hung up. Zazi called the police and gave his location. In Chelsea, the task force finally got confirmation: Zazi was back in pocket. Papadacos let Borelli know.

"Let's not lose this fucking guy again," Borelli said.

• • •

At LaGuardia, evidence-response specialists assigned to the task force searched the Impala. They found Zazi's rental agreement, a suitcase, a water bottle, and, on the floor of the front passenger side, the laptop. The one thing they didn't find was the mysterious jug that the Port Authority officer had failed to identify on the George Washington Bridge. FBI headquarters was finally satisfied that the jug was unimportant.

In most cases, the bureau would take the computer to a lab for analysis. But the agents had been instructed to proceed as though the investigation hadn't been blown. Everything they touched would have to be replaced exactly as they'd found it, in hopes Zazi wouldn't suspect the FBI had been there.

The agents photographed the laptop and handed it to Trenton Schmatz, an FBI computer forensic expert. Schmatz removed the hard drive and attached it to a device called a Logicube Talon. In a few hours, the gadget would create an exact copy of Zazi's computer.

Zazi was growing increasingly frustrated and worried. He had gone to the 109th Precinct, but the officers told him they didn't have any information about his car. He'd missed his flight and didn't have his luggage, his laptop, or a place to stay. With few alternatives, he went to Abu Bakr for the fourth of the five daily prayers, known as *Maghrib*. He knew he could spend the night there. As soon as he walked in, he saw his friend Ahmedzay. He told Zazi he had flushed the TATP down the toilet. Zazi shrugged. He was tired and hungry. And ready to get out of New York.

Using the hard-drive copy, FBI agent Craig McLaughlin surfed the contents of Zazi's laptop. Zazi had bookmarked a website, Hydrochloric Acid Lab Safety Supply. His search history showed that he'd been looking for places in New York to buy hydrochloric acid, also known by its industrial name, muriatic acid. He'd searched the website of the big-box hardware chain Lowe's, looking for a store in Queens.

It was late. Borelli was exhausted. McLaughlin's analysis would take a while and Zazi appeared to be down for the night. The car was still out at LaGuardia. Borelli decided to catch a few hours of sleep. Papadacos promised to call if anything came up.

Borelli left but wasn't halfway to his apartment on Fifty-first Street in Manhattan when his phone rang.

"Hey, you need to come back here," Papadacos said.

Within a few minutes, Borelli was in his Chelsea office, talking to Papadacos. McLaughlin had discovered nine images on the computer. They looked like photos of handwritten notes illustrating chemical formulas. The notes mentioned acetone and hydrogen peroxide, chemicals that any counterterrorism agent knew could be used to make a bomb.

Papadacos handed Borelli a sheaf of printouts. He looked them over, picked up the phone, and called the FBI's operations center in Washington. He needed a chemist right away—an explosives specialist. It was about 1:00 a.m. He told them to wake someone up.

David McCollam, one of the FBI's top bomb experts, got the call. Check your email, an agent told him. McCollam opened an attachment and read a one-page, handwritten note that he recognized as information on bomb making. He called Borelli, who wanted to know what those sketches meant. McCollam explained that they were recipes. With those notes, he said, you could make TATP.

Borelli thanked the chemist and hung up. For the first time since hearing that Zazi was speeding toward New York, he had something solid: Zazi had been trying to manufacture explosives. He must have gone to Pakistan and learned how to make a bomb in an al-Qaeda training camp. That still left Borelli, Papadacos, and the task force wondering what Zazi had intended to do with his weapons. What was his target?

It was now Saturday, September 12. Borelli had gotten only a few hours of sleep the whole week. He left the office, drove back uptown, and walked into his apartment building. He nodded to the doorman, took the elevator upstairs, stripped off his suit, brushed his teeth, set his alarm to buzz in a couple hours, and got in bed. Within minutes, he was asleep.

11

FLIGHT

NEW YORK
Saturday, September 12, 2009

Zazi woke before sunrise, as worshippers gathered at Abu Bakr for *Fajr*, the first of the daily prayers. The day began with a call from his father and, finally, some good news: The police had found his rental car. Because his father was the primary renter, he'd been the one to get the call. All Najibullah had to do was head to the 109th Precinct and pick it up.

He caught a ride from the mosque to the precinct, saving him a five-block walk in the light rain. A gentle breeze swept over Queens. As Zazi climbed the five steps toward the precinct doors, he feared he'd be arrested right there—the terrorist who showed up at the police station. But no alarms sounded when he entered, and the police didn't swarm when he checked in. If the officers of the 109th suspected anything out of the ordinary about Zazi's car, they didn't show it. Ten minutes later, Zazi had the keys to the Impala. He was free to go.

At the FBI office in Chelsea, Don Borelli's excitement at seeing Zazi's bomb diagrams the night before had given way to a dull reality. Everyone was sure that Zazi was a terrorist, and that he'd attended a terrorist training camp in Pakistan and taken a bomb-making course there. They were convinced that Zazi had come to New York to launch an attack, but because of either the bungled bridge stop or the Afzali tip-off, he'd abandoned his plans.

Yet they couldn't prove any of this. It wasn't illegal to have bomb-making instructions. The recipes for TATP and other explosives were easily found online. Sending an email to an al-Qaeda address wasn't illegal, either. Maybe the FBI could charge him with providing support to a terrorist group, but everyone knew that was a stretch. The government had a flimsy case against Zazi and nothing on Medunjanin and Ahmedzay. So while Zazi might have felt lucky to leave the police precinct free of handcuffs, the truth was that arresting Zazi that morning was never considered.

Agents figured that if they gave Zazi breathing room, he'd try to cover his tracks and perhaps make a mistake. Maybe he'd call somebody and say something incriminating. Perhaps he'd lead the surveillance team to the bomb. The obvious risk, however, was that Zazi *would* cover his tracks and wriggle his way out of the bureau's grip completely.

At that moment, though, the most immediate concern was what to do about the afternoon. Zazi had new reservations to fly back to Denver, which meant the task force needed to decide whether to let him board the flight. Borelli didn't worry that Zazi would try to blow up the plane in midair. He didn't have any weapons on him, and, after the lengthy car search, Borelli was confident Zazi hadn't hidden anything dangerous in the Impala. He would be required to remove his shoes and belt and walk through a metal detector at the airport. Still, Zazi had proven himself unpredictable. He knew the police were after him, and, whatever he'd planned to pull off in New York, he was leaving the city a failure. Even without a bomb, Zazi could try something desperate or foolish. Letting him fly was a risk.

At FBI headquarters in Washington, Art Cummings, the head of national security, figured it was a risk worth taking. Even if agents had enough evidence to arrest Zazi, which they didn't, Cummings was so committed to his wait-and-see policy that colleagues said he even disliked using government watch lists to keep suspected terrorists from boarding planes or crossing into the United States. Turn them away from the border or reject their plane ticket, and the FBI would never know what they were planning. Better to monitor closely and let them continue on their way. Cummings didn't like arresting people in national security cases until the FBI had collected all the evidence and knew everything it needed about the plot. The only exception was someone posing an imminent threat that the bureau couldn't control.

When Zazi showed up at the airport that afternoon, he would be cleared to fly.

The responsibility for controlling him fell to Ari Papadacos, the FBI supervisor beneath Borelli who had spent three days running the command center in Chelsea. Papadacos put two of his agents on standby, with orders to be on Zazi's flight. When Zazi boarded the plane that afternoon, the armed agents would be sitting nearby.

• • •

Looking over the red Impala, Zazi found everything in order. He was certain that the FBI or the police had been rummaging through his things. Who steals a car, takes it for a joyride, and touches nothing? Even the laptop on the floor of the front seat?

Zazi was done with New York. He steered the car toward the Grand Central Parkway, a tree-lined east-west highway. In a few minutes, he reached his exit: LaGuardia Airport.

Back in Chelsea, the radios chirped. Zazi was leaving early. The FBI wasn't ready.

Papadacos hurried his agents, Kevin Larkin and John Scott, out the door with one order: Get on that plane. The two agents had worked through the night and, like nearly everyone on the task force, were practically asleep on their feet.

I don't care what you have to do, Papadacos said. There is no other option.

Greg Fowler, Borelli's boss and the FBI agent in charge of the Joint Terrorism Task Force, was in the command center and saw the commotion. Not twenty-four hours after losing Zazi in the subways, it looked as though the FBI had dropped the ball again.

I thought he wasn't flying until this afternoon? Fowler asked.

Boss, we got it covered, Papadacos said. We'll be on the flight.

Zazi pulled into the Hertz parking lot shortly before 7:30 a.m. and returned the Impala, with 1,843 new miles on it. With a surveillance team in pursuit, he took a shuttle to the main terminal. He was soon at the United Airlines ticket counter, paying cash for a seat on Flight 216, direct to Denver, leaving at 9:07 a.m.

The flight started boarding in a half hour.

With sirens wailing and blue lights flashing, the FBI car sped east across Manhattan toward Queens. The drive from Manhattan to La-Guardia is a half hour on the best day, with no traffic. Once the FBI knew what flight Zazi was taking, an intelligence analyst in Chelsea booked tickets for Larkin and Scott. They pulled up to the airport and tossed the keys to a waiting surveillance agent. If necessary, the FBI was prepared to hold the plane at the gate, but that would be yet another tip-off to Zazi.

A Port Authority official met the agents inside the airport and accompanied them through security in LaGuardia's main terminal. Zazi's flight was leaving from gate C7, near the end of a more than two-hundred-yard concourse. Larkin and Scott set off running down the gangway.

The agents reached the gate just as flight attendants prepared to lock the door. They were the last two passengers on the plane.

Larkin and Scott found their seats, one row behind Zazi, across the aisle. They settled in for the three-and-a-half-hour flight to Denver. Zazi put in his earphones and closed his eyes to go to sleep.

While Zazi was airborne, the FBI almost got the break it was looking for.

Agents and analysts in Denver tracked an incoming call to Zazi's phone. The call came from an unidentified number in Pakistan, one not associated with anyone in Zazi's family.[1] They recognized the significance immediately. A week earlier, Zazi had emailed for help with his bomb. He'd included his phone number. Now it seemed that al-Qaeda was returning the call. Maybe it was a high-ranking bomb maker. What if it was al-Qaeda's chief of external operations, Saleh al-Somali himself? That call could seal Zazi's fate. Plus, with the signal from a cell phone, the CIA's drones could find a target for their missiles.

Zazi couldn't answer. His phone was off. It went to voice mail. The caller did not leave a message.

DENVER

It was clear from Zazi's father's phone conversations that he was worried about what kind of trouble his son had gotten into in New York. Steve Olson, the head of the Joint Terrorism Task Force in Colorado, figured that Mohammed Zazi would want to know right away what had happened. Since Najibullah Zazi no longer had a car, it stood to reason that his father, the shuttle driver, would pick him up at Denver International Airport. If the FBI could listen, a conversation between father and son could offer the evidence needed to make its case.

In the FBI's command center, Olson explained his idea to Captain Steve Garcia from the Colorado State Patrol. The FBI had a secret warrant to tape Zazi's conversations, but someone still had to get inside his father's car to plant a recorder.[2]

"We need somebody to make a stop," Olson said.

This was a more complicated assignment than asking a trooper to pull over Zazi for speeding and find out where he was headed, as they'd done before. Somebody needed to slip under the dashboard of Mohammed's car. And it had to be discreet.

Garcia said he'd do it. He'd been deeply involved in the case for days. It didn't make sense to find another trooper with security clearances, bring him in on a Saturday, and get him up to speed. Garcia unpinned his gold captain's bars from his uniform and, for this assignment, became a trooper again.

The Colorado State Patrol had the authority to inspect commercial vehicles, and Mohammed's shuttle van qualified. To look natural, Garcia told Olson, they needed a second person. Typically, one trooper inspected the vehicle while a second stayed with the driver and handled the paperwork. Garcia grabbed Scott Casey, one of the troopers who'd conducted the blast analysis on the Denver Art Museum. Casey had clearance and, as a former police dog handler, he had conducted many car searches alongside the highway. Casey would stay with Mohammed while Garcia planted the bug.

The recorder was about half the length of a cell phone and about as thick, with an adhesive back and a transmitter built in. It was battery operated, so Garcia didn't need to mess with wires. Just peel off the backing and stick it underneath the dash.

Neither trooper had planted a bug before. As they practiced in the FBI parking garage, the bureau's technical experts peppered them with rules: Don't put it near the vents. It was sound activated, so the whooshing of the air would keep the recorder running even when nobody was talking, running down the battery. Plus, the heater could melt the adhesive, and the bug would fall to the floor. Don't put it too close to the radio. The signal could interfere with the transmitter, and the music could drown out the conversation.

The two men set out in Garcia's unmarked Ford Crown Victoria and headed east toward the airport. From the Zazi family's apartment, the airport was a straight shot north on the E-470 toll road, which surrounds Denver on three sides like a backward *C*. Garcia drove in lazy circles near the airport, exiting and reentering the highway while on the phone with Olson back at the FBI office. An FBI surveillance team was following Mohammed Zazi. Olson had Garcia on one line and the surveillance team on another. The troopers would have plenty of warning before their target got close.

Right on schedule, as Zazi's plane touched down in Denver, his father left the apartment and climbed into his van. Olson told Garcia to be ready. When the van left the apartment complex, however, Mohammed did not head toward the highway on-ramp. He headed west on local roads toward Denver. Nobody understood. Was he going to take Interstate 225? It was a roundabout route, but maybe he had an errand to run before the airport. Whatever the reason, Garcia and Casey were on the wrong highway.

Garcia gunned the engine and motored south on the toll road, back toward the Zazi apartment. He'd get off onto local roads in Aurora and try to intercept the van. He didn't bother with sirens or blue lights. He gave it gas, sending the Crown Victoria past 100 miles per hour, flirting with 110 and 120.

Zazi's flight landed, and the FBI agents on the plane followed him into the terminal. They relayed his whereabouts to the bureau's command center, where Olson passed them to Garcia. The captain tossed the phone to Casey so that he could focus on the road.

The Crown Victoria was closing in on Mohammed Zazi when Casey got word from the FBI: Najibullah Zazi was hailing a taxi. The FBI wasn't prepared to follow the cab, and Olson needed the troopers to pick up the tail. That meant they needed to head back toward the airport.

Casey barked the new orders to Garcia, who was soon speeding back the way they'd come.

"We're looking for a cab now?" Garcia grumbled.

The assignment was unclear. Were they supposed to pull over and bug the cabbie? What good would that do? Zazi wasn't going to confess to a cabdriver. At the FBI office, Olson tried to keep everything straight.

Over the phone, the troopers could hear him shouting orders at his exhausted agents—"Matt . . . Matt! . . . *Matt!*"—and jumping from one call to the next.

The troopers had barely turned around when they were called off the chase. An FBI surveillance team had eyes on the taxi. Get back on the father's van, Olson said.

"C'mon, man, just tell us what car to stop," Garcia said, turning the car around yet again. "Pick one."

Garcia caught up with the father at a convenience store. Mohammed Zazi was inside. The troopers were stopped at a red light across the street. Garcia was ready to go.

As Mohammed got back into the van, though, Olson called off the operation. The warrant authorized the FBI to bug only Najibullah Zazi, who wasn't in the van. Pack it up, Olson said. Come back.

The FBI already had another plan. There was a crawl space between the Zazis' apartment and the building's roof, an ideal spot from which to sneak tiny microphones into the home.

NEW YORK
Sunday, September 13, 2009

Back in New York, Don Borelli spent much of Sunday the thirteenth holed up in a conference room off the command center with FBI lawyers and members of the task force from other agencies. The FBI had a list of places it wanted to search. Borelli's job was to make sure that all legal steps had been taken. At some locations, like the flophouse where Naiz Khan and his cabbie friends lived, the FBI wanted to hide a microphone. Search warrants made that easy. When agents arrived to search a home, they routinely ushered everyone outside. With privacy and time, the agents could hide microphones behind walls, inside light fixtures, or other spots that made them virtually undetectable.

After many hours behind closed doors, Borelli emerged to find the operations center packed. Borelli's boss's boss, Joe Demarest, the FBI agent in charge of all New York operations, was in full command. Demarest was a former SWAT team leader and served as a shift supervisor for the FBI's investigation into 9/11. Even subordinates who didn't care for his aggressive management regarded him as a strong battlefield general. Demarest had been out of town for the first few days of the Zazi case, but with the bureau preparing predawn raids, he was now in his element.

Hundreds of people, many in raid jackets or SWAT gear, hurried through the room. Borelli surveyed the scene and thought, "This just became an E-ticket ride"—an old Southern California term for the Disneyland passes that got you into the biggest, most thrilling attractions. When people talk about the close collaboration between the NYPD and the FBI, they are referring to moments like this.

On a whiteboard, Demarest outlined the plan for the crowd. They'd hit the flophouse, Afzali's house, and the apartments of Ahmedzay and Medunjanin. Agents were even assigned to search Zazi's coffee cart, sitting with scores of others in an overnight storage facility in Brooklyn, to make sure it wasn't going to be used to sneak a bomb into Lower Manhattan. The raids had to be simultaneous. They'd strike between midnight and dawn. People were usually asleep then and less likely to put up a fight. Fewer journalists worked at that hour, which meant more time to work before the raids were on television.

Borelli would remain in Chelsea during the raids. Demarest would lead the operation from the streets of Queens.

As FBI agents in Chelsea finished their preparations, an NYPD car picked up Ahmad Afzali in Queens and brought him to 26 Federal Plaza, the Lower Manhattan headquarters of the FBI's New York field office. Afzali didn't know what the meeting was about, but he assumed he was there to help. Given the urgency and the late hour, he was increasingly sure that Zazi and his friends were mixed up in terrorism.[3]

Afzali's NYPD handler, Daniel Sirakovsky, was there, but the imam didn't recognize the other men in suits. In a room on the twenty-eighth floor, Afzali told the agents about his life, his work history, and his role in the community. It was old news to Sirakovsky but the imam assumed his friend from the NYPD wanted him to run through the story for the FBI's benefit. Though it was late, the agents seemed in no rush.

The FBI agents, George Ennis and William Rassier, were joined by NYPD Sergeant Ray Johnson. Under questioning from the task force, Afzali became suspicious and soon realized *he* was under investigation. The imam didn't think to call a lawyer or stop the interview. He had assumed that the NYPD Intelligence Division had been working with the FBI when Sirakovsky showed up Thursday at his house. He had no idea about the blowup that meeting caused.

Again, Afzali was shown four pictures: of Najibullah Zazi, Adis Medunjanin, Zarein Ahmedzay, and Amanullah Zazi, the man he believed to be Zazi's brother. Afzali's information on the four men was dated. He'd taught them the Koran in Arabic when they were younger. Growing up, they'd played volleyball at the mosque. He told the agents that Amanullah had been a troublemaker as a young man, but that a few years earlier, he'd seen him working at a grocery store in the neighborhood.

Afzali told the FBI agents that during his visit with the NYPD three nights earlier, he'd promised to try to find out what Zazi was up to. He had called Zazi the next morning to set up a meeting. The get-together never materialized because Zazi had a flight to catch that afternoon.

The agents listened, waiting to see whether Afzali would admit to tipping off Zazi. He did not.

The interview lasted hours. After 11:00 p.m., the agents brought Afzali coffee. He told them about his meeting with Medunjanin on Friday. He explained that everything he'd done had been to help the police.

The agents let Afzali talk himself into a corner. It was among the FBI's favorite traps. Lying to the government is a federal crime punishable by up to five years in prison. People often think they can talk their way out of trouble by concocting a story.

Afzali said he realized that he'd messed up. He shouldn't have called Zazi and Medunjanin. That's probably why he noticed cars following him lately. But he wasn't in the intelligence business. He was a funeral director and an imam. What was he supposed to do, show up at Abu Bakr and start asking people what Zazi was up to? That didn't seem right. He figured he'd call Zazi and his friends directly, sit down, and talk sense into them.

Finally, the FBI asked him directly: Had he told Zazi that investigators were asking questions about him?

By now it was apparent that Afzali's NYPD contact was not in charge. The FBI agents at the table were not interested in his help. They were angry.

No, Afzali lied. He hadn't tipped off Zazi.

Afzali and the FBI agents soon were standing in his Queens home. They handed him a document entitled "Consent to Search." Afzali and his wife signed it, and the agents went to work. Wearing rubber gloves and carrying disposable forceps, they swabbed Afzali's belongings with cotton balls, which they stuffed into plastic bottles. They sealed the bottles with tape, labeled them, and placed them in evidence bags. FBI scientists would determine whether Afzali had kept explosives in his house.

The FBI handed Afzali another document, this one saying that none of his belongings had been seized. It was 3:19 a.m. About three miles away, Joe Demarest's operation was in full swing.

• • •

Adis Medunjanin and his family had broken the Ramadan fast together that night. Hours later, they awoke to FBI agents storming the apartment, guns drawn. Medunjanin, his older sister, and his parents were ordered to the floor and handcuffed. Medunjanin's sister cried. His mother, still in her nightgown, thought the armed men in body armor were soldiers.

Once the tactical team pronounced the scene safe, they ordered Medunjanin to his feet. An FBI agent named Farbod Azad had arrived to see him. Azad was a young agent, a former middle school teacher of Persian descent who'd come to counterterrorism fresh from the FBI Academy less than two years earlier. He ordered Medunjanin's handcuffs removed and asked the bearded twenty-five-year-old to take a walk.

Medunjanin followed Azad and his partner, Angel Maysonet, an NYPD detective from the task force, down to Maysonet's car. Best to get away from the commotion, they figured. Maysonet drove a few blocks north and parked near the Whitestone Expressway, where nobody was around.

Outside the car, standing in the dark alongside the highway, Medunjanin told the agents about his family's life in Bosnia. He described his two-day, $220-a-week job as a security guard in Manhattan and recounted his religious pilgrimage to Saudi Arabia. He admitted being friends with Zazi and Ahmedzay and said the three traveled to Pakistan together a year earlier. Medunjanin stuck to the script they'd agreed to at the time: He went to Pakistan to find a wife but returned home still a bachelor because the dowry was too high. He identified photos of Zazi, Ahmedzay, and the imam, Afzali.[4]

Medunjanin gave the FBI his email addresses, and they talked religion. Azad found him to be knowledgeable about Islam. For instance, Medunjanin explained that, in his view, Muslims could have checking accounts without violating the Koran's prohibition on banking interest. The conversation lasted more than two hours. As the three men leaned against the car or stood on the sidewalk, agents a few blocks away were hauling off Medunjanin's Dell computer, containing photos of al-Qaeda terrorists and a book about the eternal pleasures that awaited martyrs in paradise.

Medunjanin became confrontational when agents asked if he knew anything about a planned attack on the United States.

No, he replied, adding, "We don't want this war."

Medunjanin said that as a US citizen, he opposed the 9/11 attacks and killing civilians. It was up to Allah, however, to lead his heart the way it needed to go. And he said Americans hated Muslims. The hostility Muslims felt toward the US was because of its support for Israel, he said.

Medunjanin crossed his arms in front of him.

Why did you do that? the agents asked.

He was emulating the Prophet Muhammad, he said, crossing his arms to show strength in front of his enemies.

Medunjanin said he'd done nothing wrong and was willing to take a lie detector test to prove it. The agents said they could arrange one immediately. Medunjanin quickly changed his mind.

The scene was similar at Zarein Ahmedzay's apartment. While agents searched his things, he sat in a parked car for hours, telling his life story and repeating the rehearsed lies about the trip to Pakistan.[5] Ahmedzay and Zazi had returned home to see their wives, he said. Medunjanin went there hoping to marry.

Ahmedzay and Medunjanin had suspected the authorities might come for them. But Naiz Khan, Zazi's old friend from the neighborhood who'd offered him a place to sleep Thursday night, had no warning before the SWAT team arrived.

The agents questioned all five people living there and a sixth who'd been visiting for two weeks, sleeping on the couch. Khan was honest with the agents. He told them that Zazi had approached him in the mosque, needing somewhere to stay. He recognized photos of Medunjanin and Ahmedzay but did not know their names. Khan, like Zazi, was an immigrant from Afghanistan by way of Pakistan. The agents asked about his trips to Pakistan. Khan explained that he'd left his wife and two children behind as he tried to make a life for himself, first as a coffee cart vendor and perhaps one day as a cabdriver.

"Please, help me bring my wife here," Khan said. "And then I won't need to go to Pakistan anymore."[6]

When FBI agents searching the apartment found an electric scale and calculator in the closet, Khan was adamant: He'd never seen them. Then the agents opened a green suitcase. Inside were nine backpacks. There were enough for Zazi, Medunjanin, Ahmedzay, the five roommates, and the visitor on the couch.

Khan tried to explain. The backpacks belonged to his uncle, who also lived in the apartment. Khan's mother got them from a friend in the Bronx, whose husband got them from a wholesaler that went out of business. What were they doing in the closet? Why do a coffee cart operator and his uncle need nine backpacks? Khan said they planned to send them to relatives in Pakistan.

The story was true. But it sounded unbelievable, like the lies that Ahmedzay and Medunjanin were spinning to FBI agents a few blocks away.

Monday, September 14, 2009

It would take time for the experts to analyze the computers and for the scientists to test for explosives, but as the sun came up on Monday the fourteenth, the FBI was no closer to proving that Zazi had come to New York to launch an attack. The agents still didn't know what he and his friends had been plotting or how they fit into al-Qaeda's plans.

Now the FBI faced a new wrinkle: The driver of the white van from the rest stop in Ohio five days earlier was speeding toward New York.

While Zazi and his friends had kept FBI agents in New York and Denver occupied, the white van had been the singular focus of the FBI's Cleveland field office and its boss, Frank Figliuzzi.

Figliuzzi hadn't paid attention the night of September 9, when his surveillance team was dispatched to follow Zazi across Ohio. Cleveland was Ohio's largest FBI office, and his team was often out of town helping on someone else's case. Nobody had told Figliuzzi about the apparent predawn encounter between Zazi and the driver of the white van at the highway rest stop. So he was caught off guard when Mike Heimbach, the FBI's counterterrorism chief, called from headquarters a few hours afterward.

"Frank, what the fuck is going on?"

"I don't know what you're talking about," Figliuzzi said. "Calm down."

Before Ohio, Figliuzzi worked at headquarters running the Inspections Division, the FBI equivalent of a police department's internal affairs bureau. He knew Heimbach and could tell by the urgency in his voice that something big was going on. He promised to figure things out and call back with answers.

The license plate on the white Chevy van came back registered to a courier company located just off the grounds of Cleveland Hopkins International Airport. Like Zazi and his family, the man in the white van had easy access to an airport. If Zazi had passed him a bomb, it could be nearly anywhere by now. Figliuzzi sent an agent up to the airport to check out the company and find the white van. When the report came back, Figliuzzi's heart sank. The parking lot was full of white vans, and it wasn't clear whether they were assigned to specific drivers, meaning that the man from the rest stop might be driving a different van each day.

Since that moment, the Cleveland office, like Denver and New York, had been running a command center around the clock. Customs agents pulled all the shipping documents linked to the courier company, looking for international arrivals. Pay special attention to shipments from the Middle East, Figliuzzi told them. Anything biochemical, anything hazardous, find it immediately.

The FBI was looking for a bomb in New York, and now there was a missing courier driving around Ohio with who knew what. Until they found the driver, Figliuzzi wanted an FBI tail on every van that pulled out of that parking lot.

Figliuzzi listened again to his surveillance team's story: Zazi had returned from the rest stop bathroom, and it looked as though he and the courier had chatted. The view had been poor, but it appeared as though the courier got into Zazi's car and then disappeared from view.

Next, Figliuzzi consulted with the Ohio State Highway Patrol, which covered that stretch of I-70. By that Saturday, the FBI agents in Ohio were coalescing around a theory about what had happened in that rest stop before dawn.

This was not going to be an easy phone call.

"What's your theory?" Mike Heimbach asked.[7]

Figliuzzi paused.

"You need to know. We're hearing the area is a known spot for gay liaisons."

Now it was Heimbach's turn to pause.

"Do you want me to tell the director of the FBI that's your best theory?"

Figliuzzi said they were still working on it.

By Sunday, while Borelli was preparing for the raids in New York, Figliuzzi's agents had identified the courier. He was a young white man, and there was nothing in his background that made him an obvious threat. A surveillance team followed him as he sped around the state. Viewed as a potential terrorist, he appeared erratic and suspicious. Viewed as an innocent courier, he appeared in a rush to make deliveries.

The company was clean. None of the international shipments suggested any problems. Figliuzzi and his agents decided to approach the owner and set up a meeting with the driver. They made up a cover story and sent an agent into the office.

Sorry, the manager said. He won't be around for a few days. He's driving to New York on a delivery.

The surveillance team confirmed that, yes, the white van was heading east at high speed.

It was Zazi all over again. They could not let the van into the city without knowing whether it carried a bomb.

The FBI investigation had gone overt. After the tip-off from Afzali and the predawn raids, all the suspects knew they were being watched. There was no sense trying another ruse like the one that had failed on the George Washington Bridge.

Police stopped the white Chevy shortly before eight o'clock as it crawled toward the Lincoln Tunnel in Monday rush-hour traffic. This time, someone from the Joint Terrorism Task Force, someone with security clearances, was there to oversee it. The instructions from FBI headquarters in Washington had been explicit: Look for bottles, jugs, anything that could carry liquids. The driver allowed police and an explosives dog to search the van. Nothing.

The courier showed police his shipping documents. He was delivering an eight-by-three-foot sign to Macy's department store at Herald Square in Manhattan, where the Thanksgiving parade ended each year. He showed them the package. Investigators photographed the van, its contents, and the thoroughly confused courier. Fifteen minutes after being stopped, he was on his way.

It was another dead end. The agents were getting frustrated and exhausted.

Borelli had gone home to shower and to catch an hour or two of sleep after the raids. When he returned, he met with one of the team leaders, who mentioned casually the backpacks seized from Khan's apartment.

Backpacks? Nobody had told Borelli about backpacks.

The backpacks were noted in a summary of the raids that was sent to headquarters. As happened with the water jug and the white van, everyone up the chain of command got agitated. They wanted to know why the backpacks weren't on their way to the FBI laboratory in Quantico.

"There was a closetful of backpacks and nobody thought they mattered?" Heimbach barked.

The blame fell first on Joe Demarest, the top agent in New York, who promised to take care of it. Borelli was next. Though Demarest had led the raids out in Queens, Borelli had been in charge of logistics. Demarest said he should've had a plan to react to the backpacks.

"You got twenty-five years in the FBI!" Demarest shouted in a room off the command center. "I can't believe you fucked this up!"

Borelli apologized.

An al-Qaeda-trained bomber was slipping through the FBI's grasp. Borelli was demoralized. In Denver, FBI agents watched and eavesdropped on Zazi to no good end. The top FBI agent there, Jim Davis, wondered if they'd ever catch a break.

12

PEOPLE DIE TO COME HERE

DENVER
Tuesday, September 15, 2009

Zazi saw reports about the raids on television. Every news channel carried the story. His friend Naiz Khan described FBI agents storming his apartment with guns. Reporters said the investigation focused on a man from the Midwest who'd driven to New York for the weekend.

Soon after returning to Denver, Zazi had opened his laptop and noticed something odd. The battery was fully charged. It hadn't been when he used it before putting it in the rental car.[1] The mysterious car thief had charged his computer. He took the laptop to the garage, unscrewed the base, and removed the hard drive. He destroyed the drive with a knife and threw it away.

Things had been quiet in Denver since then. The television made clear, however, that his problems had not gone away. Reporters said that the FBI and the Department of Homeland Security had issued a bulletin warning police nationwide about homemade bombs, specifically TATP. New York newspapers said the FBI was asking about someone named Najibullah from Colorado.

Zazi needed a lawyer.

From a shared office across from a strip mall on the outskirts of Denver, Arthur Folsom defended drunken drivers and handled divorces and minor drug cases. In fact, the thirty-seven-year-old with wispy brown hair was in the middle of fighting his own marijuana possession charge. Since graduating from the University of Denver College of Law, Folsom had never tried a federal criminal case. His law firm's website featured five links dedicated to lawyer jokes.

Zazi arrived early that morning without an appointment, hoping to speak with one of the other lawyers in the office, who'd helped a friend incorporate a business. That lawyer was in court, so Folsom ushered Zazi into a conference room and listened to his story. Zazi said his friends in New York were up to something. He suspected that the FBI had searched his car. They may have found some old chemistry notes that looked suspicious but were harmless.[2] Folsom gave his new client a stack of business cards to hand out to anyone who asked questions. He told Zazi to keep quiet.

• • •

Zazi's uncle Naqib Jaji had worried about the chemicals in his garage for months. He and his wife had taken in their nephew when he first arrived in Colorado looking for work in January 2009. Zazi had grown a beard and was quicker to steer the conversation toward religion than the boy Naqib had known growing up. Naqib would occasionally see his nephew on the computer looking at videos. One appeared to be about the Taliban. Another showed tanks exploding.[3]

One night in July, Zazi entered the modest suburban house through the garage rather than through the front door as he normally did. Suspicious, Naqib went to the garage and looked around. Inside the refrigerator there, he found lab goggles, a scale, a mask, nail polish remover, and what looked like bleach.

Naqib called his nephew downstairs.

"What the hell is this?" he asked.

Zazi explained that he and his wife had been unable to have a baby. The last time he visited her in Pakistan, he said, a doctor gave him a recipe for a medicine that would help. Zazi waved a piece of white paper as proof. He swore that's what the chemicals were for.

Naqib remained suspicious. Fertility medicine from bleach and nail polish remover? His nephew had been adamant, though. He decided to pray, asking God to deliver the young man and his bride the baby they wanted so badly.[4]

Zazi had moved in with his parents when they arrived in Aurora a few weeks later, leaving the chemicals behind. Now he was back from an unusual trip to New York, and an imam had called saying that the FBI was asking questions. The raids in Queens were big news. Naqib remembered the chemicals in his garage. He feared his nephew had been trying to cook up a bomb.

His wife, Rabia, delivered the message to her brother, Mohammed Zazi: There were chemicals in the garage. If anything happened, if the government came looking for them, Rabia said, she and her husband weren't responsible.[5]

"If you can do anything," she said, "do something about it."

Mohammed Zazi was furious. Why was he hearing about this only now?

"What kind of sister are you?" he protested.

Mohammed said his wife, Bibi, and his nephew Amanullah would take care of it.

The morning that Najibullah Zazi went to the lawyer's office, Bibi and Amanullah made the short drive to his aunt and uncle's house. Zazi's mother and aunt poured the bleach down the toilet of the upstairs bathroom, filling the house with fumes. They ran the fan and opened the windows, but it did little to lessen the sharp odor.

Downstairs, Amanullah cut the mask and goggles to pieces with a knife. The women did the same with the now-empty plastic bottles.

They stuffed the debris into a plastic bag. They realized they couldn't leave it on the curb with the trash. The FBI was probably watching. They had to get rid of the bag discreetly.

Amanullah had an idea. They stuffed the bag into Bibi's eight-year-old son Osman's backpack. When the family returned to its third-floor apartment, Bibi opened the backpack and handed her boy the plastic bag. Here, she said. I'll give you five dollars if you throw this in the trash outside.[6]

If the FBI were watching, perhaps agents would merely see a boy taking out the garbage after school.

• • •

Reporters began showing up that afternoon, knocking on the apartment door and asking questions. Najibullah Zazi did not keep quiet as his lawyer had instructed.

"This looks like it's going toward me, which is more shocking every hour," he told the *New York Times* over the phone.

"I live here, I work here," he told the *Denver Post*, standing in the doorway of his apartment. "Why would I have an issue with America? This is the only country that gives you freedom—freedom of religion, freedom of choice. You don't get that elsewhere. Nobody wants to leave America. People die to come here."

Folsom told reporters it was a misunderstanding.

"If the feds are that interested in him," he explained to Denver's ABC affiliate that afternoon, "why is it they haven't served a search warrant?"

As Folsom spoke, Jim Davis and Steve Olson at the FBI in Denver were, in fact, preparing those documents. Now that Zazi had a lawyer and the attention of the national media, the agents realized there was little chance they would catch him doing something incriminating. They would raid Zazi's apartment and his uncle's house the following day.

Davis watched and read the interviews with a mixture of bewilderment and worry. He was stunned that Zazi was talking to reporters.

Zazi's demeanor, however, worried him. He didn't have the cold stare of Mohamed Atta, the hijacker who piloted a jet into the World Trade Center's North Tower. He appeared nervous but earnest. Standing on the balcony outside his apartment, wearing a blue striped button-down shirt and denying any link to al-Qaeda, Zazi was believable.

He reminded Davis of Richard Jewell, the security guard who for a time was under investigation for a bombing in Atlanta's Centennial Olympic Park during the 1996 Summer Olympics. Investigators leaked his name to reporters, making him a public suspect in a blast that killed one person and injured more than a hundred. Jewell maintained his innocence, and, when the FBI finally exonerated him two months later, the Justice Department had to apologize.

Zazi was a terrorist, but if the FBI couldn't build a case, he could end up looking like a post-9/11 Richard Jewell, a Muslim man forced into the spotlight by the bureau and a victim of calumny.

The night before the raids, Davis and Olson shared the same fear. What if they didn't find anything?

Wednesday, September 16, 2009

Zazi was on the national news again Wednesday morning, September 16, as reporters camped outside his apartment and staked out Folsom's law office. Neither could leave without facing a barricade of microphones and tape recorders.

In New York, Ray Kelly reassured people that the city had never been safer thanks to the police.

"We're the best protected city in world," he said. "There are no guarantees, as we live in a dangerous world. Certainly 9/11 showed that to us, and we can see developments throughout the world that underscore that. But we are doing more than anyplace else, and we'll continue to do that."

Folsom believed his client when he said he was merely a shuttle driver swept up in a terrorism investigation. Folsom professed Zazi's innocence at every opportunity, but until he knew what evidence the FBI had, he was defending Zazi against whispers and rumors.

The attorney called the FBI. Zazi, he said, wanted to clear up things. If the FBI was interested, Folsom would bring Zazi downtown that day.

The FBI was interested.

Nobody knew what to make of the divorce lawyer who fell into a terrorism case and now promised to offer up his client to the FBI. It went against every rule in the cat-and-mouse game that agents and defense attorneys usually played. Jim Davis was convinced that Zazi wouldn't show. His lawyer might not have a clue, but Zazi did. Maybe Folsom had some inkling that the FBI was planning a raid, and this was an attempt to buy time. Surely he would think better of it and cancel the meeting.

Davis and Steve Olson led two FBI teams to Aurora, one for Zazi's apartment, the other for his uncle's house. Whether or not Zazi showed up for the meeting, the raids would go as planned.

Shortly before two o'clock, Folsom and a colleague arrived at the federal building in downtown Denver with Najibullah Zazi and his father. They checked in at the reception desk and were told to leave their cell phones in a storage locker. Security rules, the FBI explained. No outside cell phones allowed.

It was a lie. The FBI didn't want anyone to tell Zazi that his house was being searched. Once the phones were locked up, Davis and Olson got the word: Hit the houses.

Zazi left his father in the reception area and followed his lawyers toward a conference room, where they sat across from an agent named Eric Jergenson. He had a shaved head and the build of a farmhand. A native of Oshkosh, Wisconsin, he kept miniature Green Bay Packers and University of Wisconsin Badgers football helmets on his desk. Jergenson had entered the FBI Academy in 2002, inspired like so many of his peers to join the fight against terrorism.[7]

Every FBI investigation has a case agent who drives it and makes decisions. When the Zazi affair began, Jergenson was the case agent, but that was on a piece of paper. The investigation was so high profile that Olson and Davis ran things in Colorado, with all of FBI headquarters in Washington weighing in. That changed when Zazi walked into the building. Top FBI officials don't conduct interviews. Jergenson was up.

The FBI was certain that Zazi was a terrorist. Yet the bureau had no idea with whom or for whom he was working. Zazi's arrival at the FBI was an all-too-real variation on the philosopher's ticking-time-bomb scenario, which first appeared in Jean Lartéguy's 1960 French novel *The Centurions*, in which a soldier beats an Arab dissident into confessing.

For decades, scholars have used the ticking bomb as a thought experiment. One prisoner knows the location of the hidden device. How far is the jailer willing to go to extract the information? Who would allow the innocent to die to protect the rights of a terrorist? Doesn't the jailer have an ethical obligation to do everything in his power?

The fictional scenario presaged a post-9/11 principle: "To protect our people, we need more than retaliation, we need more than a reaction to the last attack," President George W. Bush said in 2006. "We need to do everything in our power to stop the next attack."

"Everything" meant tactics that previously would have been off-limits, such as eavesdropping on Americans without warrants, holding people in offshore prisons without charges, and, in New York, spying on Muslim college students and taping sermons.

The ticking-time-bomb scenario assumes that the jailer must go to extreme lengths. Since 9/11, the word *interrogation* has conjured images of hooded men being whisked to secret CIA prisons in Asia or Eastern Europe. There the CIA shaved their heads and faces, stripped them, and stood them for photographs. Subjected to constant light and noise, the naked prisoners were shackled in uncomfortable positions to keep them from sleeping. They were slapped, doused with water, thrown against the wall, and locked in small boxes. Most notoriously, CIA contractors strapped three prisoners to boards and poured water over their cloth-covered faces. Waterboarding simulates drowning and is so terrifying and agonizing that the United States prosecuted and executed Japanese soldiers for waterboarding American prisoners during World War II.[8] When the International Committee of the Red Cross interviewed the detainees about the CIA's tactics, the humanitarian group—responsible under international law for protecting prisoners—declared them to be torture.[9]

By contrast, FBI agents traditionally acted more like Hector Berdecia at the NYPD, bringing White Castle hamburgers and building rapport in the years before he ran the Demographics Unit. The bureau had a long history of success with that strategy, but in the aftermath of 9/11, it struggled to find its place in the newly proclaimed war on terror. Prosecuting terrorists in federal courts seemed weak; a throwback to a time before America was at war. In the months after 9/11, when Don Borelli was dispatched to Islamabad, he and his government colleagues set up a system for fingerprinting and photographing suspected al-Qaeda operatives flushed out of eastern Afghanistan by the US invasion and captured. Borelli assumed that he was building a foundation for criminal trials in the United States someday.

In February 2002 the CIA identified a Pakistani microbiologist named Dr. Rauf Ahmad, who was working with al-Qaeda.[10] Ahmad had been working on biological weapons for al-Qaeda and had spelled out those efforts in letters to Ayman al-Zawahiri, the Egyptian who served as Osama bin Laden's deputy. Borelli and a pair of CIA officers met him at a suburban safe house, where Pakistani intelligence held him more as a houseguest than as a prisoner. In a second-floor sitting room, Ahmad rang a bell, and a servant fetched tea and cookies.

"Would you like some?" Ahmad asked his visitors in English.

The Americans listened as Ahmad, a midlevel government scientist, spun a story. He supported al-Qaeda, yes, but he would never hurt anybody. They talked amicably for two days as Ahmad dug himself deeper. On the third day, Borelli and the CIA officers confronted him with documents.

Without warning, Ahmad sprang to his feet and yanked off his sweater. At first, the Americans thought he was going for a bomb or a gun. Then they sensed that he felt physically constricted by his own lies. He was trying to unburden himself.

Once he regained his composure, he began answering questions, admitting what they already knew: He had been recruited to be al-Qaeda's chief scientist in charge of weapons of mass destruction. He had been instructed to make anthrax. He pointed out the location of a laboratory he'd set up in Kandahar. He detailed everyone he had met in al-Qaeda and how he gained entrée into the organization. For Borelli, it was the biggest confession of his career. When it was over, he did what he'd been trained to do. He got Ahmad to sign a statement admitting everything he'd just said, for the court case.

Court cases, however, were out of fashion. The most important terrorism suspects were dragged into the CIA's secret prisons. Hundreds of terrorists and sympathizers—even some without any ties to terrorism—went to the military's prison at the Guantánamo Bay Naval Base in Cuba. The new judicial system there allowed hearsay and coerced statements, which supposedly would make prosecutions easier. Nearly a decade after the attacks, the Guantánamo military commissions had proven a morass. They had not produced significant victories. The 9/11 masterminds had yet to go to trial, their cases stalled from years of fighting over the government's untested legal system. FBI agents believed that, had the plotters been sent to federal court, they would have already been tried, convicted, sentenced, and executed—all without treating them like the soldiers they believed they were.

Once President Barack Obama came into office, with his promise to close Guantánamo and transfer detainees to the United States to stand trial, his Republican rivals portrayed federal court as a weak venue favored by a weak administration. Obama wanted to read terrorists their Miranda rights and give them attorneys, even if it meant missing out on information that could save lives.

So Zazi's case would be watched closely across Washington, not only among law enforcement but also at the White House and in Congress. If the case fizzled, it would provide more ammunition to those who argued that terrorism suspects—even those living inside the country—should be shipped to Guantánamo, where people could be held indefinitely without the rigorous evidentiary requirements of federal court.

The FBI doubted it could prove Zazi was part of a bomb plot. The agents were certain they could not prove Medunjanin's or Ahmedzay's involvement. Still, Jim Davis never considered sending anyone besides Jergenson into the conference room with Zazi. Though Jergenson had only about seven years on the job, he'd stood out for deftly recruiting and handling a valuable counterterrorism informant.[11] The Midwesterner was friendly, patient, and respectful. He never played the bad cop. Olson joked that Jergenson was everybody's best friend.

"So, here we are, I guess," Jergenson said, casually kicking off his interview. He wore a short-sleeve button-down shirt with neither a jacket nor a tie, and he leaned back slightly in his chair.

"There's been a lot on the news, everything else," he continued. He chuckled a bit, and Zazi did too. "What I think we can do today, if it's possible, with all of us here, is that we just have an open discussion, if that's possible. Maybe we can clear the air a little bit. I mean, nothing to hide here."

Zazi nodded, liking the direction of the conversation. Jergenson wanted to sort out this misunderstanding.

Folsom said he didn't know why Zazi was under suspicion:

"Quite honestly, we're not sure, other than the fact that Mr. Zazi stayed at the house of one of his friends that was somebody that apparently was being under investigation in New York."

Jergenson nodded reassuringly, as if that sounded reasonable. He ignored Folsom's query and began questioning Zazi.

Nobody knew how long Folsom would let his client talk. So Jergenson's goal was to catch Zazi in a lie. If nothing else panned out, at least they could charge him with a crime. That was the priority. Just catch him lying.

• • •

SWAT team members stormed Zazi's apartment, followed by bomb technicians in white plastic coveralls. Zazi's mother, sister, and cousin Amanullah were there. The FBI escorted them to separate cars to wait. The apartment was barely furnished and hardly decorated. There were no couches or chairs, only pillows and rugs. Dinner preparations had begun, and the house smelled of meats and spices.

Evidence teams worked slowly. In one bedroom, they found a Hewlett-Packard desktop computer resting on the beige carpet. There was no desk. The area was a jumble of wires, and the monitor was perched atop the computer tower. Anyone who used it would need to sit on the floor. The keyboard rested upon a small cardboard box to make typing easier.

Steve Olson was standing on the landing one floor below Zazi's apartment when Agent Chris Skillman approached him. As they had done inside Afzali's apartment in Queens days earlier, FBI agents were swabbing for traces of bomb-making materials.

"There's a five-gallon Igloo cooler in the closet. It's full to the brim," Skillman said.[12] "It looks like TATP."

Olson hurried downstairs to the FBI cars where Zazi's family members waited. In Islamic culture, it would be considered inappropriate for him, a man, to question Zazi's mother or sister alone. He knocked on the window where Amanullah sat.

What's in the cooler?

"I don't know, but you'd better test it," Amanullah replied. His response had an ominous tone.

Everyone back! Olson ordered. Widen the perimeter. Push the journalists and curious onlookers back another hundred yards. Evacuate all the apartments in the building and those nearby.

While agents hurried people out of their homes, Olson heard a sound. A school bell was signaling the end of classes at Canyon Creek Elementary a hundred yards or so up the road. Olson himself had once lived in this apartment complex. He knew that many of the children about to pour out of the school doors would head for these apartments.

The bomb team would have to move fast. The cooler, the kind used to dispense water or juice on the sidelines at sporting events, was made of heavy yellow plastic, with a red top and a spigot at the bottom. The bomb technicians knew they were looking for TATP, so when they'd first unscrewed the cooler and spotted enough white powder to blow up the entire apartment, they'd wasted no time emptying the building. Looking more closely, though, they saw that the powder didn't contain crystals. It was smoother and lighter. The bomb technicians tested it.

It was all-purpose flour. Zazi's mother used it for making bread.

• • •

Zazi couldn't keep his story straight. Most defense attorneys would take that as a sign to call off the interview. But Folsom was too caught up in the moment. One colleague who would later see the hours of video taken from a camera hidden in the conference room remarked that the attorney looked as though he'd been invited to celebrate a Super Bowl victory with the Denver Broncos. The FBI saw it too. However, instead of ending the interview when Zazi's story became too contradictory, Folsom would ask for a moment alone with his client. He and Zazi would speak privately and the interview would resume.

The interrogation stopped intermittently. After sundown, when Zazi was allowed to break the Ramadan fast, the FBI brought him a McDonald's Filet-O-Fish sandwich.[13] The agents were shocked that the interview was still going on. Zazi seemed to want to confess. The more they kept him talking, the better the chance he would. Despite the perception that suspects clam up under questioning, the truth was that roughly 80 percent of them agree to talk to police, even after having been told they have the right to remain silent.[14] The FBI knew that terrorism suspects were even more likely to confess. Once a plot was foiled, confessing was their only chance at glory.

After nearly six hours, as Jergenson's questioning had become more pointed, Zazi's responses veered toward the preposterous. He viewed lying to the FBI as part of his jihad, but he wasn't very good at it.

When Jergenson asked whether he owned a scale, Zazi said no. He said his family had one that his mother and sister used to weigh ingredients for cakes and biscuits.

"Have you ever used the scale?" Jergenson asked.

"No, I haven't," Zazi replied. "I don't need to use scales."

"While in New York, did you see a scale?"

"Yes, I did," Zazi said.

"Where did you see a scale?"

"In my luggage."

Zazi laughed a bit, nervously. He explained that, while packing for New York, he'd asked his little brother to zip up his suitcase for him. His brother must have packed the scale.

Jergenson listened, nodded, let Zazi tie himself in knots. Finally, he reached for copies of Zazi's handwritten bomb-making notes. He handed the nine pages to Zazi as Borelli had done years earlier with the al-Qaeda scientist in Pakistan.

Where are these from? Zazi wanted to know.

Jergenson explained that the FBI had searched his family's home and discovered the notes on his computer.

Zazi knew Jergenson was lying. He had destroyed his hard drive.

Zazi's posture changed. He crossed his arms. He tried to explain the drawings, saying that he'd once downloaded a religious book from the internet. These drawings had automatically arrived too, he said.

"As soon as I see it, I say, 'This is not something that I need to see or has to be in my computer.'" Zazi explained. "Right away, I delete it."

Zazi's father was not faring much better. An FBI agent had begun chatting with Mohammed Zazi in the reception area. Over the hours, the conversation had migrated into one of the conference rooms, where an FBI agent and an Aurora police detective assigned to the Joint Terrorism Task Force took over. The elder Zazi told them about his family and identified photos of his son's friends. When shown a photo of Ahmad Wais Afzali, the New York imam who'd called him days earlier, Mohammed Zazi was adamant: "No, I don't know that person." He said he never got a phone call from New York about his son.

About ten o'clock, Folsom and the Zazis called it a night. Najibullah Zazi let the FBI take his fingerprints and samples of his handwriting and DNA. Agents gave the men a ride, saving them a trip through the gantlet of reporters who'd been waiting outside the office all day.

They agreed to return the next day and pick up where they'd left off.

Thursday, September 17, 2009

Najibullah Zazi was now the biggest story in the US intelligence community. FBI agents reconfigured the conference room's hidden camera to send a video feed into an adjacent room. Everyone wanted a seat. The Justice Department sent prosecutors from Washington and New York. FBI agents arrived from New York. The CIA sent an analyst. They crammed into the room, many of them forced to stand and watch the feed on a small monitor.

Mike Heimbach, the FBI's counterterrorism chief, knew that Washington's post-9/11 briefing culture would work against him. The people in the room would spend the day emailing their bosses blow-by-blow accounts of Zazi's interview. If the FBI brought charges against Zazi, all those emails and reports could be used as evidence at trial. Defense attorneys would pick apart inconsistencies, weakening a case that for the first time seemed within the FBI's reach.

"Whoever you let in that room, make sure that they understand that there is singular reporting," Heimbach told Davis that morning. "We're not creating records anywhere else."

Chauffeured by the FBI, Folsom and Zazi returned to the federal building around noon.

By now Folsom knew that his client had not been in the wrong place at the wrong time, as he'd been telling reporters. In one of their private conversations during an interview break the day before, Zazi had confessed to training in Pakistan to fire weapons, build bombs, and carry out suicide missions.[15]

Folsom's new strategy: Cut a deal.

That was fine by the Justice Department. The FBI had a solid case against Zazi for lying. It had few details about the plot, however, and nothing against his friends Adis Medunjanin and Zarein Ahmedzay. Most important, officials in Washington worried that Zazi had an al-Qaeda contact inside the country. Arresting him might leave the bulk of a US terrorist cell intact.

The government presented Zazi with what's known as a proffer letter. It was a promise: If Zazi told the FBI about his plot, prosecutors wouldn't use his statements against him. It was similar to an immunity deal, except for one important distinction: FBI agents could use Zazi's words as tips, confirm them independently, and use *that* evidence against him. Proffer agreements are often a first step toward plea deals and agreements to testify against others. Suspects use their proffers to preview the story they'd tell. Lawyers called it "Queen for a Day," after a 1950s–1960s TV game show in which women received prizes after confessing their life's sorrows.

Zazi's time on the throne was marked by fits and starts. To Jergenson's most pressing question—whether an attack against the United States was imminent—Zazi insisted it wasn't. He admitted to receiving terrorism training in Pakistan. And as the day went on, he identified locations on maps, showing the FBI where he'd been. He told Jergenson about buying acetone and hydrogen peroxide at beauty supply stores. He admitted spending days at the Homestead Studio Suites in Aurora, cooking TATP on the stove.

He said he had come to New York to finish his bomb and carry out an attack.

Nearly two weeks after seeing the cryptic "the marriage is ready" email, the FBI had cracked the code. Zazi was a suicide bomber trained and directed by al-Qaeda to strike inside the United States.

Zazi refused to discuss Medunjanin or Ahmedzay. And for reasons the FBI could not figure out, he would not talk about what happened to his computer's hard drive.

At one point during the session, Robert Mueller called Jim Davis for an update. The FBI director and the special agent in charge of the Denver office had rarely spoken before this investigation. Mueller was not one for idle chatter. In 2008, after Mueller called to promote him to special agent in charge of the Denver office, Davis looked at his cell phone. The call had lasted seventeen seconds, including, "Please hold for the director." Since the Zazi case began, the two men talked regularly. Mueller called Davis for unscheduled updates. Once, he'd called after Davis had sneaked home to walk his dogs, a beagle and a Labrador mix. He hoped all through the call that the hound would not start howling.

Davis told Mueller that the proffer session was going well. His agents would try to confirm the beauty supply purchases and the hotel visits. Davis joked about Zazi's refusal to discuss the hard drive. The young man had admitted being an al-Qaeda terrorist, Davis said, "but he draws the line at obstruction of justice."

"Why is he talking to us?" the director asked. "Is there any chance that he's drawing our attention away from something?"

Davis thought that was a good question, but he didn't have a good answer.

Zazi did have a strategy. After the first interview, he knew he was in trouble. Jergenson had his bomb notes. He knew about Medunjanin and Ahmedzay and the Pakistan trip. They'd found the scale. It was only a matter of time until they pieced together the whole plot. Zazi decided to take the blame for everything.[16]

In Queens, Borelli's agents visited Medunjanin and Ahmedzay. The two men stuck to their stories about their trip to Pakistan. Medunjanin told the FBI that he had been in Peshawar the entire time. But when agents showed him a map of the city, he struggled to point out land-marks or say for sure where he'd stayed. He was adamant that neither he nor his friends had attended a terrorist training camp.[17]

Friday, September 18, 2009

By the third day of Zazi's interview, his admission was all over tele-vision. Too many people knew, and the news of an al-Qaeda-trained terrorist operating inside the United States was too big to contain. The leaks had become streams. Journalists learned about Zazi's comments almost as soon as he made them. Folsom fumed. He was getting threats, and he feared for his client's safety.

In a post-9/11 era of information sharing in which four million people hold security clearances, the US government has more secrets than ever.[18] It is harder than ever to keep them.

Jim Davis started that morning with an earful from Mike Heim-bach at FBI headquarters. Apparently the CIA analyst in the overflow room had sent a cable to his bosses in Langley. The CIA had put its own competing version of the Zazi interview in writing. The cable had reached Heimbach's desk, and he was furious. He'd given Davis specific instructions not to let this happen.

"Get control of this," he ordered.

Now it was Davis's turn to be furious. The six-foot-ten FBI agent erupted in front of everyone, threatening to wring the analyst's neck. The analyst tried to explain, but Davis had lost it.

"Get him the fuck out of here!" he shouted. "I don't want to see him anymore!"

He meant only that he wanted the analyst out of his sight. But after his rare display of fury, his colleagues assumed he wanted the analyst tossed from the building. The CIA man received an escort to the door.

In the interview room, Jergenson pressed Zazi anew for details about Medunjanin and Ahmedzay. Zazi had incriminated himself, but his cooperation was useful to the government only if it helped them make cases against others.

Still, Zazi refused.

Jergenson increased the pressure. Immigration officials on the Joint Terrorism Task Force had reviewed Zazi's father's immigration documents. He'd sworn to the government that his nephew Amanullah was his son. That was immigration fraud. The government could deport Zazi's entire family.

Still, Zazi refused.

While he stonewalled, sixteen FBI agents and a pair of ATF agents with bomb dogs descended on the Homestead Studio Suites not far from Zazi's apartment. With the manager's permission, agents in white coveralls searched room 207. From the hood above the stove, the agents removed the filters. If anyone had been working with acetone, the scientists at the FBI's laboratory would be able to detect it.

Back in New York, word was spreading that Zazi had been tipped off to the FBI investigation. It would take a month before reporters figured out that the NYPD had approached Ahmad Afzali and that Paul Ciorra had been transferred, but it was already clear that the case had been a flashpoint in the historically strained relationship.

"Not true," Ray Kelly shot back at a Manhattan news conference when asked about the troubled partnership.

After three days of interviews in Denver, Jergenson had made progress. The FBI finally felt it had a case. Zazi, however, still would not open up about his friends in New York.

They agreed to meet again the next day, but the FBI was reaching the point of diminishing returns.

Saturday, September 19, 2009

Folsom knew that another day of questioning would mean more focus on Medunjanin and Ahmedzay. Zazi needed to decide what he was going to do. His proffer was most valuable to the government if he told the whole story, which meant that he could get a deal for himself in return. In a phone call Saturday morning, Zazi told his lawyer that he would not turn on his friends. His religion prohibited it.

"I'd rather spend life in prison than eternity in hell," he said.[19]

Very well. Folsom would cancel their meeting with the FBI. He told Zazi to spend the next hours with his family. Hug them. He might never touch them again.

"When the knock on the door comes," Folsom added, "don't resist."

At the FBI, the question now was whether to arrest Zazi or to wait. The government had a surefire case in Colorado against both Zazi and his father for lying to the FBI. On conference calls among officials in Denver, New York, and Washington, agents and prosecutors debated the merits of waiting. Federal lawyers in New York had begun work on terrorism charges against Zazi. The filters from the hotel room would be back from the lab soon. Police and FBI agents had a good lead on the beauty supply store where Zazi had bought his chemicals. It would take time to get Zazi's emails and his bomb-making notes declassified for use in court. It might make sense to wait to arrest Zazi until that evidence could be revealed and the New York case was ready.

By waiting, there was also the chance that Medunjanin and Ahmedzay would slip up. If Zazi appeared to have talked his way out of trouble, perhaps his friends would get on the telephone and incriminate themselves.

Zazi continued to talk, but not to the FBI, which he seemed to be taunting. He gave an interview to the *Denver Post* that morning and denied news reports that he'd admitted being part of al-Qaeda.

"If it was true, they wouldn't allow me to leave," Zazi said. "I don't think the FBI or the police would allow anyone who admits being a terrorist to go free for one minute."

Jim Davis felt the same way.

"He walks into my office, tells my guys he's a fucking al-Qaeda operative, and he gets to go home?" Davis said repeatedly to whoever would listen. "We can't have that."

Besides, Zazi was the ringleader and they weren't going to get anything more out of him. It was time to act. In New York, Borelli and his bosses agreed. So did FBI headquarters. While Denver was taking down Zazi, New York would arrest Ahmad Wais Afzali, the NYPD Intel informant who had seemingly wrecked the investigation and lied about it.

That night, under a moonless sky, Denver FBI agents gathered outside Cherokee Trail High School in a sunken parking lot set back from the main road. An unseasonably warm day had given way to a cool night. As they waited for a federal judge to sign Zazi's arrest warrant, Davis briefed his team.

"Take the dad first," he said. "I want him to see his dad handcuffed."

Davis wanted a spectacle for the throng of reporters outside the house. He wanted Zazi to know what he'd caused with his plotting and lying.

"He needs to recognize that we are done with the 'Come on in when you have time and we'll buy you cheeseburgers,' " Davis said. "I want him to feel the pain of this."

As they prepared to leave, Steve Olson told the agents, "Let's be visible, very loud. Lights and sirens."

The journalists didn't need a light show to know the FBI was coming. The leaks from the investigation had already alerted them. Just as Davis was pulling out of the parking lot, he got a call from Denver's NBC affiliate. The reporter wanted confirmation that the FBI was on its way to arrest Zazi. Another called Zazi at home and, with the FBI listening in, told him he was about to be arrested and asked for comment.

Davis opted against battering the door off its hinges. His agents, wearing blue FBI windbreakers, not riot gear, knocked instead. Once his team was inside, Davis scaled the three flights of outdoor stairs leading toward Zazi's apartment. When he got to the second floor, agents going down passed him, escorting Mohammed Zazi, who wore a gray T-shirt, black wind pants, and silver handcuffs.

Najibullah Zazi had been waiting for the FBI, standing in the middle of his empty living room, trying not to look threatening. He was still there when Davis entered the apartment, only now he was handcuffed behind his back. He wore jeans, a short-sleeve, checked button-down shirt, and a look of resignation. Davis saw neither anger nor defeat. The men did not speak.

Jergenson led him down the stairs, into the bursts of flashbulbs. Zazi did not respond as reporters shouted questions at him.

As the SUV rolled away with Zazi, the agents left the window down so that the nation could get a good view of a terrorist on his way to jail.

• • •

Amanullah Zazi, who introduced his cousin to al-Qaeda and had returned to Denver soon after, surprised the government by calling the FBI in November 2009. He said he was bored and needed money, a conversation that grew into a cooperation agreement with the government. He filled the gaps in his cousin's story. Amanullah pleaded guilty to conspiring to obstruct justice and helping others get terrorism training. He was sentenced to forty months in prison and then faces possible deportation.

Months later, on January 7, 2010, FBI agent Farbod Azad and Detective Angel Maysonet returned to Adis Medunjanin's apartment in Queens. This time they did not bring a SWAT team. They respectfully removed their shoes and showed him a warrant to seize his passports. His sister fetched them from a closet, and Medunjanin signed a receipt acknowledging that the FBI was taking them.

Maysonet looked at the form.

You didn't sign it "Mohammed?"

Mohammed was the nom de guerre Medunjanin had chosen in Pakistan for his al-Qaeda training.

Medunjanin, startled, didn't say a word. The FBI knew.

After Azad and Maysonet left, Medunjanin began pacing. He called

Robert Gottlieb, the lawyer his family had hired. His sister could tell something was wrong, but Medunjanin told her to go back to bed.

Two hours later, Medunjanin cracked. He got in his car and sped up the Whitestone Expressway, taking the car over ninety miles per hour and swerving between lanes. He called 911.

"Police operator sixteen-seventy-three."

"This is Adis!" he screamed. "We love death more than you love life!" [20]

"Hello? Do you need the police, fire department, or the ambulance?" the bewildered operator asked.

Then in Arabic, Medunjanin shouted the Muslim declaration of faith four times: *"La ilaha illallah, Muhammad-ur-Rasulullah!"* There is no God but Allah, and Muhammad is His messenger.

The line went dead. Medunjanin tried to kill himself, slamming head-on into another car. He didn't die. He jumped out of the car and hopped the median before FBI surveillance agents caught him. In the hospital, he spoke to the FBI for four hours, admitting that he'd been trained as a suicide bomber. He seemed both proud and relieved. He implicated Zarein Ahmedzay, who was arrested driving a cab in Manhattan.

A month later, Najibullah Zazi, facing a potential life sentence on charges of conspiracy to use a weapon of mass destruction, pleaded guilty to terrorism charges. He admitted plotting to bomb New York's subway system.

"This was one of the most serious terrorist threats to our nation since September 11, 2001," Attorney General Eric Holder announced. "This attempted attack on our homeland was real, it was in motion, and it would have been deadly."

Ahmedzay pleaded guilty to terrorism charges in April 2010. He and Zazi testified at trial against Medunjanin, who, despite his confession, tested his luck in court. Jurors deliberated about a day before convicting him. A judge sentenced him to life in prison. Medunjanin told the judge, "I had nothing to do with any subway plot or bombing plot whatsoever. I ask Allah to release me from prison."

As this book went to print, Zazi and Ahmedzay awaited sentencing.

Amanullah Zazi testified against his uncle Mohammed, who was convicted of obstruction and sentenced to four and a half years. He went to prison convinced his son was innocent.

"You have a delusion about your son," the judge told him. "He and his coconspirators were going to commit horrific crimes." [21]

Ahmad Afzali, the Queens imam who tipped off Zazi to the investigation, pleaded guilty to lying to the FBI and was deported. He was last living in Qatar after fleeing violence in revolutionary Syria.

The hapless courier driving the white van in Ohio took a polygraph and passed. He was not involved in the plot. FBI agents still don't know what, if anything, happened in the rest stop parking lot.

In Pakistan, Saleh al-Somali and Rashid Rauf, two of the senior al-Qaeda operatives in Pakistan who'd hatched the plan, were killed in CIA drone strikes. Adnan Shukrijumah, who persuaded Zazi and his friends to accept the suicide mission, was indicted but remains at large, presumably in northwest Pakistan. The New York attack was one of three that al-Somali and his cohorts had planned. The others targeted England and Norway. Authorities thwarted those too.

The drone strikes, which inspired Zazi and his friends to become suicide bombers, continue.

EPILOGUE

Osama bin Laden was killed in a CIA-led raid in 2011. Al-Qaeda's core no longer has the ability to mount sophisticated terror attacks on the scale of 9/11. Small cells of Americans like Zazi, however, represent a persistent concern.

On April 15, 2013, two brothers with homemade backpack bombs attacked the Boston Marathon, killing four and injuring hundreds. The young Muslims were born in the Caucasus region in the southern-most part of Eastern Europe and emigrated to the United States as children. Angered by the wars in Iraq and Afghanistan and fueled by the same radical internet sermons that inspired Zazi, they built the sort of pressure cooker bombs that al-Qaeda's online propagandists have encouraged.

Almost immediately, the NYPD's proxies suggested that the attack might have been prevented had Boston police used Cohen's clandestine tactics. In New York, officials reinforced the idea that being safe required Americans to change their views on privacy and civil liberties.

"We live in a complex world where you're going to have to have a level of security greater than you did back in the olden days, if you will," Mayor Michael Bloomberg said. "And our laws and our interpretation of the Constitution, I think, have to change."

Completely ignored during these debates was the fact that New York's spying programs had already faced their test.

Spotting homegrown terrorists before they strike is the reason that NYPD Commissioner Raymond Kelly revamped the Intelligence Division and hired David Cohen. The hunt justified the Demographics Unit, the use of informants, secret recordings of sermons, surveillance of religious leaders, and infiltration of advocacy groups.

When it mattered most, those programs failed.

In August 2011 we were finishing a story for our employer, the Associated Press, timed to coincide with the ten-year anniversary of 9/11. It focused on the transformation of the NYPD Intelligence Division since the 2001 terrorist attacks. Its expansion had been well documented in the media, but we uncovered new details, such as the existence of the Demographics Unit and its use of mosque crawlers and rakers. We had hoped to interview Cohen and Kelly, but the NYPD refused. Instead, Paul Browne, the deputy commissioner for public information, said he'd address our questions if we provided a list of topics. The telephone interview with Browne took place on August 18. We asked about the Demographics Unit.

"There is no such unit," Browne said. "There is nothing called the Demographics Unit."

We asked whether any unit by that name had ever existed, even informally.

"No," Browne said.

We turned to each other in surprise. Then we asked about mosque crawlers.

"Somebody has a great imagination," Browne said. "There is no such thing as mosque crawlers."

After the call, we wondered why Browne denied what we knew to be true. Sources with firsthand information of the secret programs had discussed them in detail with us. We'd expected the department spokesman to simply decline to comment or defend them. Browne chose differently. That fueled our curiosity. We kept investigating and began publishing stories.

Browne called the stories "fiction." Kelly said his investigators "simply follow leads."

"We're going to follow those leads wherever they take us," he said. "We're not going to be deterred, but we're certainly not singling out any particular group."

Mayor Bloomberg said religion played no part in the city's counterterrorism efforts.

We learned that these comments were untrue.

The Demographics Unit, for instance, neither followed leads nor generated any. It mapped Muslim businesses, mosques, and people.

Was any of it illegal? We don't know. As this book shows, the NYPD and its lawyers interpreted the Handschu guidelines as allowing them to investigate entire mosques as terrorist organizations and to monitor people's political views if they spoke Pashto. The fact that some terrorists had been members of Muslim student organizations was enough to justify monitoring entire groups.

The NYPD says it's all been legal. And it might be right.

The Justice Department declined to open a civil rights investigation, privately telling the FBI that there were no obvious victims. White House Homeland Security advisor John Brennan visited NYPD headquarters and said the department wasn't doing anything illegal and had struck the right balance to keep the city safe.

"It's not a trade-off between our security and our freedoms and our rights as citizens," Brennan said. The Handschu lawyers have gone back to court to get the NYPD's tactics declared improper. Muslims in New York and New Jersey have sued. Regardless of the outcome, the NYPD's programs are likely to join waterboarding, secret prisons, and warrantless wiretapping as tactics of our time that will be debated for years.

• • •

Zazi's plot failed because of good partnerships, good intelligence, and good luck. NSA officials intercepted the "marriage is ready" email and passed it to the CIA, which shared it with the FBI. Before 9/11, there was no guarantee that would have happened. It certainly wouldn't have happened as quickly as it did. The Joint Terrorism Task Force model in Denver and New York worked, building criminal cases and generating intelligence. The investigation was bolstered by partnerships with the Colorado State Patrol and the NYPD detectives assigned to the task force, relationships that have grown stronger over the years.

Going alone, as Cohen favored, didn't work. For all the information that Cohen gathered on Americans—where they ate and prayed, what they thought of drones, where they watched sports, and which barber cut their hair—the NYPD Intelligence Division was a nonfactor in the investigation.

Somehow, though, the Zazi plot contributed to Intel's growing mythology. In May 2012, before he left the NYPD's analytical ranks for a consulting job, Mitchell Silber wrote an opinion piece for the *Wall Street Journal*: "How the NYPD Foiled a Plot to Bomb the Subways."[1]

The NYPD added Zazi to a list of schemes it claimed to have thwarted since 9/11. By the time we started writing about the Intel Division, that tally had swelled to fourteen.

"We have the best police department in the world, and I think they show that every single day, and we have stopped fourteen attacks since 9/11, fortunately without anybody dying," Bloomberg declared.[2]

"Under Commissioner Ray Kelly's leadership, at least fourteen attacks by Islamic terrorists have been prevented by the NYPD," Representative Peter King of Long Island said.

The numbers were false.[3] Every government agency promotes itself, but the NYPD's combination of publicity and secrecy prevented people from assessing whether its intelligence programs worked and are worth the cost in money and trust.

New Yorkers had no idea they were paying for something that, at the most important moment, had proven useless. When the US intelligence community errs, there is congressional oversight. The police department faced no questions about what went wrong in the Zazi case. Nobody was called to testify about why the Demographics Unit hadn't provided early warning, why investigators infiltrating student groups didn't spot the trio of terrorists, or why the many informants and undercover officers hadn't triggered alarms. Nobody asked whether such programs were worth continuing.

The same would be true in May 2010 when Faisal Shahzad, a naturalized US citizen from Pakistan who believed the nation was at war with Islam, tried to detonate a car bomb in Times Square. The NYPD's $150 million electronic surveillance system, with more than two thousand cameras, failed to spot the smoking Nissan Pathfinder. Only a design flaw kept the bomb from detonating. A Muslim street vendor noticed it and alerted police.

Since 9/11, more secrets than ever have been kept from Americans in the name of keeping them safe; a government of the people has inched toward becoming a government kept from the people. In Washington, the administration uses its classification stamp to withhold information. In New York, the police department, with no authority to keep documents classified, routinely denies the release of basic information: crime reports, organizational charts, mug shots, and more.

Were it not for a few whistle-blowing NYPD officials with access to Intelligence Division files, it's not clear when or if any of these programs would have been disclosed. We still don't know what other domestic intelligence programs were created, what information they collected, whether they worked, or whether they're still in use.

And there's no system in place for anyone outside the NYPD to find out.

• • •

As this book goes to print, Raymond Kelly still runs the New York Police Department. Following our stories, he said he had changed nothing about the department's intelligence-gathering practices.[4] It's not clear whether he'll have a job after the 2013 mayoral election to replace Bloomberg, who faces term limits. David Cohen is still deputy commissioner for intelligence. Deputy Chief Jim Shea is no longer on the Joint Terrorism Task Force but remains with the NYPD. Paul Ciorra, the department's good soldier, never publicly complained about his transfer following the blowup over Afzali's phone call. In 2012 he was promoted to the rank of inspector. Hector Berdecia retired from the department and took a job with the federal government, allowing him to spend more time with his family.

The Demographics Unit was renamed the Zone Assessment Unit in 2010 over fears about how the title would be perceived if it leaked out. But rakers still troll Muslim neighborhoods, filing an average of four new reports every day.[5] Today Cohen's Intelligence Division has a budget of $60 million and commands nearly six hundred officers even as al-Qaida's power diminishes.

The Muslim community is marbled by fear and isolation. The NYPD is in their mosques, businesses, and student groups. Worshippers are afraid to congregate. Young men worry that growing beards will attract police attention. People fear that talking politics, marching in protests, or attending academic lectures will land them in police files.[6]

They believe this because it happens.

"Your job is to protect us," said Tahanie Aboushi, a Manhattan lawyer. "If we are now afraid of you, the community will pull together and cut themselves off from law enforcement."

The FBI has already seen that happening. The top agent in New Jersey made headlines in 2012 when he said the NYPD's tactics were isolating Muslims and making the region less safe.

"These are people that are our friends" Michael Ward said. "These are people that have embraced law enforcement, embraced the mission that we have in counterterrorism, and you can see that the relationships are strained."

EPILOGUE

• • •

Larry Sanchez left the NYPD in December 2010 after a falling-out with Cohen, taking a lucrative job in the Persian Gulf region as a consultant. The CIA's inspector general found that Sanchez's assignment in New York had been marked by inconsistent oversight and a lack of clear rules but said no laws had been broken. He was replaced by a clandestine officer, Lance Hamilton, whose assignments in Pakistan and Jordan had made him one of the most senior operatives in the CIA.[7] Nobody ever provided a direct answer about what Hamilton was doing inside a municipal police department. After his assignment was revealed, the CIA recalled him to Langley. As far as we know, the CIA no longer has an officer embedded inside the NYPD.

The New York City Council was trying to create an inspector general to oversee the police department, someone who would subject the nation's largest police department to the kind of internal review and program oversight seen at the CIA, FBI, and other executive agencies. Bloomberg and Kelly are adamantly opposed. They say any outside oversight would make New York a more dangerous place to live.

Many FBI agents named in this book have since left the bureau.

Jim Davis became executive director of the Colorado Department of Public Safety. He finally got to chase criminals. Steve Olson is close to retirement age and thinking about his second career, one that will help put his children through college.

Art Cummings, Mike Heimbach, Jim McJunkin, and Brenda Heck joined the corporate world, leaving behind a legacy of helping to reshape the bureau to fight terrorism after 9/11. Greg Fowler, the head of the New York task force, became special agent in charge of the FBI's Portland, Oregon, office. His boss, Joe Demarest, runs the cybercrime division at FBI headquarters in Washington. Ari Papadacos and Bill Sweeney are still fighting terrorism.

Robert Mueller faced mandatory retirement in 2011, but President Obama asked him to stay two more years. Congress extended Mueller's term, making him the second-longest-serving FBI director behind J. Edgar Hoover. Mueller's term expires September 4, 2013.

• • •

Don Borelli went on to retire from the FBI, accepting a position as vice president with a Manhattan consulting firm. When the Zazi investigation finally slowed down, Borelli took a week off for his forty-ninth birthday. He flew to New Mexico with a bottle of whisky and went fly-fishing.

ACKNOWLEDGMENTS

This book grew out of a series for the Associated Press, where we have been given the two great luxuries in American journalism: time to piece together stories and the space to tell them. Supporting investigative journalists is rarely easy and often expensive but we are fortunate to have the backing of many wonderful bosses. AP president Gary Pruitt, Executive Editor Kathleen Carroll, and Senior Managing Editor Mike Oreskes have been unwavering. Ted Bridis is our editor, defender, and friend. Sally Buzbee, AP's Washington bureau chief, is one of the industry's great champions of investigative reporting.

As journalists and, later, as authors, we relied on the support and contributions of talented colleagues, including Christopher Hawley, Tom Hays, Peter Banda, Maria Sanminiatelli, Nahal Toosi, David Stringer, Justin Vogt, Justin Pritchard, James Risen, David Caruso, Mark Mazzetti, Julie Tate, Michael Powell, Charles Dharapak, John Doherty, Len Levitt (who has been tilting at windmills longer than any of us), and the incomparably talented Eileen Sullivan.

This book would not have been possible without the trust and help of many current and former officials from the NYPD, FBI, CIA, the Justice Department, Colorado State Patrol, and elsewhere. We received help along the way from Mike Kortan, Richard Kolko, and Beth Lefebvre from the FBI; Lance Clem at the Colorado Department of Public Safety; Preston Golston at CIA; Robert Nardoza at the US Attorney's Office for the Eastern District of New York.

Defense lawyers Robert Gottlieb, Justin Heinrich, Steve Zissou,

ACKNOWLEDGMENTS

Robert Boyle, Ron Kuby, Michael Dowling, and Deborah Colson were generous with their time. The Handschu lawyers—Martin Stolar, Jethro Eisenstein, Paul Chevigny, and Franklin Siegel—summoned boxes from warehouses to help us understand a fight that has spanned decades.

We are grateful to Melanie Pearlman and Christina Gradillas at the CELL; Adrienne Schwisow; Landon Nordeman; Umair Khan; Fahd Amed; Daniel Baker at FlightAware; and chefs Robert Berry, Justin Smillie, and Richard King, who kept our sources and us well fed with some of New York's best food.

Several people named in this book helped us greatly. Many more could not be named, either here or elsewhere, but provided invaluable documents and insight into the NYPD's inner workings and the race to stop Najibullah Zazi. For that, we thank you.

We are indebted to our agents, Gail Ross and Howard Yoon, and to Matthew Benjamin and his team at Touchstone, who visualized the story we wanted to tell and supported this book at its earliest stages.

Stephen Merelman and Amy Fiscus provided deft edits. They lived inside our sentences and our brains, leaving both sharper and wiser. Their insights and suggestions made this book immeasurably better. We are lucky to have such friends, mentors, and colleagues.

We owe much of our success to our loving parents.

And, of course, we are forever thankful for the support of our wives, Becky and Allison, who put up with so much during two years of reporting. We love you.

NOTES

Two: A Spy in New York

1. Leonard Levitt, *NYPD Confidential: Power and Corruption in the Country's Greatest Police Force* (New York: Thomas Dunne Books), pp. 41–42.

2. Kelly's Vietnam service record includes participation in Operations Harvest Moon, Blue Marlin, Dagger Thrust, and others.

3. Jim Rutenberg, "Torture Seeps into Discussion by News Media," *New York Times*, November 5, 2001, www.nytimes.com/2001/11/05/business/media/05TORT.html?pagewanted=all.

4. *The September 11 Detainees: A Review of the Treatment of Aliens Held on Immigration Charges in Connection with the Investigation of the September 11 Attacks* (Washington, DC: US Department of Justice, Office of the Inspector General, April 2003), www.justice.gov/oig/special/0306/full.pdf.

5. The phone call is described in Christopher Dickey, *Securing the City: Inside America's Best Counterterrorism Force—The NYPD* (New York: Simon & Schuster, 2009), p. 36.

6. Interview with a former colleague who witnessed the event.

7. Interview with a former colleague.

8. Interviews with former CIA officials who know and worked with Cohen.

9. Interview with Melvin Goodman.

10. Interview with John Deutch.

11. The "Jordans" anecdote and the sentiment in the Near East Division were described in an interview with longtime officer Robert Baer and confirmed by other former Directorate of Operations officers.

12. Gordon Lederman, *Memorandum for the Record (MFR) of the Interview of David Cohen of the Central Intelligence Agency conducted by Team 2* (Washing-

ton, DC: National Commission on Terrorist Attacks upon the United States, June 21, 2004), http://media.nara.gov/9-11/MFR/t-0148-911MFR-00164.pdf.

13. Ibid.

14. *The 9/11 Commission Report: Final Report of the National Commission on Terrorist Attacks upon the United States* (New York: W. W. Norton & Company, 2004), pp. 111–12.

15. Email to the authors from Boston University spokesman Colin Riley: "[Cohen] received a Master's Degree in Government on 5/29/1966."

16. The best insider's account of the NYPD Intelligence Division of that era is Anthony J. Bouza, *Police Intelligence, The Operations of an Investigative Unit* (New York: AMS Press, 1976). The mission creep is described on pages 163–64.

17. Defendants' Answers to Plaintiffs' Interrogatories, Handschu v. Special Services Division, United States District Court, Southern District of New York, 71-CV-2203, document filed on December 22, 1977.

18. Affidavit of Rosemary Carroll, Handschu v. Special Services Division, United States District Court, Southern District of New York, 71-CV-2203, March 18, 1981.

19. Details of the FBI and CIA spying operations are taken from six books that make up the *Final Report of the Select Committee to Study Governmental Operations with Respect to Intelligence Activities,* particularly book 3, *Supplementary Detailed Staff Reports on Intelligence Activities and the Rights of Americans* (Washington, DC: U.S. Government Printing Office, 1976), available at www.intelligence.senate.gov/pdfs94th/94755_III.pdf.

20. *Final Report,* bk. 3, p. 695.

Three: Heading East

1. Lord Carlisle of Berriew, QC, *Operation Pathway: Report Following Review* (London: Institute of Race Relations, October 2009), www.irr.org.uk/pdf2/Carliles_report_Pathway.pdf. This document links email to "Al Qaeda's operations outside Pakistan." Al-Somali was al-Qaeda's external operations chief at the time. The Justice Department has publicly linked the email address to al-Somali through a courier.

2. McHale testimony from *Hearing on 9/11 Health Effects: The Screening and Monitoring of First Responders, Before the Subcommittee on Government Man-*

agement, Organization, and Procurement of the Committee on Oversight and Government Reform, House of Representatives, One Hundred Tenth Congress, First Session, September 10, 2007 (Washington, DC: U.S. Government Printing Office, 2009), available at www.napo.org/washington-report/McHaleTestimony.pdf.

Four: Demographics

1. Adam Goldman and Matt Apuzzo, "Authority for NYPD-CIA Collaboration Questioned," Associated Press, January 20, 2012, http://online.wsj.com/article/AP99d50ace043148fbbe3d296b37c3c5aa.html.

2. The content of these discussions and the immediate post-9/11 concerns were described in interviews with former senior NYPD officials directly involved in transforming the department at that time.

3. Terry McDermott, "A Perfect Soldier," *Los Angeles Times*, January 27, 2002, http://articles.latimes.com/2002/jan/27/news/mn-25005.

4. Ibid.

5. Stevenson Swanson, "9/11 Haunts Hijacker's Sponsors," *Chicago Tribune*, March 7, 2003, http://articles.chicagotribune.com/2003-03-07/news/0303070298_1_mohamed-atta-hijacker-world-trade-center.

6. John Cloud, "Atta's Odyssey," *Time*, September 30, 2001, www.time.com/time/magazine/article/0,9171,176917,00.html.

7. Tim Golden, Michael Moss, and Jim Yardley, "Unpolished Secret Agents Were Able to Hide in Plain Sight," *New York Times*, September 23, 2001, www.nytimes.com/2001/09/23/national/23PLOT.html.

8. John Hooper, "The Shy, Caring, Deadly Fanatic," *Observer* (UK), September 23, 2001, www.guardian.co.uk/world/2001/sep/23/september11.education.

9. United States v. Zacarias Moussaoui, criminal no. 01-455-A, prosecution trial exhibits, government exhibit ST00001, stipulation (regarding flights hijacked on September 11, 2001; September 11, 2001, deaths; al-Qaeda; chronology of hijacker's activities; Zacarias Moussaoui; and the Computer Assisted Passenger Pre-Screening System [CAPPS]), filed March 1, 2006. Available at www.vaed.uscourts.gov/notablecases/moussaoui/exhibits/prosecution/ST00001A.pdf.

10. Cohen's interest in Reid's time in Paris was described in an interview with a former senior federal intelligence official who discussed Reid's case with Cohen.

11. Cohen's description of raking coals was described in interviews with former NYPD officials involved in the genesis of the program.

12. Sam Roberts, "Police Demographics Unit Casts Shadows from Past," *City Room* (blog), *New York Times*, January 3, 2012, http://cityroom.blogs.nytimes.com/2012/01/03/police-demographics-unit-casts-shadows-from-past.

13. The Israeli inspiration was described in two interviews: one with a former NYPD official and a second with a former senior US intelligence official who spoke to Sanchez about the program.

14. *International Religious Freedom Report 2004: Israel and the Occupied Territories* (Washington, DC: US State Department. September 15, 2004), http://www.state.gov/j/drl/rls/irf/2004/35499.htm#. Quoted: "Tensions continued to remain high due to the institutional, legal, and societal discrimination against the country's Arab citizens."

15. Chris McGreal, "Facility 1391: Israel's Secret Prison," *Guardian*, November 13, 2003, www.guardian.co.uk/world/2003/nov/14/israel2.

16. Department of Justice, Office of Legal Counsel, "Memorandum for Alberto Gonzales Re: Standards of Conduct for Interrogation under 18 U.S.C. sections 2340–2340A," August 1, 2002, www.justice.gov/olc/docs/memo-gonzales-aug2002.pdf.

17. Joel Greenberg, "Israel Affirms Policy of Assassinating Militants," *New York Times*, July 5, 2001, www.nytimes.com/2001/07/05/world/israel-affirms-policy-of-assassinating-militants.html.

18. The origin of the term was described in interviews with former NYPD officials. Its official use was documented in an NYPD PowerPoint presentation obtained by the authors and published by the Associated Press. It is available at http://wid.ap.org/documents/nypd-demo.pdf.

19. The list of ancestries of interest was revealed in an NYPD PowerPoint presentation obtained by the authors and published by the Associated Press. It is available at http://wid.ap.org/documents/nypd-demo.pdf.

20. Matt Apuzzo and Adam Goldman, "With CIA Help, NYPD Moves Covertly in Muslim Areas," Associated Press, August 23, 2011, www.ap.org/Content/AP-in-the-News/2011/With-CIA-help-NYPD-moves-covertly-in-Muslim-areas.

21. NYPD Intelligence Division Analytical Units presentation, obtained by authors. The relevant excerpt, published by the Associated Press, is available at http://wid.ap.org/documents/nypd-demo.pdf.

22. Details of the meeting with the foundation leadership were recounted in interviews with someone present for the discussion.

23. This was included in the 2003 copy of the *New York City Police Foundation Journal*, an annual fund-raising document summarizing the foundation's successes and highlighting its major donors.

24. Dzikansky described his drinking problem in his book (coauthored with Robert Slater) *Terrorist Cop: The NYPD Jewish Cop Who Traveled the World to Stop Terrorists* (Fort Lee, NJ: Barricade Books, 2010), pp. 227–31, and in interviews with the authors.

25. Concerns over Dzikansky's role and his involvement in favors for the Israelis were spelled out in interviews with NYPD and FBI officials and corroborated by NYPD surveillance documents obtained by the authors.

26. The conversation was recalled by a former US official in attendance.

27. Kelly's acknowledgment that no tips were generated from the program came in public remarks recounted in Len Levitt, "Kelly and AP: Ray's Pants Are on Fire," *The Blog, Huffington Post*, January 14, 2013, www.huffingtonpost.com/len-levitt/kelly-and-ap_b_2472012.html.

28. The details of this meeting, including what was said, were described in interviews with Henoch.

29. NYPD Intelligence Division, *Strategic Posture 2006*. Document obtained by authors and available at http://nypdconfidential.com/other/120604-intel.pdf.

30. NYPD Intelligence Division, Demographics Unit, *N.Y.P.D. Secret: Syrian Locations of Concern Report*, available at http://hosted.ap.org/specials/interactives/documents/nypd/nypd-syria.pdf. Document obtained by authors and published by the Associated Press.

31. NYPD Intelligence Division, Demographics Unit, *Secret: Albanian Locations of Concern Report*, available at http://hosted.ap.org/specials/interactives/documents/nypd/nypd-albania.pdf. Document obtained by authors and published by the Associated Press.

32. Eileen Sullivan, "White House Helps Pay for NYPD Muslim Surveillance," Associated Press, February 27, 2012, available at www.newsday.com/news/new-york/white-house-helps-pay-for-nypd-muslim-surveillance-1.3560418.

33. Supervisor, Demographics Unit to Commanding Officer, C.A.R.U., memorandum, "Supervisors Conferral with Detective," January 26, 2006, available at http://wid.ap.org/documents/nypd-memo.pdf. Document obtained by authors and published in redacted form by the Associated Press.

34. NYPD Intelligence Division, Demographics Unit, *N.Y.P.D. Secret: Newark, New Jersey, Demographics Report*, available at http://hosted.ap.org/specials/interactives/documents/nypd/nypd_newark.pdf. Obtained by authors and published by the Associated Press.

35. Rocco Parascandola and Corky Siemaszko, "NYPD Report on Muslim Shops Includes Stores Owned by Jews, Catholics," New York *Daily News*, March 9, 2012, www.nydailynews.com/new-york/nypd-wrongly-listed-businesses -muslim-linked-part-surveillance-article-1.1036538.

36. Adam Goldman and Matt Apuzzo, "NYPD: Muslim Spying Led to No Leads, Terror Cases," Associated Press, August 21, 2012, www.ap.org/Content/AP -In-The-News/2012/NYPD-Muslim-spying-led-to-no-leads-terror-cases. See also deposition of Thomas Galati, Handschu v. Special Services Division, United States District Court, Southern District of New York, June 28, 2012, 71-CV-2203, available at www.nyclu.org/files/releases/Handschu_Exhibit4 (GalatiEBTredacted)_2.4.13.pdf.

37. Ibid, p. 119. Galati: "Sometimes these officers, when they go, they go to places that they may like the food and go back for that reason, and I know that that has happened."

Five: Accidental Tourists

1. "Afghanistan and the United Nations," UN News Centre, www.un.org/News/dh/latest/afghan/un-afghan-history.shtml.

2. Sarah Talalay, "Afghans in US Look Homeward: Soviet Pullout Arouses Hopes, Wariness—No Indifference," *Christian Science Monitor*, May 13, 1988, www.csmonitor.com/1988/0513/aghan.html.

3. Ibid.

4. Ibid.

5. Dexter Filkins, "Afghans at Queens Mosque Split Over bin Laden," *New York Times*, September 19, 2001, http://www.nytimes.com/2001/09/19/nyregion/nation-challenged-new-york-mosque-afghans-queens-mosque-split-over -bin-laden.html

6. Ibid.

7. Michael Wilson, "From Smiling Coffee Vendor to Terror Suspect," *New York Times,* September 25, 2009, http://www.nytimes.com/2009/09/26/nyregion/26profile.html?pagewanted=all&_r=0.

8. Ibid.

9. FBI interview with Adis Medunjanin (FBI 302). Made public in United States v. Medunjanin, United States District Court, Eastern District of New York, 10-cr-00019.

10. Zarein Ahmedzay testimony, trial transcript, United States v. Medunjanin, United States District Court, Eastern District of New York, 10-cr-00019, p. 199.

11. FBI interview with Adis Medunjanin (FBI 302), January 7, 2010. Made public in United States v. Medunjanin, United States District Court, Eastern District of New York, 10-cr-00019.

12. Steve Coll, *The Bin Ladens: An Arabian Family in the American Century* (New York: Penguin Press, 2008).

13. "Haqqani's Close Relatives Killed in US Missile Strike," Dawn.com, September 8, 2008, http://archives.dawn.com/archives/39967.

14. Najibullah Zazi testimony, p. 546. Trial transcript, United States v. Medunjanin, United States District Court, Eastern District of New York, 10-cr-00019.

15. Ibid., p. 549.

16. Zarein Ahmedzay testimony, ibid., p. 164.

17. Peter Bergen, "Bin Laden: Seized Documents Show Delusional Leader and Micromanager," CNN, May 3, 2012, http://www.cnn.com/2012/04/30/opinion/bergen-bin-laden-document-trove.

18. Page 1 Adis Medunjanin FBI 302 1/22/2010. Made public in United States v. Medunjanin, United States District Court, Eastern District of New York, 10-cr-00019.

19. Zazi's considering jumping from the bridge was told to the authors in interviews with current and former officials, who were briefed on government interviews with Zazi.

Six: Zone Defense

1. The details of this investigation were pieced together in interviews with a former senior NYPD intelligence official, as well as with other former NYPD and federal officials.

2. Interview with former NYPD analyst. This phenomenon was not unique to Hezbollah. Documents obtained by the authors, including one entitled "Hamas Case Recap," show NYPD efforts to monitor Hamas: "The investiga-

tion consists of fifteen main subjects and nearly seventy-five associates. The subjects can be categorized as Hamas leader/recruiters, members or associate-sympathizers. Our main subjects all have the common thread of being extremely religious and are more radical in their feelings of Hamas."

3. Galati deposition, p. 35, available at www.nyclu.org/files/releases/Handschu_ Exhibit4(GalatiEBTredacted)_2.4.13.pdf.

4. NYPD Intelligence Division, Intelligence Analysis Unit, *N.Y.P.D. Secret Intelligence Strategy Report: US-Iran Conflict: The Threat to New York City*, May 15, 2006, available at www.documentcloud.org/documents/288719-nypd -iranian-intel.html?key=9a9ba0d2ea8a33e7dce6.

5. Details of the meeting were recounted by a former official in attendance who took notes. Though the authors did not review the notes, the official did.

6. Seidel has identified himself as the station chief in Jordan during that time, both in public comments and on his LinkedIn profile.

7. NYPD Intelligence Division, presentation, "Integrating Collection, Analysis and Operations," circa September 2006. Obtained by authors. The strategy is spelled out under the heading "Our Philosophy": "NYPD plays 'zone defense,' not 'man to man'/strategically arrayed resources enable pre-emption". It was fleshed out in interviews with former intel officials.

8. Patrick Murphy affidavit, p. 3. Filed in Handschu v. Special Services Division.

9. Listening posts are mentioned in a number of NYPD documents, including the *N.Y.P.D. Secret: Syrian Locations of Concern Report*, available at http:// hosted.ap.org/specials/interactives/documents/nypd/nypd-syria.pdf.

10. The recruiting process was described in interviews with former NYPD detectives and supervisors and with former NYPD informant Shamiur Rahman, whose story was described in Adam Goldman and Matt Apuzzo, "Informant: NYPD Paid Me to 'Bait' Muslims," Associated Press, October 23, 2012, http:// bigstory.ap.org/article/informant-nypd-paid-me-bait-muslims.

11. Michael A. Sheehan, *Crush the Cell: How to Defeat Terror Without Terrorizing Ourselves* (New York: Three Rivers Press, 2008), p. 193.

12. Adam Goldman and Matt Apuzzo, "With Cameras, Informants, NYPD Eyed Mosques," Associated Press, February 23, 2012, www.ap.org/Content/AP-In -The-News/2012/Newark-mayor-seeks-probe-of-NYPD-Muslim-spying.

13. Pinkall's attendance and failure at the Farm were described by former intelligence and law enforcement officials.

14. The activities of the undercovers are taken from the NYPD's internal documents including Cohen's daily briefings on the activities of the SSU. They were also described in interviews with two former senior NYPD Intel officials and a former SSU detective.

15. Handschu v. Special Services, "Defendants' Answers to Plaintiffs' Interrogatories," December 22, 1971. The NYPD said it was possible to open an investigation based solely on rhetoric, but, because of its record keeping, it was impossible to say if or how often that happened.

16. Memorandum from FBI headquarters, quoted in *Final Report of the Select Committee*, book 3, *Supplementary Detailed Staff Reports*, p. 18, www.intelligence.senate.gov/pdfs94th/94755_III.pdf.

17. Galati deposition, p. 86: "Most Urdu speakers from that region would be of concern."

18. TIU Watch List. NYPD document, 2004. Obtained by authors.

19. Galati deposition, p. 66.

20. Statements of Rhetoric, Masjid Al-Ikhwa. Terrorism Interdiction Unit, circa 2004. Document obtained by authors.

21. Interviews with a former NYPD intelligence official who attended a meeting with Parker.

22. Apuzzo and Goldman, "With CIA Help," www.ap.org/Content/AP-in-the-News/2011/With-CIA-help-NYPD-moves-covertly-in-Muslim-areas.

23. Apuzzo and Goldman, "NYPD Keeps Files on Muslims Who Change Their Names," Associated Press, October 26, 2011, http://www.ap.org/Content/AP-In-The-News/2011/NYPD-keeps-files-on-Muslims-who-change-their-names.

24. Dates of Interest. Masjid Al-Ikhwa. Terrorism Interdiction Unit. Circa 2004. Document obtained by authors.

25. Quintan Wiktorowicz, "Anatomy of the Salafi Movement," *Studies in Conflict & Terrorism* 29, no. 3 (April–May 2006): 207-39, http://ipac.kacst.edu.sa/edoc/2006/157374_1.pdf.

26. Steven D'Ulisse, "Integrating Collection, Analysis and Operations." Presentation, September 2006. Obtained by authors.

27. NYPD Intelligence Division, *Strategic Posture 2006*, www.nyclu.org/files/releases/Handschu_Exhibit7b_(StrategicPostureredacted)_2.4.13.pdf.

28. Mitchell D. Silber and Arvin Bhatt, *Radicalization in the West: The Homegrown*

Threat (New York Police Department, 2007), p. 70, www.nypdshield.org/public/SiteFiles/documents/NYPD_Report-Radicalization_in_the_West.pdf.

29. Goldman and Apuzzo. "With Cameras," www.ap.org/Content/AP-In-The-News/2012/Newark-mayor-seeks-probe-of-NYPD-Muslim-spying.

30. NYPD Intelligence Division, *Strategic Posture 2006*, www.nyclu.org/files/releases/Handschu_Exhibit7b_(StrategicPostureredacted)_2.4.13.pdf.

31. Ibid.

32. NYPD Intelligence Division, Cyber Intelligence Division, *Weekly MSA Report*, November 22, 2006, http://hosted.ap.org/specials/interactives/documents/nypd-msa-report.pdf.

33. Mitchell D. Silber, "Who Will Defend the Defenders?" *Commentary*, June 2012, www.commentarymagazine.com/article/who-will-defend-the-defenders/.

34. Mitchell D. Silber and Donald Powers, letter, entitled "Request to Conduct a Preliminary Inquiry Concerning Dennis Christopher Burke and Certain of His Associates," March 27, 2008.

35. NYPD Intelligence Division, Intelligence Collection Coordinator, *Deputy Commissioner's Briefing*, April 25, 2008, http://hosted.ap.org/specials/interactives/documents/nypd/dci-briefing-04252008.pdf.

36. Memo to Kelly from Cyber Intelligence Unit, May 12, 2008. Obtained by authors.

37. The X Team is mentioned in NYPD documents, including an organization chart that lists it as part of the Special Case Unit. Its function was described in interviews with former NYPD officials.

38. Surveillance Request. Technical Operations Unit. December 9, 2008. Obtained by authors.

39. Sheehan, *Crush the Cell*, p. 175.

40. Interview with former law enforcement official who'd attended the meeting.

41. This conclusion was described by a former law enforcement official involved in the discussions.

42. Associated Press reporter Eileen Sullivan first heard about this conversation from a source. In the reporting of this book, the authors then corroborated it in an interview with a former official who'd attended the briefing.

43. The story of Mueller in Newark is told frequently in FBI circles. It was confirmed by three current and former FBI officials with direct knowledge of the discussion.

44. Interviews with three former federal prosecutors with direct knowledge of the decision.

45. Craig Horowitz, "Anatomy of a Foiled Plot," *New York Magazine*, December 6, 2004, http://nymag.com/nymetro/news/features/10559/.

46. Mitchell D. Silber, "Who Will Defend the Defenders?" *Commentary*, June 2012

47. FBI officials would not discuss Aziz, but the authors have obtained numerous NYPD documents related to Confidential Informant 184. Separately, Aziz has identified himself as a longtime NYPD informant in Martin Mawyer with Patti A. Pierucci, *Twilight in America: The Untold Story of Islamic Terrorist Training Camps Inside America* (Lynchburg, VA: PRB Publishing, 2012). Aziz's assignment, travel, NYPD handler, immigration status, and criminal record match those described in the CI 184 documents.

48. *Deputy Commissioner's Briefing*, April 9, 2008.

Seven: Ostermann

1. Now known as the Counterterrorism Education Learning Lab.

2. The details of this briefing were described in interviews with Davis, Ritter, Carpenter, and Colorado State Patrol major Brenda Leffler.

3. *Federal Support for and Involvement in State and Local Fusion Centers* (Washington, DC: United States Senate Permanent Subcommittee on Investigations, Committee on Homeland Security and Governmental Affairs, October 3, 2012), available at http://www.hsgac.senate.gov/download/?id =49139e81-1DD7-4788-A3BB-d6e7d97dde04.

4. Interviews with Davis and Shepard.

5. Details about the informant and the search for explosives residue were confirmed in interviews with Davis, Olson, and Lambert.

6. The 5,500 figure comes from interviews with current and former counterterrorism officials.

Eight: Mosques

1. Details from inside the meeting were described in interviews with a former law enforcement official.

2. Interview with Ahmad Wais Afzali.

3. Author interview with Fatimah Zulaika Rahim.

4. Ibid.

5. Details of this call are described in Afzali's handwritten statement to federal agents on September 17, 2009.

6. Afzali recounted this meeting in an interview with the FBI on September 14, 2009. It was memorialized in an FBI document known as a 302.

7. Afzali has remained consistent in his interviews with the federal government—memorialized in a sworn personal statement and his FBI 302—that Sirakovsky told him to find out more about Zazi. Though some of his statements were false, the government has never alleged that this one was. Further, NYPD detectives did not need Afzali to identify Zazi's picture. They knew who he was. They needed Afzali for information. Sirakovsky denies this, however, and says that his only instruction to Afzali was for him not to tell anyone about their conversation.

8. Ervin Dyer, "Mosque Members Denounce FBI Raid as Desecration," *Pittsburgh Post-Gazette*, July 8, 2006, www.post-gazette.com/stories/local/neighborhoods-city/mosque-members-denounce-fbi-raid-as-desecration-441219.

9. *Domestic Investigations and Operations Guide (DIOG)* (Washington, DC: Federal Bureau of Investigation, October 15, 2011, http://vault.fbi.gov/FBI%20Domestic%20Investigations%20and%20Operations%20Guide%20%28DIOG%29/fbi-domestic-investigations-and-operations-guide-diog-2011-version/fbi-domestic-investigations-and-operations-guide-diog-october-15-2011-part-01-of-03/view.

10. Ibid.

11. Interviews with current and former US law enforcement officials.

12. Andrea Elliott, "Why Yasir Qadhi Wants to Talk About Jihad," *New York Times Magazine*, March 17, 2011, http://www.nytimes.com/2011/03/20/magazine/mag-20Salafis-t.html?pagewanted=all&_r=0.

13. Bill de Blasio, public advocate for New York City, http://advocate.nyc.gov/sites/advocate.nyc.gov/files/deBlasioFOILReport_0.pdf.

14. Modified Handschu Guidelines, second revised order and judgment, August 6, 2003, 288 F. Supp. 2d 411.

15. Ibid.

16. These figures come from NYPD documents from the time, including minutes from Handschu meetings and requests for approval to open terrorism enterprise investigations.

17. TIU Watch List, NYPD document, 2004. Obtained by authors.

18. Fred Burton and Scott Stewart, "Tablighi Jamaat: An Indirect Line to Terrorism," Strafor Global Intelligence, January 23, 2008, www.stratfor.com/weekly/tablighi_jamaat_indirect_line_terrorism.

19. Handschu Committee Minutes, May 12, 2009. Obtained by authors.

20. Andy Newman with Daryl Khan, "Brooklyn Mosque Becomes Terror Icon, but Federal Case Is Unclear," *New York Times*, March 9, 2003, www.nytimes.com/2003/03/09/nyregion/brooklyn-mosque-becomes-terror-icon-but-federal-case-is-unclear.html?pagewanted=all&src=pm.

21. Michelle Goldberg, "My Arab Street," *Salon*, March 7, 2003, www.salon.com/2003/03/07/al_farooq.

22. Len Levitt, "Intel at Inception," *The Blog, Huffington Post*, December 10, 2012, www.huffingtonpost.com/len-levitt/intel-at-inception_b_2271152.html.

23. United States v. Al-Moayad, United States District Court, Eastern District of New York, 03-1322, government exhibits Bates stamped 3500 MA-1 and 3500 MA-4.

24. Ibid.

25. TIU Watch List, NYPD document, 2004. Obtained by authors.

26. The meeting and the request to bug the mosque were described in interviews with former law enforcement officials.

27. Interview with former law enforcement official.

28. William Glaberson, "Focus Changes in Terror Case Against Sheik," *New York Times*, January 20, 2005, www.nytimes.com/2005/01/20/nyregion/20sheik.html?pagewanted=print&position=&_r=0.

29. Opinion of US Court of Appeals for the 2nd Circuit, decided October 2, 2008, United States v. Al-Moyad, 05-4186.

30. *Deputy Commissioner's Briefing*, March 9, 2009. "New Imam @ Al Farooq." Obtained by authors.

31. Interview with Shamiur Rahman. The authors also reviewed Rahman's cell phone photos sent to the NYPD.

32. Interviews with former law enforcement official.

33. Counterterrorism Intelligence Package, 2004. NYPD document obtained by authors.

34. Interview with former law enforcement officials involved in or briefed on the taping.

35. NYPD Intelligence Division, Central Analysis Research Unit, *N.Y.P.D. Secret Intelligence Note: NYC Mosque Statements on Danish Cartoon Controversy*, February 9, 2006, http://hosted.ap.org/specials/interactives/documents/nypd/nypd_cartoons.pdf.

36. Goldman and Apuzzo, "With Cameras," www.ap.org/Content/AP-In-The-News/2012/Newark-mayor-seeks-probe-of-NYPD-Muslim-spying.

37. Ibid.

38. Ibid.

39. NYPD Intelligence Division, Intelligence Analysis Unit, *N.Y.P.D. Secret Intelligence Note: DD5S Referencing 10/11/06 Plane Crash into Building at 524 72nd Street*, October 16, 2006, http://hosted.ap.org/specials/interactives/documents/nypd/nypd_planecrash.pdf.

40. Eileen Sullivan, "NYPD Spied on City's Muslim Anti-Terror Partners," Associated Press, October 6, 2011, www.ap.org/Content/AP-in-the-News/2011/NYPD-spied-on-citys-Muslim-anti-terror-partners.

41. Andrea Elliott, "A Muslim Leader in Brooklyn, Reconciling 2 Worlds," *New York Times*, March 5, 2006, www.nytimes.com/2006/03/05/nyregion/05imam.html?pagewanted=1&_r=0&ei=5088&en=b4ea067a0c307d39&ex=1299214800&partner=rssnyt&emc=rss.

42. Ibid.

43. Sullivan, "NYPD Spied," www.ap.org/Content/AP-in-the-News/2011/NYPD-spied-on-citys-Muslim-anti-terror-partners.

44. Elliott, "A Muslim Leader," www.nytimes.com/2006/03/05/nyregion/05imam.html?pagewanted=1&_r=0&ei=5088&en=b4ea067a0c307d39&ex=1299214800&partner=rssnyt&emc=rss.

45. William K. Rashbaum, "Trial Opens Window on Shadowing of Muslims," *New York Times*, May 28, 2006, www.nytimes.com/2006/05/28/nyregion/28tactics.html?pagewanted=all.

46. Ibid.

47. Ibid.

48. William K. Rashbaum, "Detective Was 'Walking Camera' Among City Muslims, He Testifies," *New York Times*, May 19, 2006, www.nytimes.com/2006/05/19/nyregion/19herald.html?pagewanted=all.

49. Andrea Elliott, "To Lead the Faithful in a Faith Under Fire," *New York Times*, March 6, 2006, www.nytimes.com/2006/03/06/nyregion/06imam.html?pagewanted=all&_r=0.

50. NYPD Intelligence Division, Strategic Intelligence Unit, *Briefing Report, Buffalo, New York,* January 2, 2009, http://nypdconfidential.com/columns /2012/120227.pdf.

51. Ibid.

52. Sullivan, "NYPD Spied," www.ap.org/Content/AP-in-the-News/2011/ NYPD-spied-on-citys-Muslim-anti-terror-partners.

53. "Abu Hamza Jailed for Seven Years," BBC News, February 7, 2006, http://news .bbc.co.uk/2/hi/uk_news/4690224.stm.

54. NYPD Surveillance Request, November 7, 2008. Document obtained by authors.

55. NYPD Surveillance Request, November 7, 2008. Document obtained by authors.

56. *Deputy Commissioner's Briefing,* October 24, 2008. Document obtained by authors.

57. *Deputy Commissioner's Briefing,* May 12, 2008. Document obtained by authors.

58. Ibid.

59. Modified Handschu Guidelines, second revised order and judgment, August 6, 2003.

60. *Deputy Commissioner's Briefing,* October 24, 2008. Document obtained by authors.

61. The authors reviewed Rahman's text message history with Hoban.

62. Goldman and Apuzzo, "Informant: NYPD Paid Me," http://bigstory.ap.org/ article/informant-nypd-paid-me-bait-muslims.

Nine: The American Who Brings Good News

1. Office of the Inspector General, report 02-38, *A Review of the Federal Bureau of Investigation's Counterterrorism Program: Threat Assessment, Strategic Planning, and Resource Management* (Washington, DC: Office of the Inspector General, September 2002), http://www.justice.gov/oig/reports/FBI/a0238 .htm.

2. *National Commission on Terrorist Attacks upon the United States, Law Enforcement, Counterterrorism, and Intelligence Collection in the United States, Prior to 9/11,* Staff Statement 9, p. 6. http://govinfo.library.unt.edu/911/staff_state ments/staff_statement_9.pdf.

3. Interviews with Davis and Olson.

4. Interview with current and former law enforcement officials.

5. David Kris and J. Douglas Wilson. *National Security Investigations and Prosecutions. 2007* Thomson/West. Cited at §19:5.

6. Ashlee Vance and Brad Stone, "Palantir, the War on Terror's Secret Weapon," *Bloomberg Businessweek*, November 22, 2011, www.businessweek.com/maga zine/palantir-the-vanguard-of-cyberterror-security-11222011.html.

7. Department of Justice Office of the Inspector General, Oversight and Review Division, *A Review of the Federal Bureau of Investigation's Use of Exigent Letters and Other Informal Requests for Telephone Records,"* January 2010, p. 46, www.justice.gov/oig/reports/FBI/a0238.htm.

8. Interview with former senior CIA official.

9. *American Al Qaeda: The Story of Bryant Neal Vinas,* CNN, May 15, 2010, http://www.cnn.com/SPECIALS/bryant.neal.vinas/.

10. Vinas testimony, United States v. Medunjanin, United States District Court, Eastern District of New York, 10-cr-00019.

11. *American Al Qaeda.*

12. "U.S. Muslims Desecrate American Flag: Video Shows Group on Street Corner Declaring Islamic Dominance," WorldNetDaily, June 8, 2005, www.wnd .com/2005/06/30701.

13. "Islamic Thinkers Society Calls for Genocide and Jihad on 34th Street," Militant Islam Monitor.org, April 25, 2006, www.militantislammonitor.org/ article/id/1867.

14. *American Al Qaeda.*

15. NYPD Intelligence file entitled "Mahmoud Al-Ayyoub," Undated. Obtained by authors.

16. *American Al Qaeda.*

17. Ibid.

18. Ray Kelly, "Defying the Inevitable," *New York Post*, September 11, 2007.

19. Robert Windrem, Richard Engel, and Sam Singal, "A New Breed of 'NYPD Blue': Six Years After 9/11, NYC Sets 'Gold Standard' in Counter-Terror Efforts," NBC News.com, September 11, 2007, http://www.msnbc.msn.com/ id/20730904/ns/nbcnightlynews/t/new-breed-nypd-blue/#.UJ8uouOe8wg.

20. The authors reviewed a March 2009 document in which Vinas recounted for FBI and Belgian authorities his al-Qaeda training.

21. "NYPD Transformed Since 9/11 Attacks," New York *Daily News*, September 10, 2008, http://articles.nydailynews.com/2008-09-09/news/17905319_1_ police-commissioner-raymond-kelly-share-intelligence-al-Qaeda.

22. *Deputy Commissioner's Briefing*, April 15, 2008. Obtained by authors.

23. NYPD Intelligence document entitled "Memorandum for the Record," April 18, 2008. Obtained by authors.

24. Ibid.

25. "Documents Captured by the United States Army in an Al-Qaeda Safe House in Pakistan Expose the Ambivalent Relations Between Al-Qaeda and Iran . . ." Meir Amit Intelligence and Terrorism Information Center, June 14, 2002, www.terrorism-info.org.il/Data/articles/Art_20348/E_109_12_196531746 .pdf.

26. Interview with former senior CIA official.

27. Vinas testimony in Medunjanin trial, United States v. Medunjanin, United States District Court, Eastern District of New York, 10-cr-00019.

28. *American Al Qaeda.*

Ten: In the Wind

1. Accounts of the blowup between Shea and Ciorra were described in interviews with officials who witnessed it.

2. The Iranian Mission operation was described in Adam Goldman and Matt Apuzzo, "Consequences for Security as NYPD-FBI Rift Widens," Associated Press, March 20, 2012, www.ap.org/Content/AP-In-The-News/2012/ Consequences-for-security-as-NYPD-FBI-rift-widens. The consideration of charges against NYPD officials was described in interviews with former FBI, CIA, and Justice Department officials.

Eleven: Flight

1. Interviews with Davis and other law enforcement officials.

2. The bugging operation was described in interviews with Garcia, Olson, and Casey.

3. Details of the interview were memorialized in an FBI document known as a 302. It was obtained by the authors.

4. Details of the interview were taken from Azad's testimony in Medunjanin's trial, United States v. Medunjanin, United States District Court, Eastern District of New York, 10-cr-00019; and the FBI's September 14, 2009, interview report obtained by authors.

5. United States v. Medunjanin, trial transcript, p. 191.

6. Karen Zraick, "A Man Under Watch, but Not Under Wraps, in a Terrorism

Case," *New York Times*, October 8, 2009, www.nytimes.com/2009/10/09/nyregion/09surveil.html?pagewanted=all&_r=0.

7. The conversation and other details about the Ohio operation were described in interviews with Figliuzzi and other current and former law enforcement officials.

Twelve: People Die to Come Here

1. Garrett Graff, "Homegrown Terror: Najibullah Zazi and Colorado's Terrorist Ties," *5280* (magazine), November 2011, www.5280.com/magazine/2011/11/homegrown-terror.

2. Ibid. Folsom is now deceased. His recollection of this first meeting is based on Graff's article.

3. United States v. Mohammed Wali Zazi, United States District Court, Eastern District of New York, 10-CR-60, transcript, p. 648.

4. Naqib Jaji testimony, ibid.

5. Amanullah Zazi testimony, ibid.

6. Ibid.

7. Meg Jones, "Oshkosh Native, FBI Agent Recalls Meeting Terrorist," Milwaukee *Journal Sentinel*, April 25, 2012, www.jsonline.com/news/wisconsin/terror-within-inches-ac55b80-148988495.html.

8. John Frank, "History Supports McCain's Stance on Waterboarding," PolitiFact, December 18, 2007, http://www.politifact.com/truth-o-meter/statements/2007/dec/18/john-mccain/history-supports-mccains-stance-on-waterboarding.

9. *ICRC Report on the Treatment of Fourteen "High Value Detainees" in CIA Custody* (International Committee of the Red Cross, February 2007), http://assets.nybooks.com/media/doc/2010/04/22/icrc-report.pdf.

10. George Tenet, *At the Center of the Storm: My Years at the CIA* (New York: HarperCollins, 2007), p. 278.

11. Interviews with Davis and Olson.

12. Interview with Olson.

13. Graff, "Homegrown Terror," www.5280.com/magazine/2011/11/homegrown-terror.

14. Mark A. Godsey, "Reformulating the *Miranda* Warnings in Light of Contemporary Law and Understandings," *Minnesota Law Review* 90, no. 4 (2005–06): 781.

15. Graff, "Homegrown Terror," www.5280.com/magazine/2011/11/homegrown
-terror.

16. Zazi testimony in United States v. Medunjanin, p. 704 ("I knew beforehand,
sir, that I'm screwed, and I was just trying to go and pretend that anything
would happen, just blame me for it").

17. Medunjanin 302, transcription date September 18, 2009. Obtained by authors.

18. Greg Miller, "How Many Security Clearances Have Been Issued? Nearly
Enough for Everyone in the Washington Area," *Washington Post*, September 20, 2011, www.washingtonpost.com/blogs/checkpoint-washington/post/
how-many-security-clearances-has-the-government-issued-nearly-enough
-for-everyone-in-the-washington-area/2011/09/20/gIQAMW3OiK_blog
.html.

19. All quotes and details from the phone call are described in Graff's article in
5280.

20. A tape of Medunjanin's 911 call was released at his trial.

21. Mosi Secret, "Prison for Father Who Lied About Terror Plot," *New York
Times*, February 10, 2012, http://www.nytimes.com/2012/02/11/nyregion/
mohammed-wali-zazi-sentenced-for-lying-about-subway-bomb-plot.html.

Epilogue

1. Mitchell D. Silber, "How the NYPD Foiled a Plot to Bomb the Subways," *Wall
Street Journal,* May 4, 2012, http://online.wsj.com/article/SB10001424052702
304743704577380403870893454.html.

2. Ibid.

3. Justin Elliott, "Fact-Check: How the NYPD Overstated Its Terrorism Record," ProPublica, July 10, 2012, www.propublica.org/article/fact
-check-how-the-nypd-overstated-its-counterterrorism-record.

4. James Freeman, "The Political War on the NYPD," *Wall Street Journal*, April
5, 2013, http://online.wsj.com/article/SB10001424127887323501004578388
311774675612.html.

5. Matt Apuzzo and Adam Goldman, "NYPD Messages to Muslim Informant:
'Get Pictures,' " the Associated Press, May 20, 2012.

6. http://www.law.cuny.edu/academics/clinics/immigration/clear/Mapping
-Muslims.pdf.

7. Though the CIA maintains that Hamilton's name is classified, the authors were
told this by several NYPD officials, including some who do not have security

clearances. He worked in an unclassified office and identified himself to colleagues as a CIA officer. Asked about Hamilton's job in 2011, NYPD spokesman Paul Browne said, "It sounds right that he's a special assistant to Cohen on loan from the CIA." He subsequently emailed to clarify that nobody by that name worked for the NYPD.

INDEX

INDEX

INDEX

Civil Liberties Union, New York, 48
civil rights/liberties: case against
NYPD for violation of, 279; and
FBI investigations of mosques, 179;
FBI-NYPD Intelligence Division
relationship and, 148, 149–50;
Handschu guidelines as safeguard for,
50; need for change in views about, 277;
and terrorism enterprise investigations,
180
Clinton, Bill, 32, 36, 39, 66
Cohen, David: accomplishments of, 154,
190, 191, 196, 213; and Ahmadinejad
motorcade, 23–24; appointment as
NYPD deputy commissioner for
intelligence of, 30, 39–40, 278, 282;
and approval and renewal of
investigations, 197; Atta case study and,
69, 71, 72; Berdecia assignments and,
79, 80; big-net strategy of, 141; Borelli
and, 121, 124; Burke investigation
and, 143; and changes in NYPD
Intelligence Division, 138, 147, 148;
CIA career of, 30–36, 37–39, 47, 50,
65, 66; CIA relationships with, 83, 150;
creation of Intelligence Division and,
17–18, 19–20, 81; and demographics
of New York City, 69; FBI-NYPD
Intel relationship and, 18, 19, 123–25,
150; FBI relationship with, 24, 25,
66, 83, 123–25, 149, 217, 228–30;
Handschu guidelines and, 50–52,
74, 78, 142, 143, 144, 145–46, 148,
179–80, 181, 183, 197, 212; Hezbollah
case and, 121–25; and identification
of terrorists, 128, 129–30, 132, 133,
140, 141; immigration information
and, 188; JTTF relationship with, 81,
151, 153–54, 183–86, 228–30; Kelly
meetings with, 30, 66; "management
by fear" philosophy of, 35; mosque
investigations and, 179, 181, 182,
183–86, 187–88, 194, 195; name-change
program and, 135, 136; and NYPD
officers in foreign police departments,
83, 181; NYPD vision of, 49, 69;
oversight of, 142, 209; personality
of, 68–69; power and responsibilities
of, 24, 26, 181, 197; and pressures on
NYPD Intel detectives, 134; profiling

and, 72; and recruiting for NYPD,
74–76; refusal to put NYPD people
on JTTF, 125; refuses interview with
Apuzzo and Goldman, 278; reputation
of, 35–36, 37–38, 39; Rutgers case
and, 24–25; Sanchez and, 66–67, 69,
83, 283; September 11, 2001 and, 150;
Shehadeh case and, 18, 229–30; and
shutting down Intel cases, 196–97;
Siraj investigation and, 151, 152, 153;
60 Minutes interview of, 190; and
uniqueness of Intelligence Division,
147; Vinas investigation and, 212, 213,
216–17; Zazi investigation and, 25–26,
155, 173, 176, 209, 228–29, 280
colleges/universities: identification of
terrorists at, 139–41; See also Muslim
student groups
Colorado Information Analysis Center
(CIAC), 161–63
Colorado State Patrol, 10–11, 160–61, 163,
166, 239–40, 280
Columbia University, 41, 44, 140
community policing strategy, Kelly's, 28
CompStat computer system, NYPD, 196
Computer People for Peace, 44
Counterterrorism Center, CIA, 210
Counterterrorism Division, FBI, 6,
170–71, 202, 219
"Critical Mass" bike rides, 144
Crown Heights (Brooklyn) riot (1991), 28
Cummings, Art, 58, 59, 61, 64, 168, 201,
229, 236–37, 283
Curveball (Iraqi defector), 84
Customs Service, U.S., 26, 188
Cutter, John, 48, 68
Cyber Intelligence Unit, NYPD, 141

Davis, Jim: and briefings at FBI
headquarters, 170; and Denver Art
Museum threat, 157–61, 163, 165–68,
172; Heimbach relationship with,
171; post-Zazi investigation career of,
283; professional background of, 160,
163–65; and raid on Zazi apartment,
248; reputation of, 170; Zazi arrest and,
271–72, 273; Zazi confession and, 268;
and Zazi email account, 54, 55; and
Zazi-FBI interview, 258, 262, 266, 269;
Zazi investigation and, 54, 55, 57, 59,

310

INDEX

ABOUT THE AUTHORS

MATT APUZZO and ADAM GOLDMAN are investigative reporters for the Associated Press in Washington, D.C. They shared in the 2012 Pulitzer Prize for Investigative Reporting for a series on the New York Police Department's clandestine spying program targeting American Muslims. Together Apuzzo and Goldman have uncovered the location of an overseas CIA prison, revealed widespread cheating on FBI exams, and showed how the CIA's haphazard disciplinary system resulted in promotions for officers who kidnapped and killed the wrong people. They have shared the Goldsmith Prize for Investigative Reporting, a George Polk Award, the Paul Tobenkin Memorial Award, and the Edgar A. Poe Award from the White House Correspondents' Association. Apuzzo has covered organized crime, corruption, and law enforcement in Massachusetts, Connecticut, and Washington. Goldman has covered crime and government for newspapers in Virginia and Alabama. He reported from Las Vegas and New York for the AP.